Charles... sc

For 'brahim and Jane
w/ my best wishes.

R— Watt

CONVICTS AND ORPHANS

CONVICTS AND ORPHANS

Forced and State-Sponsored Colonizers in
the Portuguese Empire, 1550–1755

———————

TIMOTHY J. COATES

STANFORD UNIVERSITY PRESS

Stanford, California 2001

Stanford University Press
Stanford, California

© 2001 by the Board of Trustees of the
Leland Stanford Junior University

Published with the support of the Fundação Calouste
Gulbenkian of Lisbon.

Printed in the United States of America
on acid-free, archival-quality paper

Library of Congress Cataloging-in-Publication Data
Coates, Timothy J., 1952–
    Convicts and orphans : forced and state-sponsored colo-
nizers in the Portuguese Empire, 1550–1755 / Timothy J.
Coates.
        p.   cm.
    Includes bibliographical references and index.
ISBN 0-8047-3359-7 (alk. paper)
    1. Portugal—Colonies—Emigration and immigration.
2. Ex-convicts—Portugal—Colonies.   3. Orphans—
Portugal—Colonies.   I. Title.
JV4227.C578 2002
325'.3469'0903—dc21

                                        2001032018

Original Printing 2001
Last figure below indicates year of this printing:
10 09 08 07 06 05 04 03 02 01

Typeset by G & S Typesetters, Inc. in 10/13 Aldus

To my mother, Barbara Batchelor Watrous, who also loves the Iberian world; and to honor the memories of Professor Ursula Lamb, who many years ago started me on this path, and my aunt, Ellene Rosemund Coates, who so often encouraged me along the way.

CONTENTS

TABLES

ILLUSTRATIONS

You should decide what you want to read. Legal works and colonial
history have nothing in common.

— *A Lisbon librarian, 1990*

This study is somewhat unusual in the literature on Portuguese overseas
history. First, the use of criminals, sinners, orphans, and prostitutes as colonizers has remained unexplored in the Portuguese world. Furthermore,
since this topic is thematic and not limited to one colony, it starts in Portugal and wanders through the former empire, both in terms of geography and
time. This breaks one of the unwritten rules of Portuguese historiography.
Traditionally, the empire has been divided into Asian, African, and Brazilian
segments. I do not pretend that a topic as broad and multifaceted as penal exile will be done justice here in my short study, but it is my intention to show
that these separate imperial parts were interconnected. Furthermore, officials of the Portuguese state were quite conscious of this interdependence;
their awareness was reflected in how agencies of the Crown, in particular
the judicial system and the Overseas Council, used these figures during the
early modern period. When viewed over a short time span or in terms of one
colony only, it is difficult, if not impossible, to see the larger imperial system
at work.

Portuguese Asia, the former Estado da India, is my main focus. Goa and
the Asian empire formed the so-called First Empire and were the center of
Portuguese economic and colonizing efforts during the sixteenth century.
This process continued in fits and starts throughout the seventeenth century,
although by 1700, Portuguese Asia had ceased to be the center of the empire
and became only one of many regions in crisis. Given these circumstances,
the Estado da India is the logical area with which to begin this study. However, this is not to say that this work centers on Portuguese Asia exclusively.
The former African colonies of São Tomé and Angola are critical to any investigation of exile in the Portuguese world. Brazil, in particular Maranhão,
is another important secondary area. After some investigation, it became obvious to me that the early modern Portuguese state believed these figures offered promise and contoured the legal system to fit imperial needs. Another
aspect of my argument is that at some point in the first half of the seven-

teenth century, forced colonization was not required to populate most areas of Brazil.

After citing examples of internal exile used in metropolitan Portugal, I have selected data that represent virtually every part of the former Portuguese Empire: exiles in the Moroccan garrison forts; others sent to São Tomé and Angola; prostitutes and colonizing families conducted to Mozambique; criminals sent as soldiers to Goa; demographic and ethnographic data on both Goa and Macau; criminals exiled to Sri Lanka and the Molucca Islands (in modern-day Indonesia); Azorean families paid to relocate to Pará; and others relocated to Brazil's Maranhão and to the highlands of Mozambique. Orphan girls entered this muddied picture once they started arriving in Salvador and Goa from Lisbon, and they were used by the Crown all over South Asia. Reformed prostitutes formed a third layer to this process and were relocated in South Asia, Mozambique, and Portuguese America.

This process of forced (in the case of criminals or sinners) or state-sponsored colonization (in the case of others) was an internal Portuguese concern. Readers who search for a comparative history of Asia, Africa, or South America (or for that matter, Europe) will be disappointed. This is not a history of those areas, nor is it a comparative study of interaction outside of the former Portuguese Empire, although from time to time the discussion of some interaction is inevitable. Comparison has been conducted in terms of one colony in light of another or change in one colony over time. The perspective adopted is that of the Crown and its agents, with a sympathetic eye toward these European colonizers and the hardships they endured.

The ideal study of forced colonization in the Portuguese world would cast an even wider net to include Gypsies and New Christians and would extend until the punishment of exile ended in the mid-twentieth century. However, including these last two groups would have made this already dangerously broad topic even more so. And extending it to recent times would have made this study unrealistic and unwieldy. I have made a couple of comments about both of these groups, especially Gypsies. I trust that this outline of the Portuguese early modern penal process will provide a starting point for others who may want to investigate the colonizing roles played by either New Christians or Gypsies or the continued use of exile as punishment in the nineteenth and twentieth centuries.

In terms of the time frame involved, I had originally envisioned a narrower study of the century between 1550 and 1650. By the end of this period, the Estado da India sank into an economic depression from which it never really recovered, and Brazil became Portugal's preeminent colony. Discussion of this shift would have been supported by an analysis of the Portuguese state's use of exiles and others as forced colonizers. A parallel argument would have been based on shifting locations within the Estado da India of imperial dowries awarded to orphan girls and other women. Readers will note the outlines of these arguments in this work, but they are not its main thrust, at least not to the extent I had first planned. After almost three years of research in the archives, it became apparent that neither the exile nor the dowry documentation could be limited to the period between 1550 and 1650. Documentation on exile as punishment in Portugal begins with the High Middle Ages and continues until this practice was abandoned in 1954.[1] Neither exile nor penal servitude in Portugal has begun to be investigated. This means that, in addition to the mass of data uncovered on these topics, there is no secondary literature that links critical, interconnected issues, such as the galleys, penal exile, crime, and military recruitment, or most of the institutions at the center of this process, such as the judiciary. The studies that do exist typically do not even mention forced colonizers. For example, studies of the Inquisition dwell on other aspects and hardly mention that exile was that institution's principal punishment. The two inquisitorial studies that break from this pattern are recent and focus exclusively on colonial Brazil. Laura de Mello e Souza's stimulating work on the Portuguese Inquisition is cast in the mold of religious punishment, demonology, and purification by the crossing of the waters of the Atlantic. Her work concentrates on cases of exile to Brazil as punishment for sin, not as a rational process of colonization. Indeed, forced colonization to colonial Brazil, although popular with the metropolitan tribunals of the Inquisition, was the exception and not the norm, especially after the 1690s. My friend and colleague, Geraldo Pieroni, has also investigated exile to Brazil as punishment by the Inquisition; his work is immediately relevant to this study. However, my contention remains that it is impossible to discern the overall system (used by both the Catholic Church and Portuguese state) unless one examines all regions of the empire over a long span of time. This study concentrates on the state's courts and relevant aspects of inquisitorial exile during two centuries in order to define the broad contours of this system. The evidence has led me to conclude that, in spite of its piecemeal and fragmented nature, exile was an extremely rational system, coordinated by both church and state, for colonization, emergency manpower, and social control.

Another example of problems with sources can be found in the standard reference on Portuguese galleys by Barros. This work provides excellent technical insight on the construction of galleys, but it does not say one word about the men who worked in them or the system providing labor. In spite of its popularity with scholars of other early modern nations (especially France), little has been written on crime and criminality in early modern Portugal. The dowry data provide a secondary, but still compelling, argument, but they also transcend the 1550–1650 boundaries. The result of this situation is the deliberately vague use of *early modern* in this work. The real focus of this study is the period from 1550 to 1755. Not only was the bulk of data uncovered for that era, but those two centuries encompass much of the early modern era in the Portuguese world, from the stern Counter-Reformation views and decrees of Kings D. João III and D. Sebastião, through the so-called Greater Seventeenth Century, to the reign of King D. José I and the Enlightenment in Portugal.

This extended two-hundred-year view of forced and state-sponsored colonization ends with the rise to power of the Marquês of Pombal. During the mid-eighteenth century the system described here was transformed into a more modern and rational one. In a series of related moves, the criminal justice system turned away from sentences of public works (including galleys). At the same time, the military made strides toward professionalization, a change that severed its link with the criminal justice system. As a result, 1755 is a logical point to end this study.

The sources for this work are listed in the Bibliography, but perhaps a word or two about them might be in order. Archives where research was conducted included both the predictable as well as the lesser known. Not surprisingly, the Arquivo Histórico Ultramarino (AHU) in Lisbon and the Historical Archives of Goa (HAG) proved to be the two most pertinent to this study. In the case of the former, I was fortunate to be able to review much of their pre-1700 documentation and did not limit myself to one former colony. In the case of the HAG, during my year in Goa I was able to consult virtually all their pre-1750 documentation.

Many other archives in Portugal contain relevant materials. The Arquivo Nacional da Torre do Tombo holds masses of documentation, but these humble figures were not likely to appear in much of the official correspondence unless they were making an appeal, a general pardon was issued, or in case something went terribly wrong, such as losing a ship. This left documentation from two specific institutions to examine in detail. In the case of exiles, the Desembargo do Paço, a consultative body that functioned as a supreme court, revealed numerous appeals and pardons. For the orphans, the deliberations of the Mesa da Consciência e Ordens outlined several important decisions made at the highest levels of national government. This institution reflected on issues of national importance and also acted as a screening board for membership in the prestigious military orders. Much of the documentation that would have been extremely relevant, such as that from the Lisbon *misericórdia,* from Lisbon's main jail of Limoeiro, from the Office of the Secretary of Galleys in the Ministry of the Marine, or from the Casa da Suplicação (Appeals Court) was destroyed in the 1755 earthquake and fire. This may explain why a study such as this has not been attempted to date and it also may explain the lack of supporting studies.

Bits and pieces of data were located all over Portugal; archives were selected for consultation on the basis of information available from their published guides. In the United States, the James Ford Bell Library and the John Carter Brown Library were especially rich and useful collections. In Goa, India, in addition to the Historical Archives of Goa, both the Central Library of Panaji as well as the Library of the Xavier Centre for Historical Research were fruitful collections for this study. A complete list of archives that I had the good fortune to consult can be found in the reference section at the back of this study.

Since documentation on orphans usually appeared in municipal, or *misericórdia,* documents and that concerning exiles was contained in regional collections, both municipal and district archives were consulted whenever possible. In addition to these archives, the field of early modern Portuguese history as a whole is fortunate that numerous series of documents have been published in the last two centuries.

Other Early Modern States and Penal Exile

Portugal was at the forefront of a process that would be used with mixed results by a variety of other European powers. Criminal exile or transportation (as the term is used in much of literature on Great Britain) refers to coerced colonization that, by commuting the original sentence, forced a criminal to reside in one of the colonies. This system required distant, strategic, and undesirable (at least in the popular perception) outposts of a central authority. These were locales where the state wished to reinforce its often tenuous hold and where it could not attract sufficient free immigration. In short, it supported an empire. Although this may appear obvious, it explains its use by powers as diverse as France, England, and China and its absence in other regions, such as the Germanic lands.

France and England made notable efforts in the use of transportation. In the seventeenth century, both were focusing their attentions on their New World territories. England experimented with virtually all of its colonies in North America (other than those in New England) by using them as exile locales. The concept of forced colonization in England "had been considered in [Queen] Elizabeth's time, was in regular use by 1615, and became common in the course of the seventeenth century."[2] England also directed forced colonizers to its island holdings in the West Indies, principally Barbados and Jamaica. During the course of the seventeenth century, forced colonizers in British North America were blended with indentured servants. Nevertheless, British use of penal exiles was modest before the passage of the Transportation Act of 1718.[3]

The questions of exile and penal servitude as punishments are issues receiving increased attention in the literature on early modern European powers. I found a fundamental beginning in the 1939 study by Rusche and Kirchheimer that presented many of the basic arguments and dilemmas of early modern crime. Verlinden's work is extremely important, not only for European colonization as a whole but also for the early administrative foundations of the Portuguese case in particular. Crime, criminals, and criminality in general are interconnected issues with a growing literature such as the work by Weisser that was quite instructive.

The British use of forced colonization has been the most closely studied and provided a useful comparison at several stages in my work through the works by Smith, Shaw, Hughes, and Ekirch.

The French Crown had equally severe problems in populating its New World colonies throughout the seventeenth and the beginning of the eighteenth century. French convicts were increasingly sent to the French West Indies in the 1680s; at the same time, a soldier could have the length of his duty shortened if he agreed to remain there.[4] Convicts, orphan girls, and even children banished from France by their parents helped to provide a French presence in the West Indies in the late 1600s.[5] Frenchmen in Louisiana, like the Portuguese in Goa, seemed to prefer indigenous women over the handful sent from Europe.[6] They also shared with the Portuguese the goal of returning to their homeland "as soon as they had amassed some wealth."[7] The failure of voluntary immigration to Louisiana made the French Crown resort to force in order to colonize it. Salt smugglers (in 1717) were later joined by prostitutes and runaway soldiers in Louisiana, which became a quasi-penal colony.[8] In 1719, the French began a system of "compulsory indentures," assigned to galley prisoners as well as vagabonds, who were given these compulsory five-year contracts.[9] Galley prisoners, counterfeiters, and other convicts were sent to Cayenne, the French colony on the mainland of South America.[10] French women in the New World were in especially short supply; in 1721 thirty cartloads of "young women of middling virtue" were deported to the Mississippi Colony.[11] The French began to use criminals and prisoners as soldier-colonizers in French Canada.[12] By the middle of the eighteenth century, "the French found that *degredados* were more trouble than they were worth . . . and abandoned the practice of exiling its criminals to North America but the English persisted."[13]

Bamford's investigation of the French galley system was particularly useful for this study, as were the works by Allain on French policy and Boucher on French America.

During the sixteenth and seventeenth centuries, the Spanish used penal labor closer to home in their galley system, in the mercury mines at Almadén, or in one of their North African presidios. It was during the second half of the eighteenth century that the Spanish Crown extended penal servitude to its New World colonies; in the effort to reenforce its defenses in the Caribbean, Spanish convicts were principally directed to the garrisons in Havana and San Juan (Puerto Rico).[14] Pike provided a succinct model of this process in her work.

At this same time, the Chinese began a systematic effort to colonize Xinjiang (Chinese Turkestan) by transporting criminals and their families to this remote frontier region.[15] The Chinese case, while similar to the European use of transportation, developed from a long-standing legal tradition of internal exile and amnesty. The Ottomans also used state-sponsored relocation as a tool to rationally control and distribute their population. In early modern times, Cyprus was an exile location for many criminals from the Turkish mainland.[16]

Nor was Portugal the only power attempting to control the lives of its orphans. In the case of England, the city of London, in its 1580 provisions, was already directing the marriage of young orphan girls.[17] Within one hundred years, part of the city's regular duties was "to preserve the Orphans' Estates, take care of their education, dispose of them to Trades and Matches suitable to their Qualities and Estates, which was accordingly done for a long while."[18] In the town of Glaucha (Saxony) by the late seventeenth century, widows were being sheltered as were twelve orphans who were also being schooled at a public orphanage.[19] The French Crown also initiated a system using its orphans and women of questionable virtue to populate Quebec. By 1663, the first batch of such women had been recruited in France and left for French Canada.[20] In his exhaustive study on these French orphans, Dumas lists a total of 774 women who emigrated to Canada in the decade from 1663 to 1673.[21]

The Chinese example aside, what makes these cases from other powers all the more intriguing is that they occurred *well after* the Portuguese had firmly established a penal exile system of their own.

In spite of this, neither exile nor penal servitude has attracted attention in the literature on Portugal and its empire. More often than not, criminal exiles and orphans were simply not considered suitable material for inclusion in official histories. A good example of this attitude can be seen in the chronicle written by Bernardo Pereira de Berredo on Maranhão. Although he was the former governor of this province, where exiles and others were forced to relocate and where they formed an important segment of the European population, he mentions soldiers a few times and ignores *degredados* (male criminal exiles) completely. Most histories of the island of São Tomé fail to mention that *degredados* provided the vast majority—if not 90 to 95 percent—of the European population during early modern times. To a certain extent, this situation is understandable since *degredados* were hardly Lusitanian "heroes of the sea." Their story, many must have felt, was unedifying and even uncomplimentary. Nevertheless, historians from the earliest chroniclers to recent scholars at least mention exiles as being omnipresent throughout the empire. Few have gone beyond this to question what imperial role they may have played. Two important works break with this standard: Boxer's *Seaborne Empire* and Bender's *Angola Under the Portuguese*. Both have chapters on penal exiles and their colonial impact, Boxer for the early modern period and Bender for modern Angola. However, to date, there has not been any study that focuses on criminality, exile, and empire building in the Portuguese world.

In spite of this situation, several other works on Portugal and aspects of her empire are fundamental for this study. On Portugal itself, many of João Lúcio de Azevedo's works (in spite of their age) retain their relevance. The same could be said of Jaime Cortesão. Works by Oliveira Marques are essential references for the framework of empire. In terms of historical and cultural geography, Orlando Ribeiro and Stanislawski are indispensable. For Portuguese Asia, I have found the works of Boxer, Magalhães Godinho, Pearson, Subrahmanyam, Teotónio de Souza, and Winius to be especially useful.

Three institutions are central to this study. Although they have not been examined adequately, several studies laid the groundwork that made my work possible. Central to criminality, social welfare, and state-control are the institutions of the high court (*relação*), the Santa Casa de Misericórdia (charitable lay brotherhood), and the municipal council (*câmara*). These institutions, as well as several others important to this study, are defined and discussed here in the Introduction. Gama Barros is a fundamental reference for the beginnings of the early modern period in Portugal and is a point of departure for examining all structures crafted by the Portuguese state. For the courts, Schwartz's investigation of the high court of Salvador is a unique and important study of this central institution. Interest in social history in Portugal is growing, and the *misericórdia* is beginning to receive increased attention. For example, Guimarães Sá published her important new study (*Quando o rico se faz pobre*) of the *misericórdia* in its imperial setting in 1997. Nevertheless, Russell-Wood's study of the city of Salvador, *Fidalgos and Philanthropists*, remains a model study of one chapter. In the case of Goa, Ferreira Martin's work, now almost a century old, is still useful.

City councils were the subject of Boxer's *Portuguese Society*, the only study that viewed them in their powerful colonial roles until the 1998 publication of *O Município no Mundo Português*. Also important in terms of institutional studies are works such as Borges Coelho.

Boxer's *Women* and Sanceau's *Mulheres Portuguesas* are the only two works that concentrate on Portuguese women in the empire. Women, both Portuguese and foreign, have not been the subject of a great deal of scrutiny, in spite of the possibilities offered by the documentation. I suspect that this situation will change in the near future, since the field is completely open for such lines of inquiry. Women in Portuguese society in Europe have been the subject of a small but growing body of literature that made an impact with the 1985 publication of *A Mulher na Sociedade Portuguesa*.[22] More so than any other individual, Silva Correia should be credited for questioning the impact of female Portuguese emigration to the colonies during early modern times. He investigated these themes in a multivolumed work on India as well as in several smaller works on other colonies. Unfortunately, his work contains a number of fatal flaws in the use and interpretation of data, and its lack of organization makes it extremely difficult to consult.[23]

The outline of this work follows a certain logic, which is perhaps best stated now in order to clarify my objectives. The Introduction presents an overview of early modern Portuguese society; Chapters 1 through 5 trace interlocking aspects of the rather complex Portuguese legal system that was so fond of exile as a punishment. To accomplish this, Chapter 1 examines the legal foundations behind exile and the system that collected criminals. Chapter 2 discusses the roots of internal exile in the High Middle Ages, the galley system, and the early application of exile to North and West Africa. Chapters 3 and 4 are descriptive in nature and present the lion's share of archival discoveries on convicts and their imperial reality. Chapter 5 begins with individual pardons and collective shifts in exile locations throughout the seventeenth century and concludes with a brief analysis of how the state molded this system to suit its needs. Chapter 6 shifts gears slightly to discuss interwoven aspects of single women, the early modern Portuguese state, empire, and colonization. Chapters 7 and 8 outline how the state linked dowries to its empire. Finally, I offer some concluding remarks and include general demographic figures to discuss the imperial impact these figures may have had.

ACKNOWLEDGMENTS

No topic such as this grows in a vacuum, and this study is no exception. My interest in forced colonization began during my graduate course work in the Department of History at the University of Minnesota. The Center for Early Modern History within that department proved to be a dynamic and stimulating environment in which to study. I first began researching the orphan girls and their dowries. Criminals and sinners were later included in my project at the suggestion of my former adviser, Professor Stuart Schwartz, in order to balance the role played by these orphan girls. During my eight years at Minnesota, Professor Schwartz frequently assisted and guided me; without his kind support and advice, this work could have never been completed.

In addition to Professor Schwartz, Professors Carla Rahn Phillips and James Tracy were instrumental in my orientation to the early modern globe. They assisted me in the exploration of ideas of criminality, in the pursuit of opportunities to research the subject area, and eventually in the coherent presentation of my findings. Professor Joseph Schwartzberg of the Geography Department at Minnesota provided insights on South Asia that both encouraged me to visit Goa, India, and gave me a greater understanding of the peoples and cultures of that region during my year there. I was also fortunate to be able to work closely with Professor Michael Pearson while he was the Union Pacific Visiting Professor of Early Modern History at Minnesota.

This decade-long project would never have lifted off the ground without the advice and assistance of many others who have also been most generous with their time and suggestions. It now gives me the greatest pleasure to be able to thank them in writing. Professors Dauril Alden, Janaína Amado, Glenn Ames, Charles Boxer, Caroline Brettell, William Donovan, Robert Garfield, Isabel dos Guimarães Sá, José Jobson Andrade de Arruda, Laura de Mello e Sousa, Fernando Novais, Katia M. de Queirós Mattoso, Muriel Nazzari, Geraldo Pieroni, Luís Reis Torgal, Joel Serrão, and Chandra R. de Silva were all instrumental in helping me frame questions and issues. I thank all of them for the time they took to answer my questions and discuss issues related to this work.

The bulk of the research for this study was conducted during the two-year period from October 1989 to September 1991. Without the generous support from several institutions, it would have been impossible to undertake the research. I am greatly indebted to the Calouste Gulbenkian Foundation for the fellowship awarded me for 1989–1990 to support my year of archival research in Portugal. In addition, the Graduate School of the University of Minnesota was most generous in providing me with supplementary grants throughout that period, as was the History Department in awarding me the Samuel Dienard Memorial Research Fellowship in 1989 and again in the fall of 1992. Special thanks are also due to the Instituto Português do Património Cultural for allowing me to consult the priceless library at the National Palace in Mafra and to the Santa Casa de Misericórdia of Évora for permission to consult their historical records. My year of research in India was made possible by a fellowship awarded by the American Institute of Indian Studies. I am indebted to both the institute and to the Xavier Centre for Historical Research in Alto Porvorim, Goa, which generously agreed to sponsor me in India.

Research was conducted at numerous archives and libraries in the United States, Portugal, India, and China. The assistance, so freely given, of many librarians and archivists made my work considerably easier. I would like to thank all the directors and staffs, but in particular Dr. Carol Urness of the James Ford Bell Library of the University of Minnesota for her support; the interlibrary loan staff of the University of Minnesota Libraries for their patient tracking down of numerous obscure items; Dr. Thomas Amos of the Hill Monastic Manuscript Library of St. John's University; Senhor Leão of the Arquivo Histórico Ultramarino in Lisbon; Senhor Constantino Borges Caramelo of the Arquivo Distrital de Évora and Senhora Laura Caeiro Domingues of the Manuscript Section of the Biblioteca Pública de Évora, who made my stay in their beautiful city both pleasant and rewarding; Dr. Alberto de Oliveira Marinho, director of the Biblioteca Municipal de Elvas, who took such a helpful interest in my work in that fascinating city; and to Dr. Isabel Abecasis, director of the Library of the Palácio Nacional de Mafra, as well as the assistant librarian, Dr. Paulo Jorge Barata. The three of us spent two pleasant weeks working together in the Mafra Library, and their numerous efforts on my behalf are greatly appreciated. In Goa, I would like to thank Dr. Shirodkar, director of the Historical Archives of Goa, and

Mr. Rivankar, director of the Reading Room. Special thanks are also due to Mr. Rivankar's staff for their prompt and courteous attention during my year there. Dr. Lourdes Bravo da Costa, director of the Rare Books Collection of the Central Library of Panaji, was also extremely helpful and knowledgeable about that rich collection.

Special thanks are also due to both Dr. Teotónio R. de Souza, former director of the Xavier Centre of Historical Research, and Dr. Charles Borges, S. J., the center's new chief. Dr. Souza made many helpful suggestions while I was conducting research in Goa; I trust that this will be the "source book" that we both envisioned. Both he and Dr. Borges took a personal interest in my work and did much to make my research in Goa profitable and my time there enjoyable. In Providence, Rhode Island, I would like to thank the staff of the John Carter Brown Library, especially Daniel Slive and Susan Danforth.

In addition, I would like to express my gratitude to Dr. Maria Clara Farinha, assistant director of International Services of the Calouste Gulbenkian Foundation (now retired), and Mr. L. S. Suri, associate director of the American Institute of Indian Studies in New Delhi, for their personal attention to my progress and well-being while I was a grantee of their respective institutions.

This study was made possible by the efforts of several old friends, who contributed in a variety of invaluable and much appreciated ways. João Gata, Paula Korsko, Helena Simas-Lima, and Silas Oliveira all helped, and for their assistance I am grateful. Our mutual friend, Gregory Lucas, the former director of the Centro de Estudos Norte Americanos, and Carlos Manuel Silva Dias, the centro's executive secretary, are due my sincere thanks for their assistance in Lisbon. I never would have reached India without the prompt intervention of Mr. Das, cultural affairs attaché of the Indian Embassy in Lisbon, who procured my research visa just in the nick of time. During my year there, Michael Maeorg and I spent many a pleasant evening on my porch in Goa discussing issues in our respective research; his anthropological background provided numerous insights about Goan society that I would have otherwise overlooked. Professor Rocky Miranda has also been most helpful, both in Goa and afterward in Minneapolis. I am also grateful for the editing work done by Jason Masciantoni and Joseph Coady, which helped transform this manuscript into its final form. To Professor Francis Dutra I owe a tremendous *obrigado* for his attentive reading of my manuscript and his numerous helpful corrections.

Two follow-up visits to Lisbon since 1991 were made possible by the generosity of the Luso-American Development Foundation, the Fundação Oriente, and the National Commission for the Commemoration of the Portuguese Discoveries (CNCDP). I am especially grateful to Jorge Manuel Flores, Fernando Dores Costa, and Clara Boléo of the CNCDP for their interest in this work, shown by having it translated and published by the CNCDP in 1998.[1] I am also grateful to Dr. Miguel Tamen for his sustained interest in seeing this work published in English. A second grant from the Fundação Oriente and assistance from the Graduate School of the College of Charleston and my department allowed me to travel to Macau to consult the archives in December and January 1996–1997.

On a final note, I have attempted to follow the usual conventions of spelling and reference. Modern place names listed in *Webster's* ninth edition are used (for example, Alentejo rather than Alem-Tejo, Sri Lanka in place of Ceylon). The city of Salvador da Baía de Todos os Santos is referred to as Salvador, while Bahia refers to the lands surrounding it. Authors and titles of references are unaltered. Abbreviations (other than those listed in *Webster's*) are detailed in a separate list located in the reference section. Portuguese kings are referred to by their Portuguese names (for example, João rather than John). The three Habsburg monarchs of Portugal are referred to as they were known in Spain (for example, King Filipe II is Filipe I of Portugal), since this is the English-language convention.

CONVICTS AND ORPHANS

Introduction

One of the hallmarks of the early modern period (approximately 1450–1750) was the development of strong, centralized governments that came to direct a wide variety of activities that earlier had been either beyond their reach or not of such intense concern. As a result of this centralizing of authority, early modern states began a new, more visible and intrusive relationship with their citizens. This is a study of one such relationship: how the early modern Portuguese state punished and rewarded its citizens by relocating them at home and overseas to suit its own domestic and imperial requirements.

I examine two methods the state used to reach these ends: penal exile and dowries. Penal exile was largely directed through the courts and coordinated by the Overseas Council. Imperial dowries were a solution to several issues: rewarding past services to the Crown; protecting daughters orphaned by such service; attending to pressing social needs at home in the form of an increasing number of such needy women; and stabilizing the colonial presence of a Portuguese elite, either born in the European homeland or directly descended from those who were.

Populating distant colonial cities and staffing remote garrisons placed a heavy burden on the demographic resources of any early modern power. In a country as small as Portugal, these demands required flexible and inventive responses by royal agencies. The Portuguese developed their system of penal exile from a Roman model, in use in the Mediterranean in the fifteenth century (notably by Venice on Crete). In turn, this Portuguese system, which incorporated orphan girls, prostitutes, and other marginal figures as colonizers, supplied a blueprint for other European powers. This is a study of that process: how it strengthened the royal agencies that conducted it; and how it bound together the many regions of the Portuguese world as a result.

National Councils

The lives of convicts and orphans, in spite of their humble status, were directed by several of the highest and most powerful bodies in the land. The Overseas Council, or Concelho Ultramarino, directed and coordinated all imperial policies in the colonies, including relocating penal exiles and rewarding orphan girls with dowries of state offices. Created shortly after the restoration of independence in 1640, the Overseas Council divided its workload into three parts: on Mondays, Tuesdays, and Wednesdays it dealt with issues relating to Asia; on Thursdays and Fridays it concentrated on Brazil; and on Saturdays it deliberated African matters.[1]

The legal counterpart of the Overseas Council was the Desembargo do Paço, founded by King D. João II (1481–1495). Its major function was that of supreme court, but it also appointed judges and advised the Crown on a range of legal matters. Penal exiles frequently appealed to the Desembargo do Paço to have their sentences reduced or modified. Directly below the Desembargo do Paço was the Casa da Suplicação, or Appeals Court, in Lisbon. Under it were the high courts, scattered throughout the empire in Porto, Salvador, and Goa.

The final national institution of special importance to this study is the Mesa da Consciência, first established in 1532 by King D. João III to debate national policy and advise the Crown on issues of national importance. These duties were expanded in 1563 to include screening candidates for membership to the prestigious military orders. Thus, this newer body acquired the title of Mesa da Consciência e Ordens.[2] It was this last institution that, on occasion, discussed the merits (and even the ethics) of sending orphans overseas.

The Demography of Early Modern Portugal

Demographic information for much of the early modern period is notoriously scanty. Nevertheless, in the past twenty years research on the available data has revealed a great deal about the population of Portugal in early modern times.

Estimates based on the 1527 hearth tax of King D. João III place Portugal's population between 1.1 and 1.4 million. By 1641, the population had decreased by approximately twenty thousand. A new hearth census ninety years later in 1732 showed the overall population to have been around 2.1 million, growing to 2.9 million by the end of the eighteenth century.[3]

The Portuguese population was (and remains) unevenly distributed throughout the country. The Minho (northwestern Portugal) had the greatest density; the eastern and southern interior areas were the most sparse. In terms of cities, Lisbon in 1527 had a population of 50,000 to 60,000.[4] Porto and Évora were more or less equal in size with 15,000 inhabitants each. The other major cities in the kingdom had populations of around 5,000 and included Guimarães, Coimbra, Santarém, Setúbal, and Beja.

The Portuguese population remained relatively static from 1527 to 1641. In the same period, the population of Lisbon tripled to around 165,000.[5] From 1641 to the end of the eighteenth century, the overall totals increased sharply. Population figures are not available for Lisbon; because of the earthquake in the middle of the eighteenth century, any figures for the capital during that period would not be indicative of any overall trend. It would seem that it followed the national pattern. In 1864, Lisbon had grown to 190,000 — an increase of only 25,000 in 250 years.[6]

Early Modern Portugal

Portugal occupies approximately one-fifth of the Iberian Peninsula. With the exception of the Olivença issue, the border has remained virtually unchanged (with some very minor exchanges of land) since the completion of the Portuguese *reconquista* (the reconquest of the Iberian Peninsula from

TABLE 1

Distribution of the Population of Portugal in 1527
(Population density per square kilometer
[percentage of national population])

	Littoral	Interior	Total
North	47.6 (23.3%)	10.0 (7.4%)	25.0 (30.7%)
Center	12.3 (8.5%)	10.7 (12.7%)	11.3 (21.2%)
Lisbon Region	26.1 (15.7%)	16.2 (7.6%)	23.2 (23.3%)
South	15.5 (5.3%)	12.0 (19.5%)	12.5 (24.8%)
Total	25.4 (52.8%)	11.8 (47.2%)	

SOURCES: Akola Meira do Carmo Neto, "Demografia," in Serrão, *Dicionário de História de Portugal*, 2:281–86; and Alves Morgado, 337.

Moslem forces), which ended in the late thirteenth century.[7] One reason behind this permanence is in the basic topography of Iberia. Of the five major rivers draining the peninsula—the Ebro, Guadalquivir, Guadiana, Tejo, and Douro—the last three listed (and their tributaries) form 70 percent of Portugal's eastern border and drain into the Atlantic after crossing the Portuguese countryside. The eastern border, in addition to being well-defined by these rivers, is characterized by what Stanislawski labels "limited desirability." The historical result has been that areas on both sides of this frontier have been lightly populated.[8] The northern border has been more problematic, in spite of the Minho River defining part of it. The separation of Galicia from Portugal has been based on political rather than geographical, linguistic, or cultural factors. Nevertheless, Portugal was one of the first European nations to assume its present dimensions; by 1249, Portugal (more or less as it is recognized today) emerged among the various Iberian kingdoms. With the exception of the sixty-year period from 1580 to 1640, when it was ruled by the Spanish Habsburg kings, Portugal has remained independent. Even in this period that past historians have labeled the "Spanish captivity," Portugal was but one of several kingdoms ruled from Madrid, while it managed to retain a degree of autonomy. One of the means by which independence was maintained after 1640 was to recruit criminals and Gypsy men for the army, when the need arose.

The Portuguese countryside and general topography are traditionally divided into two very broad sections, defined in detail by Orlando Ribeiro: an

TABLE 2
North-South Cultural and Geographical Distinctions in Portugal

Variable	North	South
Topography	mountainous	flat
Rainfall	uneven, very high or low	more uniformly low
Vegetation	oak (various)	oak and pine
Population Density	dense littoral	uniformly sparse
Size of Land Holdings	small	large
Major Cities	numerous, 9–10	few, 4–5
Major Non-Latin Influences	Celtic and Germanic	Arab
Differences in Dialects	yes	yes
Housing Materials	stone common	adobe, brick
Crops	grapes, maize, and rye	wheat, oats, and rice
Major Subdivisions	Minho, Tras-os-Montes, and Beira	Alentejo, the Algarve

SOURCES: Ribeiro, *O Mediterrâneo*; and Stanislawski, esp. 204–11.

Atlantic north and a Mediterranean south.[9] The dividing line is approximately 40° north latitude, just south of the university town of Coimbra. Table 2 outlines the major differences between these two regions.

Topography and rainfall are two of the major differences between these regions. The North is characterized by numerous small hills, rising to 3,000 feet in some areas. The South is essentially a broad plateau ranging from 600 to 1,200 feet in height. The rainfall distribution is equally disparate. Some areas of the Minho and Beira Alta (north and southeast of Porto, respectively) receive in excess of 30 inches. The interior areas of the North are relatively dry. Rainfall in the South does not exceed 25 inches other than in limited regions in the low hills separating the Alentejo from the Algarve (Serras da Monchique and Calderão), which are wetter.

The North-South division of the country has other cultural manifestations. The style of houses and materials used in their construction, dialect differences (not only North-South but intraregional), the importance of family structure, traditional music, dress, and cuisine are but several of many possible examples.[10] Stanislawski has also shown significant differences in topographical names: southern Portugal has 5 to 10 percent Arabic and Arabized names; most of the North has more than 5 percent—the Minho more than 40 percent—Germanic place names.[11]

This North-South division is not totally uniform. Ribeiro actually states that Portugal has three distinct regions; he considers the Tras-os-Montes region as a separate transmontane north (that is, northern interior Iberia). Within the North, there has been a long-standing separation of the Minho from Beira. In the South, the Alentejo is separated from the Algarve by low-lying hills. For historical reasons, throughout the early modern period the Algarve was considered a separate kingdom. Its reduced rainfall is perhaps its most outstanding characteristic when compared to the neighboring Alentejo or other regions of the country.

The imbalance in population density is another striking difference between the North and South. From the first records available, the North has consistently been the most densely populated region of the country. The South, the interior areas in particular, traditionally has been underpopulated. This pattern is, in part, due to the North to South incorporation of territory during the *reconquista*. Other factors include the distinct differences in the size of landholdings, the lower fertility of the southern soil, and reduced rainfall. Most urban centers of importance during the early modern period were located along the littoral, although the southern cities of Évora and Beja broke with this pattern.

It is sufficient here to state that these distinctions defining the North-South dichotomy of the Portuguese landscape did (and do) exist and were based on numerous factors, including those mentioned above. What were the effects of this division on the daily lives of ordinary people? In a 1580 description of the foodstuffs available in Lisbon, two Venetians commented that the ordinary people ate a lot of sardines and a type of coarse bread, because prices of other foods were too high for most people.[12]

A steady supply of wheat in sufficient quantities has been the major problem confronting Portuguese agriculture since the late Middle Ages. Wine was never mentioned as being in short supply. Quite to the contrary, Portugal has been closely associated with grapes and wine production since Roman times. The Roman name for (northern) Portugal was Lusitania, so named to honor Lusus, a companion to Bacchus. Wine has been one of the few agricultural commodities produced in surplus throughout the medieval and modern periods.

"In general, medieval agrarian production did not surpass national consumption," observes Peres.[13] Fruit, wine, and salt were the only items produced in surplus and, consequently, for trade. Although this Portuguese surplus was modest, the kingdom appears to have been more or less self-sufficient until the late fourteenth century. At this time, one first hears complaints of a lack of wheat in Porto and in Lisbon.[14]

The reasons for the lack of grains, a basic element of nutrition for the common people, were more complex than one might at first believe.[15] It is true that the Portuguese landscape is not well suited for grain, particularly wheat, cultivation. Irregular rainfall and inappropriate soil were two overriding factors. Wheat tends to be cultivated in the South. This has been the traditional pattern since the thirteenth century. However, the Alentejo's climate is too exposed to extremes (large seasonal fluctuations in rainfall) and is too arid overall (without irrigation) to produce more than one annual wheat crop.[16] Portuguese farmers practiced a birotational system (rather than the more common trirotational system used in northern Europe) since the birotational pattern fit Mediterranean rain patterns better. It was less productive. Cattle, providing critical manure for fertilizing fields, were limited by the availability of additional grazing lands. In addition, the seed yield was low: 3.89 for wheat, 3.82 for barley, 2.43 for oats.[17] Considering that Slicher van Bath, in his authoritative study on early modern European agriculture, considers three to be a workable minimum yield, it is clear that there was a precarious balance between production and consumption. These factors combined to produce an annual grain harvest that fell short of basic national needs as the population slowly increased.

Two additional factors reinforced and maintained this low yield from the wheat-growing South: the pattern of large landholdings and low population. Southern property holdings awarded by the Crown during the *reconquista* reflected medieval patterns. Vast estates were given to the church (monasteries, religious orders, convents), the military orders, and to the nobility. Other areas were retained by the Crown and given to cities.[18] The monastery of Alcobaça, for example, received 40,000 hectares. "The City of Tomar was founded by the Templar Order on lands given to it by King D. Sancho I. The monk-knights of Calatrava [known as 'of Évora' in Portugal] received [the city of] Aviz in 1211."[19] The result of this process was large, unproductive, absentee estates in the South. The comparatively few workers available (taking into consideration the initial low density of the population and the demographic decline during the fourteenth century) were then faced with the reality of "working other people's lands," moving to Lisbon—the major urban area in the country—or making their fortunes overseas in one of the colonies.[20] Commoners in the North confronted a different set of circumstances, which also tended to drive many off the land. Small, unproductive landholdings typical of the North became smaller still when divided by inheritance to the surviving children. Without any additional lands available in the crowded North, emigration was the path taken by many from the Minho and Beira.

Unlike most of Europe, slaves were used in Portugal and began to be imported as early as 1441. Many were directed to agricultural work in the South for the reasons mentioned above. In Saunders's study of slavery in early modern Portugal, the known residences of Africans in fifteenth and sixteenth century Portugal indicate an overwhelming presence in the South (twenty of twenty-six towns and cities listed).[21] Saunders has pointed out that people of all classes owned black slaves and used them for a variety of tasks. Black servants became an important status symbol for the larger and richer households in Lisbon. "By the mid-sixteenth century up to ten percent of the population of Lisbon, Évora, and the Algarve was black slaves."[22] An odd twist then developed: Portuguese emigrated or were exiled to the colonies, including many coastal areas in Africa, while many Black Africans were enslaved and bolstered the *metropole*'s decreasing labor force.[23] The fears of losing additional labor and prospective soldiers were reasons that, by 1646, the Crown became concerned with the number of people leaving the kingdom and required a license for any who wished to do so.[24]

Many Portuguese were aware of the causes of their manpower and wheat shortages and made suggestions to remedy these problems. These issues surfaced in the correspondence between the city of Lisbon and the Crown. The city council suggested how and why so much money was leaving the country, the reasons for the constant lack of wheat, and what remedies were at hand for this sad state of affairs—collect vagrants and other unemployed persons to work the large, unproductive landholdings in the South and mint special coins that could not be taken out of the country.[25] Complaints in a similar vein continued until the 1630s and then begin to slowly taper off. This is not to say they disappeared altogether; complaints about the lack of wheat continue well through the eighteenth century.

Under the circumstances available to it, the Portuguese Crown went to great lengths to solve an essentially unsolvable problem. In the fifteenth century, it tried to participate in, if not control, the nearby North African grain trade by capturing a series of port cities, beginning with Ceuta in 1415. However, this backfired when the North Africans refused to cooperate under terms dictated by the Portuguese; these ports developed into little more than expensive liabilities. When this attempt to solve the grain problem did not work, the search for West African gold developed into a short-lived but thriving trade with São Jorge da Mina. Agricultural colonies in the Atlantic were established; in particular, several islands in the Azores became permanent sources of grain. The Crown cut its losses in North Africa and imported forced labor to the Alentejo. None of these solutions was effective in the long term. The low agricultural yield, the generally poor growing conditions, and manpower shortages made it difficult (if not impossible) to raise a sufficient quantity of wheat at home. In the long run, the reexport of highly profitable goods from the colonies, such as gold, pepper and other spices, sugar, and diamonds allowed the purchase of the wheat that could not be grown domestically. In turn, this rationale, based almost exclusively on the quest for wheat, explains much of the motivation for the formative period of Portuguese overseas discoveries.

Early Modern Portuguese Society

The uneven population distribution created a landscape where wild open spaces separated the few cities; travel by road was difficult, time consuming, and dangerous. Highway robbers were a frequent feature of the countryside; many of those apprehended were sentenced to work in the Lisbon dockyards, to the galleys, or overseas as soldiers. In the fifteenth century, bears threatened travelers, and throughout early modern times wolves roamed the countryside.[26] Wolves, in fact, were such a threat that in 1655 the Crown offered those convicted in civil cases the option of paying their fines by killing wolves: a large wolf was equal to 3 *milréis* "and an equivalent amount" would be credited for smaller ones.[27] In addition to these hazards, the roads themselves were in a terrible state. Whenever possible, the safest and easiest method of travel between cities was by sea, but sea travelers also faced the risk of corsairs. The fact that most cities were either on or near the coast only tended to reenforce this trend.

The basic social order was similar to that of many other areas of early modern Europe. The vast majority of the population were peasants, the *povo*, involved in agriculture. The remaining segments of the society were those in the religious orders and the nobility. This tripartite division was, not surprisingly, reflected in legislation. In fact, exile overseas was theoretically restricted to the nobility, and commoners were to provide manpower for the state's galleys. Members of the religious orders who committed sins or crimes were usually sentenced by religious courts, although their sentences were similar to members of the other two estates. Other privileges and rights of the nobility were jealously guarded. For example, the *povo* of Lisbon were prohibited from riding around town on horses or in coaches.[28]

Municipalities in Portugal observed a strict order of rank, reflected in their terminology. Although this distinction may be lost on the English-speaker, it was (and is) extremely important to the Portuguese. The smallest areas were known as *povoações* (hamlets), followed by *aldeias* (villages), and then *vilas* (towns). At the top of this urban pecking order were *cidades* (cities). Cities were not only larger, but many retained special privileges or rights (*foros*), sometimes expressed as exemptions granted to their inhabitants. Cities also had the right to be represented in the Cortes, or national parliament, when it was convened.

The vast majority of the locales under discussion in this study were cities, although some towns were also of importance in terms of forced colonization. These same hierarchical distinctions were carried overseas and used in the Portuguese *ultramar*. The area of jurisdiction of a town or city extended well beyond its walls to its *terra* or *termo*—the surrounding countryside. The *terra*, city, parish, and street were the defining characteristics of *patria* —where one was from. These features defined one's background and life; it was through these terms that early modern Portuguese defined themselves in the records when they needed to do so. Exile, or *degredo*, was a terrible and feared punishment precisely for this reason: it separated the criminal (or sinner) from the social and economic lifelines of family and *patria*. It is noteworthy in this context that there is little distinction in Portuguese between the terms *alone* and *lonely*. Indeed, in Portuguese being alone (*estar só*) is to express the need for company. Exile forced the convict to begin a new life, which was both these terms. Being separated from this network made *degredo* a merciful but cruel punishment, to be feared.

The Santa Casa de Misericórdia

Within these towns and cities, two institutions are at the center of this study. Although both were municipally based, each had imperial connections. The *misericórdia* (charitable lay brotherhood) and the *senado da câmara* (city council) were two influential institutions, directing many social aspects of municipal life during early modern times. The forces in Portugal that brought about the creation of the social institution known as the Holy House of Mercy, or Santa Casa de Misericórdia, are still somewhat unclear. However, it is known that this institution was first founded in Lisbon by the Queen Regent Dona Leonor de Lencastre in August 1498.[29] Other chapters of the *misericórdia* quickly spread throughout the Portuguese world.

The *misericórdia* was established as a charitable lay brotherhood directed by a board composed of an equal number of members of the nobility (*irmãos nobres*, or noble brothers) and from the lower classes (*irmãos mecânicos*, or artisans). Serving the *misericórdia* was seen as both a religious duty and as a privilege that brought status and respect within the community. Membership was excluded to all but those who met the highest moral standards, whose motivations were beyond question, and whose bloodlines did not include any New Christian ancestors, those descendants of Jews forcibly converted to Catholicism in the late fifteenth century.

Typical of these membership guidelines were those of the *misericórdia* of Porto. In their revised statutes of 1643, the number of possible brothers was increased from 150 to 250, to be equally divided between nobles and others. In order to join, a background check was mandatory; if the prospective brother were married, the investigation was extended to his wife's family. If unmarried, the brother had to be at least twenty-five, literate, and have no "Moorish" or Jewish ancestors. An eight-day waiting period was observed before anyone could join. Any brother could make a secret complaint regarding any new applicant; final voting was then conducted, using black and white beans as tokens.[30]

Russell-Wood, in his study of the *misericórdia* of Salvador, outlines the fourteen duties of this institution—seven spiritual and seven corporal works, known collectively as "the works of mercy."[31] The spiritual duties were to teach the ignorant, give good counsel, punish transgressors with understanding, console the sorrowful, pardon injuries received, suffer the shortcomings of others, and pray to God for the living and the dead. The corporal duties are what more directly concern this study and consisted of ransoming captives and visiting prisoners, curing the sick, giving clothes to the naked, feeding the hungry, giving water to the thirsty, sheltering travelers and the poor, and burying the dead.

Both the need for the various activities of the *misericórdia* as well as the increased social status attached to membership explain this institution's popularity; chapters were established throughout Portugal and in virtually all of its overseas territories. "Within the year 1498, ten branches were founded in addition to the *misericórdia* of Lisbon. Of these, eight were in Portugal and two in Madeira."[32]

Not surprisingly, the larger cities of Porto and Évora also had more active and influential *misericórdias*. These two chapters, in addition to Lisbon, were perhaps the three most important in Portugal. Within a century, almost one hundred chapters had been established in Portugal, including the Azores and Madeira. This popularity extended to the colonies. To mention only several of the more important examples, during the sixteenth century *misericórdias* were founded in Goa (ca. 1519), Santos (1543), Salvador (ca. 1552), Macau (ca. 1569), Luanda (1576), Rio de Janeiro (ca. 1582), and Mombassa (after 1593).[33] In addition to these, other chapters were begun before 1600 throughout Portuguese Asia in Colombo (Sri Lanka), Cochin, Chaul, Diu, Malacca, Ormuz, Cannanore, and São Tome of Mylapor (Map 1).[34] In the seventeenth century, additional chapters were begun in many of the remaining regions in the empire, such as in Massangano (Angola, begun before 1661), Belém do Pará, and São Luís do Maranhão, the latter two in Brazil's north.[35]

The establishment of a *misericórdia* often went hand-in-hand with the founding of a city; the *misericórdia* quickly became an empire-wide institution and an additional facet of municipal life both at home and overseas. Although these various chapters frequently corresponded with each other and had similar goals, it is important to realize that, like the city councils, each body was independent and responded to the needs of its own community with its own independent finances. In some cases, its financial clout could be considerable.

How a *misericórdia* financed itself is of more than passing interest. The case of seventeenth-century Évora is most instructive, since that city was plagued by a series of misfortunes throughout the 1600s. Nevertheless, the *misericórdia* managed to continue much of its work. Évora began a long decline when its manpower was repeatedly drained to supply imperial needs in India and Brazil. After 1640, many of the campaigns of the War of the Restoration of Portuguese Independence were fought near the city. These campaigns dragged on until the 1660s. At the same time, Portugal was undergoing major economic difficulties associated with high inflation. Nevertheless, the *misericórdia* of Évora was able to continue its work because it had diversified its sources of income. In the second half of the seventeenth century, it received foodstuffs (such as wheat and olive oil), fixed payments from rental incomes, other cash payments, and inheritances as forms of income. Real estate owned by this *misericórdia* extended well beyond a number of houses within the city walls to include plots in the countryside. This diversity allowed the *misericórdia* of Évora to provide social services to an

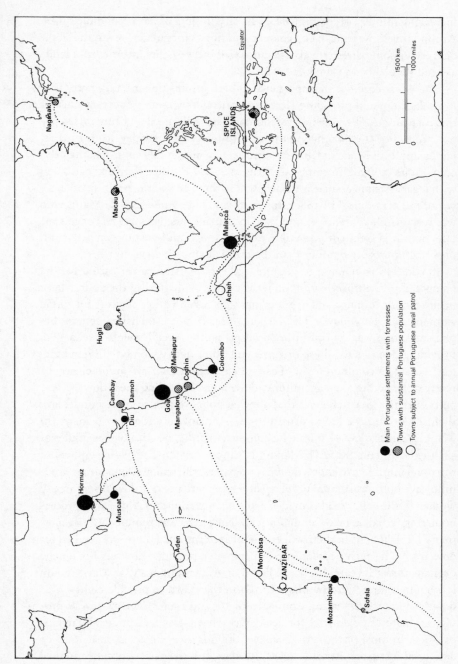

Map 1. The Portuguese in Asia. Reprinted with permission from K.N. Chaudhuri, *Trade and Civilization in the Indian Ocean* (Cambridge: Cambridge University Press, 1985). 70.

Equator

1500 km
1000 miles

Nagasaki

Macau

SPICE
ISLANDS

Malacca

Acheh

Hugli

Meliapur
Colombo
Cochin
Mangalore
Cambay
Damoh
Goa
Diu

Hormuz
Muscat

Aden

Mombasa
ZANZIBAR
Mozambique
Sofala

Main Portuguese settlements with fortresses
Towns with substantial Portuguese population
Towns subject to annual Portuguese naval patrol

increasing number of individuals in the city in spite of hard economic times. Around this same time, Goa's chapter was not as fortunate—even though it did receive some direct royal assistance that increased its income from lands around Bombay and Damão.

The *misericórdia* is of importance to both groups under study here. Visiting, feeding, and providing clothes to prisoners was an important duty of this institution. The judicial system may have sentenced and supervised penal exiles, but the *misericórdia* tended to many of their day-to-day needs. For example, in Braga the *misericórdia* spent considerable sums feeding prisoners in its city jail. In some cases, the *misericórdia* also provided prisoners with legal assistance, such as in Goa, where they created the position of "lawyer of the prisoners." In 1680, this post was held by one Luís de Matos who was responsible for both "white" and local prisoners.[36] As a result of this interaction, it is frequently possible to learn much more about convicts from *misericórdia* records, rather than the more obvious judicial sources.

In addition to tending to prisoners, the responsibility for caring for orphans fell to the *misericórdia* under the duty of sheltering the poor. Many *misericórdias* founded and operated orphanages and other shelters for single women, such as widows. The Lisbon *misericórdia* established several orphanages; one was central in imperial plans, the Recolhimento do Castelo. Providing dowries for these orphans and other needy women "of good virtue" became a common form of assistance from the *misericórdia*, either directly or by acting as an agent for endowments. Providing these dowries was perceived as a charitable act that allowed poor women to marry and "save themselves" from a life of prostitution—the only alternative for many. In Manoel Cardozo's work on the Lisbon *misericórdia*, he cites two examples of such endowments. King D. Manuel I (1495–1521) and several members of the royal family gave endowments for dowries; the widow Dona Simoa Godinho gave both substantial property and money to provide dowries for needy women.[37] Russell-Wood provides additional examples of this same process occurring in Salvador. A home for female orphans was founded in Salvador; many local citizens in their wills remembered the need these women had for dowries.[38] The *misericórdia* in São Paulo also provided dowries for female orphans under its care. In Braga, Pedro de Aguiar and his wife Maria Vieira left enough money to the *misericórdia* in that town to provide eighty-four dowries for such deserving women from 1652 to 1806.[39] The process of providing shelters and dowries for needy women was also well underway in Goa by 1600. In most of these cases above, the *misericórdia* acted on its own or simply as a trustee. In other cases the state and the *misericórdia* combined

Figure 1. Portalegre Town Hall (*câmara*). As it was during early modern times, the *câmara* continues to be one of the centers of life, especially in the smaller cities and towns of Portugal. Photo by author, 1990.

their efforts to reward orphan girls selected for dowries of positions in the state bureaucracy.

The Senado da Câmara

The second institution of importance that had a social impact at the municipal level was the *senado da câmara*. As Boxer has pointed out in his study of this institution, the city council in the early modern Portuguese Empire has not received the attention its role merits.[40] His study, in fact, forms much of what has been written on the subject.

The *câmara* was composed of several aldermen (*vereadores*) and a collection of other municipal officials who supervised aspects of city life. These included a municipal attorney (*procurador*), a representative of the guilds (*mestre*), a justice of the peace (*juiz ordinário*), a probate judge (*juiz dos órfãos*) whose responsibility was to supervise the estates of widows and orphans, a market inspector (*almotacel*), a treasurer, a secretary (*escrivão*), a

Figure 2. The Centro de Estudos Judiciários, located on or near the site of the former Limoeiro Jail. Photo by author, 1996.

constable (*alcaide*), a bailiff (*meirinho*), a doorkeeper (*porteiro*), and other minor officials.[41] A small town might have one of each of the above positions. In larger cities, two or more officials might be elected to divide the workload.

Of the officials listed above, I will return to the role played by the bailiff in the collection and transportation of criminal exiles. The office of the probate judge figures prominently in the administration of estates and the supervision of minors.

The deliberations of the city councils offer valuable insights into the daily lives and dramas played out in many cities and towns. Security, of course, was threatened by the presence of the idle poor (*vadios*), displaced farmers, Gypsies, and newcomers in the city. In addition to maintaining public order, municipal cleanliness was another primary concern of the *câmara*.

In an example of concern for public safety, the Lisbon city council in 1570 attempted to solve the "continual problem of idle and lazy persons" in that city by allowing any unemployed man or woman twenty-one days to get out of town. After that grace period, any idle folk would be exiled to one of the overseas colonies.[42] Three years later, the Crown turned its attention to Gypsies, in one of many decrees on this subject. They were formally expelled from Portugal; thirty days after the decree, any Gypsies remaining in Portugal could be sent to the galleys for life. All their goods were subject to confiscation, half going to the *câmara* where they were found and the other half to the *misericórdia*.[43] The idle poor and Gypsies continued to be the subject of legislation twenty years later.[44]

The Lisbon city council frequently complained about the number of thieves on the streets.[45] In Viana do Castelo in 1631, the local judges and aldermen decided that their city was home to an excess of "idle and lazy foreigners, both men and women" who were responsible for the recent rash of robberies in town. They decreed that these people who were not from the area (*naturais da terra*) had two days to leave town. Residents on each street would be responsible for identifying newcomers. Those who failed to leave within the two days would be taken to jail and fined 6 *milréis* before they would be allowed to leave.[46] The Crown repeatedly ordered that any *vadios* caught in houses where card games were played should be rounded up and sent to India.[47] At one point in Lisbon in 1702, robbery and street crime became so commonplace that the local judges (*julgadores dos barrios*) were allowed to offer rewards of immunity and payments up to 100 *milreis* (if necessary) in order to find the guilty, especially those who had stolen from royal councilors.[48]

In addition to law and order, keeping the city clean was another major concern for the *câmara* and one that both the local authorities and the Crown took seriously. The *câmaras* of Évora, Braga, Elvas, Goa, and Salvador were from time to time preoccupied with municipal cleanliness.[49]

Although maintaining public security and cleanliness may have been paramount, *câmaras* had a range of duties that extended from small to significant. For example, organizing and funding public festivals was one duty of the *câmara*. Many of these festivals were important focal points of municipal life. Expenses could be hefty, such as the 120 *milréis* spent by the *câmara* of Viana do Castelo for the festival to honor the birth of a prince born to King D. Filipe III in 1605.[50] The *câmara* of Évora was also concerned with the details of providing water, keeping the city's aqueduct in good order, and storing wheat.[51] The *câmara* of Goa created the post of slave catcher and had several on the municipal payrolls.[52] This same *câmara* also maintained four municipal jailers, each of whom (in 1574) was paid 400 *reis* monthly.[53] During the campaigns of the War of Restoration of Portuguese Independence, the *câmara* of Elvas (a city also in the middle of many battles in the Alentejo) paid for food and wine for both troops and religious orders.[54]

Some positions were funded by several sources, including the *câmara*.

One of these was that of tutor. The *câmara, misericórdia*, and Crown frequently pooled their resources to fund such schools, as well as orphanages, hospitals, convents, and monasteries. The Goan orphanage of Our Lady of the Mountain (Nossa Senhora da Serra) was funded by this tripartite combination, in addition to its own sources. On other occasions, the *misericórdia* alone might fund one institution, such as a widows' shelter. Many convents and monasteries were largely self-supporting, such as the convent of Santa Mónica in Goa.

The *câmara* and *misericórdia* reproduced themselves in a clonelike manner throughout the Portuguese-speaking world, making them constants in an inconstant world. The legal system and a diverse blend of national councils directed colonization that was further supported by the Catholic Church. I now turn to the punishment of exile and its legal background in Portugal and discuss the mechanics of the system that collected and directed penal exiles.

ONE

The Legal Basis of Exile as Punishment

Exiled convicts are forced to leave their native land and are deprived
of the company of their parents, family, and friends. They will spend
their lives among strangers with unfamiliar ways, and their lives will
be miserable and sad. For this reason, judges should be very cautious
in using this [sentence] and not rush to exile criminals.

—MANUEL LOPES FERREIRA, 1742

In November 1698, Manuel Francisco Villar, the owner of the ship *Menino
Jesus e Nossa Senhora da Piedade*, petitioned the Overseas Council for justice; a series of earlier misadventures had resulted in the loss of his boat and
all its contents. The captain of this ship, João Nunes Freire, picked up one
hundred criminal-soldiers from the island of Madeira for transport to Maranhão. The Overseas Council had strongly suggested that a forceful leader
be on board—someone who could command the respect of these future soldiers—since they were not volunteers.[1] Along the way, a leader did emerge,
but it was hardly the figure envisioned by the Crown. D. João de Arez, his
son, and two nephews commandeered the ship, locked the captain in the
prow, and forced the pilot to chart a course for Margarita Island in the Spanish West Indies. The governor of that island eventually sold the ship and all
its contents; the one hundred men disappeared from the documents. However, D. João de Arez was taken back to Iberia, escaped from jail and returned
to his home on Madeira. This gave the ship's owner an opportunity to seek
redress.[2]

21

In the next four chapters, I will examine how such a military and logistical fiasco could occur. First, I turn to the historical and legal foundations supporting the use of exile as punishment. The three subsequent chapters examine the beginnings of exile at home and abroad, the imperial reality of penal exile, and the remarkable flexibility this system demonstrated.

The Roman Basis of Exile (degredo) and Its Place in Portuguese Law

Portuguese legal codes from the early modern period classify exile (that is, having one's status degraded by a limitation placed on movement, labor, or speech) on the basis of seven or eight types, all of which are based on Roman law.[3] Portuguese law during much of the early modern period falls into one of three distinct periods. The *Ordenações Manuelinas* were codified at the beginning of the sixteenth century and remained in effect until the *Ordenações Filipinas* were collected and issued approximately one hundred years later in 1602. This latter collection was current throughout the seventeenth and much of the eighteenth century but was amended by *leis extravagantes*, or uncodified legislation.[4]

In both *Ordenações*, sentences of exile were classified in the order listed below, from the least to the most serious:[5]

1. Away from one's town or region. The punishment of *fora da vila* (out of town) was relatively minor. Exile could be more specific, such as "out of bishopric" or "out of nearby lands" (*terra*) but, for the purposes of this study, these can be lumped together.

2. To a monastery (for members of the clergy only); this form of exile often curtailed speech as well.[6]

3. To a designated place for a specific number of years.

4. (a) To a designated place for an indefinite period at the king's discretion, or (b) To a designated place without a stated length.

5. To the galleys, a quasi-independent system.

6. To a designated place for life.

7. From Portugal and all its colonies for life, with a concurrent loss of nationality.

Clerics, monks, and married men could all be exiled, but special exemptions were given to the nobility. In particular, nobles were not to be sentenced to the galleys.[7] In theory, *degredo* was actually reserved exclusively for the nobility and exile to the galleys exclusively for commoners. Although members of the nobility did not find themselves in the galleys, common folk more often than not found themselves overseas. In legal theory the punishment of *degredo* may have been exclusively for members of the nobility, yet in practice it was clearly extended to all members of Portuguese society.[8] Foreigners were not to be sent to the overseas colonies and were usually simply banished from Portugal.[9]

Actually, the Portuguese slightly modified the Roman definition of deportation and used the Roman legal concept of relegation: "a sentence for the condemned to remain in a place of their choosing or for a specific time or for life."[10] Denaturalization and permanent banishment from Portugal was one of the most severe weapons at the disposal of the early modern Portuguese state. Although the state seemed hesitant to use it, a few laws suggest that the punishment was not abandoned. For example, a 1645 decree made leaving the kingdom without permission or license punishable by permanent denaturalization.[11] An example from a century later (1746) shows this punishment still on the books and being used.[12] As with the use of the death penalty, all indications are that the early modern Portuguese state was unwilling to use it and only did so as a last resort. Because of its rare application, the few examples encountered virtually leap from the documents. One such case was the unfortunate Luís Francisco de Assis Sanches de Baena. In 1744 he abandoned his place of assigned exile in Miranda and moved across the Spanish border to Zamora to arrange his marriage. For this crime, he was stripped of his nationality, any honors, income, interest, and pensions. Furthermore, he was forbidden to contract any further business in Portugal.[13]

All seven of these levels of *degredo* were used by the Portuguese legal system. In a fascinating twist to this process one of the most fundamental distinctions in modern law—that between civil and criminal punishment—was deliberately blurred. When the courts deemed it expedient, criminal sentences of exile were abandoned and fines substituted. Internal exile, the most lenient form of this punishment, was an early and frequent casualty of substitution by fine.[14] In other, more practical ways, the Crown differentiated between those exiled internally and those who served its interests overseas since it clearly recognized the former and encouraged the latter.[15] Not stated, but clearly understood, was that those sentenced overseas were not free, frequently waited for extended periods to begin their exiles, and served long, sometimes indefinite, terms in the colonies.

Figure 3. The Pillory of Elvas. The pillory was a central feature in every town and city in the Portuguese world during early modern times. The *câmara*, local bishops and lords, as well as local judges, used it to punish offenders for petty crimes that did not merit exile. Photo by author, 1990.

Crimes Punished by Degredo *and the Galleys*

Broadly speaking, crimes in Portugal punished by the above-mentioned forms of exile can be classified into three types: minor, serious, and absolutely unpardonable.[16] All three were punished by exile and perhaps fines. Although this classification may strike the reader as vague, I have deliberately avoided the use of modern legal terms such as *felony* and *misdemeanor* because these legal distinctions were lacking in early modern Portugal. The courts and legal codes made a distinction along the lines of minor, serious, and very serious.

Minor infractions, such as passing notes to those in jail, usually resulted in internal exile or perhaps a few years overseas. Criminals who committed crimes in the other two categories are at the center of this study. A list of these crimes provides a fascinating insight into what authorities felt threatened the social order in early modern times: blasphemy, murder, committing an injury, kidnapping, rape, witchcraft, attacking jailers, entering a convent with dishonorable intentions, committing damage for money, injuring someone in a procession, or harming a judge. These were the crimes labeled *serious* and were frequently listed as those not forgiven in general pardons—at times when all others were.[17] Four crimes or sins fell into the last category of absolutely unpardonable: heresy, treason (lese-majesty), counterfeiting, and sodomy. At times, falsifying papers was considered counterfeiting and was included with this list; on other occasions it was omitted.[18]

The question then arises as to why those guilty of these specific four crimes or sins were singled out for special punishment. The answer to this seemingly straightforward question is actually quite complex: these crimes threatened the early modern Portuguese state at its theological, political, economic, and social foundations. A number of other early modern powers had a similar preoccupation with these specific crimes.[19]

Of these four crimes or sins, the documentation on sodomy is particularly rich. King D. Sebastião seemed to hold this sin above others as especially evil. In 1571, he passed a decree against this practice, supplementing earlier decrees already on the books, such as that of 1506 that made sodomy punishable by being burned at the stake with all the goods owned by the guilty confiscated by the Crown.[20] Statements denouncing individuals for this practice could be given freely, and neither they nor the names of any individuals would be made public, even in the trial. The person making the statement received half the goods of the guilty party and was forgiven of any wrong doing. In the event that the individual did not have any goods, the state would pay the informer 100 *cruzados* from the royal treasury. The guilty party could be tortured and the names extracted of any friends with which he committed this sin. Noteworthy here is the fact that the Crown retained the legal possibility of applying the death penalty but clearly preferred not to use it. Instead, it recommended that individuals guilty of sodomy be punished severely, preferably by being sent to the galleys.[21] In accordance with these wishes, the viceroy of India in 1571 deported Martim Afonso from the Estado da India to Lisbon, presumably to work in the galleys. In addition, in a move suggesting that Martim was found guilty after being denounced, the king ordered the confiscation of the goods that had belonged to Afonso's deceased father.[22] In 1575 it was suggested to the Casa da Suplicação that it would be a good idea to exile several *fidalgos* to the kingdom of the Congo or to Príncipe Island, as long as they were not guilty of this sin.[23] A 1606 law further modified King D. Sebastião's earlier ideas. Anyone caught engaging in this sin would be sent to the galleys for seven years. If a noble, he would be exiled to Angola for an equal period, without the possibility of appeal. If it were the second conviction for this sin, the punishment could be increased to death.[24]

Sodomy was not the only sin watched and judged in the state's courts. In a rather jaded social commentary, Jerónimo de Azevedo, the viceroy of the Estado da India in the early 1600s, wrote the Crown that "those guilty of sloth will be punished through the courts, as their serious sin merits. In regard to giving false testimony, this is a much older vice around these parts and will not be easy to get rid of."[25] Blasphemy was a sin punishable by exile or service in the galleys. Specifically, individuals who doubted the existence of God or the Virgin Mary, used either name in vain, or questioned the authority of the church faced such penalties as walking thirty times around the village pillory (an omnipresent feature in villages and towns throughout the Portuguese Empire) and payment of a fine, three years' exile in Africa, or the galleys. Questioning the power of saints could result in one year in Africa or in the galleys. Punishment varied upon the status of the sinner and the number of times sin had been committed: nobles faced one to three years in Africa and a heavy fine; and commoners could face up to three years in the galleys.[26]

Anyone who injured a judge or another official, such as a city councilman, an inspector of weights and measures, a bailiff or his secretary, doorkeeper, assistant, or a witness giving testimony, faced a possible sentence of having his hand cut off and of ten years in exile to Africa. If the injury were to someone else, exile was for four years to Africa, only. If the injury were only by word, two years to Africa would suffice. If the guilty were sent to Brazil, they should sent in chains if they were a noble or a tradesman (*mecánico*).[27] Any soldier trying to jump ship could be exiled.[28] Any soldier interfering with the state tobacco monopoly, or selling tobacco on his own, could lose credit for his years of service and be exiled to Angola for five years.[29] By the early 1600s, purchasing stolen goods was one of the many crimes punishable by time in the galleys.[30] Some crimes were less specific, such as "going astray." This landed Bartholomeu de Cabedo de Vasconcelos in jail in 1623 and was why he was exiled to India.[31] "Because of the frequency of murders, robberies, and other crimes," slaves over the age of fifteen caught wandering the streets of Goa after seven in the evening could be sentenced to life in the galleys in Goa. Although that prohibition in all likelihood had more to do with personal vendettas than a general "crime wave," the punishment is what is of interest here. The person who submitted the slave to justice officials was to be paid half the value of the slave. In the event that two or more slaves were encountered and they were armed, they were both to be killed and the person who encountered them to be paid 20 *pardáos*.[32]

Punishment to the galleys was used for a wide variety of crimes and sins. For example, any slave guilty of hitting, hurting, or wounding a Portuguese could spend the rest of his life at the oars.[33] Any subjects of the Ottoman Sultan caught in Portuguese lands were to be sent to the galleys for as long as the king decreed. This included Armenians, Arabs, Greeks, and Persians.[34]

The Inquisition and Sins Punished by Degredo

Within the confines of this study, it is notable that exile was one of the punishments most frequently used by the Inquisition during early modern times, particularly during the seventeenth century. Tribunals of the Holy Office, as it was known, were headquartered in the three Portuguese cities of Lisbon, Coimbra, and Évora. In addition, a fourth tribunal was established in Goa. Unfortunately, the bulk of the records of this last body have disappeared. Nevertheless, the cases of the three domestic courts remain and have been examined in increasing detail in the past few years. Although several excellent studies have been done on these tribunals, with the exception of Pieroni's work one issue that has gone without comment is central here: the use of exile as punishment.[35] In this case, exile was the sentence for committing a sin. Also of note is the fact that the state's judicial system and the Tribunals of the Holy Office of the Inquisition coordinated the locations of their sentences of exile as well as the supply of manpower needed by the Crown for its galleys. Prisoners in the Inquisition's jails were channeled on a system parallel to that run by the state. These two systems eventually merged in Lisbon; sinners sentenced to exile or the galleys were turned over to the jailer of exiles in Lisbon's Limoeiro jail, where the state's system also brought its criminals.

The data presented in Table 3 summarize the frequency of various sins in the 748 cases resulting in punishments of exile from the Inquisition in Portugal from 1662 to 1699. These cases represent approximately 40 percent of those before that body in this period. Of these, around one-third were women. These data have been compiled and presented here for two reasons.

TABLE 3

Sins Before the Holy Office of the Inquisition Punished
by Exile or Galley Service, 1662–1699

Sin	Percent	Number
1. Bigamy	23	167
2. Not stated or not clear	18	128
3. Witchcraft	12	87
4. Judaism	11	83
5. Giving false testimony	9	61
6. Relapsing [to Judaism]	7	50
7. Sodomy	5	41
8. Profanity and blasphemy	5	33
9. Breaking first sentence of exile	4	30
10. Soliciting [in the confessional]	2	16
11. Interfering with the work of the Holy Office	1	11
12. Pretending to be part of the Holy Office	1	8

SOURCE: BNL, códice 199, (F100) Lists of Sentences from the Lisbon, Évora, and Coimbra Tribunals.

First, the critical period of the late seventeenth century in the Portuguese world was one with far more demands on Portugal's limited manpower than were ever available. How the church and state coordinated their efforts under pressure offers yet another glimpse of their cooperation during this especially difficult period of high inflation and general economic instability. This, coupled with the War of the Restoration of Portuguese Independence (1640–1668) and, using Boxer's phrase, the "global struggle with the Dutch," make the late seventeenth century an excellent period to examine. Second, the frequency of sins committed offers its own commentary of what the Inquisition saw fit to prosecute and how.

In addition to the Inquisition, punishment for a number of sins could be reserved for bishops, particularly the Bishop of Lisbon. Within this dovetailing legal system of church and state, bishops had the right to exile persons guilty of the sins listed above (table 3) as well as a number of others, including arson, homicide (other than in a "just war"), failure to pay debts amounting to more than 200 *réis*, and creating or using false writings as holy scripture.[36] Such prisoners exiled by bishops were to be held with other *degredados* in civil jails.[37]

How the Transportation System Functioned

An intricate system supervised the collection and transportation of *degredados*. The first comprehensive royal decree passed in Portugal regarding a system for transporting criminals during early modern times appears to be that of King D. Sebastião, signed in 1575 and reissued with only one small change by King D. Filipe II in 1583.[38] This same king had organized a similar system for Spain almost twenty years earlier.[39] The manuscript version uncovered in the archives provides a great deal more detail of how the system was to operate than do the various printed versions of the law.[40] A separate *regimento* directing labor to the galleys was in effect no later than 1626.

By 1610, for administrative functions, Portugal was divided into six provinces and twenty-seven judicial districts, or *comarcas*.[41] Each superior magistrate (*ouvidor* or *corregedor*) was responsible for those sentenced to exile from his *comarca*. Criminals were forwarded to his court from each of the subdistricts headed by a *juiz da fora*, a "judge from outside" appointed by the Crown, "the lowest rank of the professional judiciary."[42] It was the duty of the *ouvidor* to arrange for the transportation of these criminals in gangs or levies (*levas*), consisting of a minimum of six criminals, to the neighboring district on the road to Lisbon. In this manner, prisoners were passed "from district to district [to reach Lisbon] from the other jails in the Kingdom, along with their documentation."[43] From time to time, the Crown issued reminders that the system was there to be followed, as it did in its letter to the *câmara* of Coimbra in 1628: "In the jails of that city there are several *degredados* who should be brought in the manner prescribed by law to this city [Lisbon] so that they can leave to complete their *degredo*."[44] The *regimento* also stipulated that the criminal was not to be detained in jail longer than three months before being transported. This was obviously intended to be a general guideline since it was possible that an individual would remain longer than three months before five other exiles appeared in jail or he would have to transported at the end of three months in a group smaller than six. Those prisoners of the upper classes, in deference to their social standing, were only chained at the foot and were not to have chains across their chests.[45] The route, according to the *regimento*, should be changed "from time to time to maintain the security of the *degredados*." This was, of course, an indication of the general peril travelers faced all over early modern Europe. In addition, "the road to Lisbon" was not as vague as the phrase might sound. A convict's associates would also have known where and how he would be transported and could have easily attempted to liberate their friend. A special jailer and several assistants conducted the men along their way to Lisbon and were paid a set salary, collected at the point of origin.[46]

Security along the route was important. The state stood to lose manpower for its galleys as well as a section of its colonial troops. This, as well as a more fundamental issue of maintaining public order, motivated the state to supervise the process closely and ensure that all exiles reached Lisbon safely—in chains. On occasion, more than a few criminals must have been able to escape the arm of the law by crossing over the border into Spain. In spite of a long history of hostility, both the Spanish and the Portuguese Crowns were willing to sign extradition agreements for such criminals, first in 1568 for parties guilty of treason and later in 1703 for murderers.[47]

As the chain gang passed through each district, any exiles awaiting transportation could be added to it. Eventually, the levy would reach the main jail of Lisbon, Limoeiro, located above the cathedral and the Alfama and below St. George's Castle. Limoeiro had been designated for this function since 1481 when this building, housing the former national mint, became Lisbon's principal civil jail.[48]

Once in Lisbon, the exiles were placed in a separate wing of the jail, under the supervision of the jailer of exiles. There is documentation to suggest that while they were in the Limoeiro jail, prisoners received some special medical attention, if required.[49] For example, in 1642 the city of Lisbon ordered that, in the best interests of the city, sick prisoners, including a group of Spaniards captured near the border, should be removed from Limoeiro and taken to the hospital (*casa da saude*).[50] The jail of Limoeiro itself was notorious for the periodic illnesses that swept through it. In 1639, for example, the Council of State suggested to the king that those convicts in Limoeiro jail departing for India be removed from "the evil odors of the Lisbon jail" to the more healthy prison in Almada.[51] The process of attending to sick prisoners continued throughout early modern times; in 1758 the Crown was placing them in the royal hospital of São João de Deus.[52]

Convicted exiles had their documents checked at every stage of the transportation process; these were eventually surrendered to the Limoeiro jailer. Exiles-to-be came into the Lisbon jail via this state-run system that collected them from all over the country. The few areas of Portugal not administered by the judiciary in *comarcas* were controlled by the military orders. Individuals sentenced to exile by one of these orders were also handed over to the head jailer in Lisbon.[53] He, in turn, was required to keep a book listing all exiles in his care; his secretary was obliged to keep an additional copy. In short,

Limoeiro jail was the critical focal point in this entire system. It was where all exiles were channeled, regardless of the type or location of the sentencing court. From Limoeiro *degredados* were either entrusted to the master of the galleys or placed on board ships embarking for the colonies.

In line with other early modern European penal practices, from time to time prisoners convicted of minor crimes were freed from jail in celebration of important national events. Such was the case in 1598, when some petty criminals were released in honor of the coronation of King D. Filipe III.[54] In 1656, in honor of the coronation of the new queen, prisoners guilty of minor crimes were freed—a decree also extended to soldiers.[55] Selected prisoners in Goa's jails were released in 1657 to honor the coronation of King D. Afonso VI.[56] Similar pardons were repeated in 1666 and 1687 in honor of entrances into Lisbon of the queen and in 1669, 1688, and 1689 for the birth of children in the royal family.[57] In 1711, prisoners guilty of "crimes of minor consideration," were given their freedom in honor of the birth of Princess D. Maria Barbara.[58] However, many exiles were not included in these fortunate groups of the pardoned. Their more serious crimes did not allow them to be pardoned so easily.

Unfortunately, only one jailer's book mandated by these requirements was uncovered in the archives.[59] This small but fascinating list of convicts, about to become exiles, offers a detailed view of a group of Limoeiro inmates during a three-year (1688–1691) period. Of the fifty-four prisoners listed, eight were women. In terms of length of their stay in jail, Manuel Jorge had been detained for the longest period, more than three years.[60] Pedro Fialho only stayed in jail one month before his sentence was delivered. Several inmates appear to have escaped when this list was compiled, notably António Francisco. Escape was not unusual; only ten years earlier Prince Regent D. Pedro himself had noted that jailers were allowing prisoners to escape in large numbers.[61] Only one convict from this list, João Rodrigues, died in jail. This was an unusually low mortality rate for early modern prisons, especially given the unhealthy state of Limoeiro. Among the crimes committed, murder was the overwhelming reason for exile: twenty-one of the thirty-four cases where the crime was stated indicated murder as the charge. In those remaining, murder and theft would be safe guesses for many, given their prominence on this list, as well as in a larger sample from 1694 to 1696.[62]

The various chain gangs outlined in the guidelines are clearly indicated in this jailer's book, specifically those from Castelo Branco (via Santarém, two different gangs, one arriving 28 April 1689 and the other 2 December 1689), from Beja (arriving 24 July 1689), and from Faro. Levies such as these were not unusual and were a feature of daily life in Iberia; Cervantes, for example, mentioned them in *Don Quijote*.[63]

One of the charitable duties the Santa Casa de Misericórdia performed was to feed and clothe indigent prisoners. There is ample evidence to suggest that, on many occasions, the deportation process itself—the chain gang from the provinces to Lisbon and departure overseas from Limoeiro—was accelerated because of these costs to the various local *misericórdias*. A gentle reminder to this effect was passed in the form of a 1604 *alvará* (royal decree) stating that prisoners under the care of the *misericórdia* should be sentenced and dispatched as quickly as possible.[64] In March 1622 alone, the *misericórdia* of Évora spent some 1$940 *réis* on food for prisoners in the city's jail, although that figure was small when compared with expenses on other forms of charity.[65] In the fiscal year 1652–1653, this same body spent 79$000 *réis* on prisoners and an additional 28$000 *réis* on their medical expenses, representing about 6 percent of its budget. The next fiscal year, the *misericórdia* of Évora spent approximately 3 percent of its total income on prisoners.[66] In 1655–1656, that *misericórdia* spent around 2 percent of its income on prisoners; in 1657–1658 that figure was almost 4 percent. The *misericórdia* of Braga also spent considerable sums on feeding prisoners in its municipal jail.[67] In Porto, the *misericórdia* made a request, which was granted, that prisoners in the local jails who had been sentenced to exile in India, and who did not leave on the annual fleet, be resentenced for exile elsewhere by the *relação* (high court) of Porto.[68] The obvious motivation was financial; the petition was made in June and the *misericórdia* would have had at least another six months before these prisoners would have left for India. In another example, the *misericórdia* of Funchal complained in 1689, "People from all the other towns on the Island [Madeira], where they have committed crimes, were being held at the jail here." It asked that these prisoners be transported back to jails in their native towns, where they committed the crimes, and that this situation (that is, expense) be avoided in the future.[69] The *misericórdia* of Goa in 1576 noted that *degredados* in the jails there "should leave at once if sentenced to a fort in India, Diu, Malacca, the Moluccas, or elsewhere in the *Estado da India*." Those few "sentenced to exile in Portugal, Santa Helena, São Tomé, or Brazil should remain in prison."[70]

Independently of the *misericórdia* and its financial burden, agents of the Crown also urged that the transportation process proceed quickly. In Lisbon in 1674, the shipment of prisoners from Porto arrived after the ships for India had left; the Crown ordered their sentences reviewed and changed because they could not be held until the next fleet.[71] In another example, for the month of May 1693, the *câmara* (not the *misericórdia*) of Elvas spent 1$600 *réis* for prisoners in that city's jail.[72] Delays of two to three years did occur and were what both the *misericórdia* and the Crown attempted to avoid, each in its own way. The *misericórdia* reminded, and the Crown attempted to accelerate the process by decree. Neither side, in spite of its best efforts, could prod a sluggish judiciary to ensure a prompt dispatch of the convicted. This situation endured through the entire early modern period. In 1734, the Crown was informed that many people were in Limoeiro jail awaiting sentencing and ordered that sentences be handed down promptly for people guilty of similar crimes and that it be notified of action taken.[73]

The ideal situation for this process was for the ships of the *carreira da India* to leave Lisbon at the end of January or early February and that a group of *degredados* be on board.[74] On numerous occasions, the Crown attempted to coordinate these two distinct processes. One such example occurred in 1632 when the Crown was making a systematic effort to get prisoners on board the boats for Brazil and India. Royal correspondence directed to the Évora city council in December asked them to send prisoners from the *comarcas* of Évora and Beja, with the usual documentation.[75] Ten years later, the Crown ordered the *corregedor da comarca* to hand over prisoners for Brazil to the *juiz da fora* of Évora, "as is done with criminal exiles" and to pay the usual expenses.[76] Unfortunately, lethargy and inefficiency in the judicial system were only reinforced by logistical problems with the navy.[77] Clearly, the judicial process of transporting these people overseas was slow and cumbersome and was only made that much more so when coupled with problems supplying and preparing the departure of the annual fleets. The Crown did eventually find an expedient manner around this problem, but not until the mid-seventeenth century.

Much of the basic logistical effort centered on the head of the Limoeiro jail. It was his responsibility to monitor ships departing from Lisbon and to match exiles with their intended destinations. He had the power to seize the sails from any ship that refused to accept *degredado* passengers. Captains were also required to report the date and destinations of planned departures to the judiciary.[78] The jailer was responsible for drawing up the updated *cartas de guia* (legal papers) for each batch of departing *degredados*. He was to keep the original and send one copy with the ship's captain; the captain's copy would be submitted to the judge in the exile locale. These papers were to include the personal and legal background on each exile: his or her name, parents, hometown, distinguishing features, crime committed, and sentence given. In spite of these bureaucratic safeguards envisioned by the Crown, intact lists of departing *degredados* are rare. The few encountered do not state all the information required in these rules, but they do include some information about each exile, indicating at least a passing familiarity with the requirements. Several examples of longer *cartas de guia* were encountered in archives, one from 1669 and 1670, a similar list from 1755, and a third from 1783.[79] Boxer has published an additional example of what he calls "a fair cross-section of several hundred entries" of such *cartas de guia* from the municipal records of Luanda in the first half of the eighteenth century.[80]

This process of transporting criminals to the colonies depended on several other key figures in addition to judges and jailers. The captain of a departing ship came to play a central role as an agent for the state. Once an exile was on board ship, the captain or pilot was charged with holding his or her papers and submitting them to the judicial or ecclesiastical authorities in the exile location.[81] This scenario is worthy of a few additional comments. On the one hand, these ships were required to accept *degredado* passengers, something they clearly may not have wanted to do. After all, these were criminals; some of them were undoubtedly dangerous—all were potential troublemakers. This accounts for the Lisbon jailer having the authority to remove sails from ships—thus forcing them to cooperate. On the other hand, ships were notoriously understaffed. More than one captain must have been tempted to enlist *degredados* as sailors. A quick perusal of the Limoeiro list shows examples of this dilemma. Some individuals appear to have been hardened criminals, such as Manuel Gomes, convicted of murdering his wife and Antonio Morou. Others such as Manuel Jorge and Manuel Boieyro were youths guilty of minor offenses; both might have made acceptable sailors. The captain was then torn between the need to obtain sufficient manpower to run his ship and the duty to act as a penal transporter for the state. The *regimento* had built-in safeguards to ensure that the state's interests were met first. Failure to turn over the *degredado* and his documents to the appropriate authorities within one year of leaving Lisbon resulted in a fine. A further check on the captain's honesty was maintained by copies of these lists kept and distributed by the secretary of Limoeiro. The secretary was required to keep, in addition to a book of exiles, a list showing exile locations, names of dispatched criminals, departure dates, and names of ships. An additional copy of this book was to be sent to the Conselho da India.[82] These provisions regarding the registry of *degredados* were repeated in 1658, suggesting (as does the lack of existing documentation) that these laws were not being followed, in spite of the Crown's intentions.[83] Clearly, the registration requirements for *degredados* were not being met. Much later, the Crown decided that papers alone were not sufficient; by the early eighteenth century, the punishment of exile was announced in public, along with the crime committed.[84]

Once in the colony, exiles were not detained and were free to roam within the confines of that district. In a decree of 1534, King D. João III specifically forbade the beating of *degredados* and stated they should be treated in the same manner as everyone else.[85] The local judge was informed of the exile's presence in his district only when the ship's captain turned over the *carta de guia*. The judge's role was to act as a probation officer, although documentation showing a judge intervening in the day-to-day life of an exile is lacking. Exiles had two restrictions placed on their freedom: (1) they were not allowed to leave the district; and (2) they were not allowed to hold any office in the state or local bureaucracy, such as on the city council. The first restriction was maintained by requiring licenses to depart and by severe punishments given to captains who disregarded them. The second was maintained in laws on the books and through frequent reminders, such as that to the governor of Cabo Verde in 1676. Paragraph seventeen in the outline of his duties specifically forbade him from allowing *degredados* to occupy any position in the bureaucracy.[86] A similar *regimento* for the governor of Angola in the same year contained the same restrictions for exiles.[87] There is ample evidence to suggest that neither restriction was followed as strictly as the law required. Shortages of qualified Portuguese to staff positions, such as those on the *câmara*, were particularly acute on São Tomé throughout most of the seventeenth century. In 1655, Cristovão de Barros Rego, governor of the island, made this complaint to the Crown and requested that *degredados* who were "so inclined that they could be useful" be sent there.[88] In one example alone, it is possible to see both restrictions being ignored. António de Sousa Falcão, in spite of his sentence of *degredo* for life to India, returned to Portugal because of a number of deaths in his family. António petitioned the Overseas Council for permission to serve in the position promised as his wife's dowry at the Fort of Damão. The Overseas Council and the king agreed that he should be allowed to occupy the post, regardless of being a *degredado*.[89]

Degredados were allowed to work and were paid for their labor. Perhaps it would be more accurate to say that a *degredado* was paid by the state as frequently as was anyone else. Increasingly throughout the late sixteenth and seventeenth centuries, the Portuguese state was a poor and tardy paymaster. For example, in 1613, the Conselho da Fazenda (Treasury Council) in Goa discussed the problems of paying isolated soldiers in Mozambique and commented on how they had not been paid promptly in some time and were lacking basic supplies.[90] This point is readily evident in the correspondence of the time, as well as developed in the literature, and needs no additional comment here. What is important in this case was that *degredados* were not slaves and, at least in theory, were paid for their labor. Those sent to the galleys were paid as well, although these insignificant payments did not provide sufficient food for galley workers.

There seems to have been some early confusion by the Crown on this point of payment of *degredados*. In 1515, Afonso de Albuquerque made payments of 1$000 *réis* (each) to two *degredados*: Gonçalo de Évora, a stonemason, and Estévão Gonçalves, a sailor. Neither man had received a salary "since they were *degredados*."[91] Nevertheless, salaries were listed for soldiers and sailors later, and many of these were *degredados*. Separating *degredados* from volunteers in Asia, while attempting to create a regiment of soldiers for example, would have been an impossible task given the state's lax supervision, the constant need for soldiers, and the equally constant shortage of Portuguese manpower. In some cases, *degredados* were clearly identified as such, yet received payments along with the other soldiers in a fort or troop. One early example of payments made to *degredados* can be found at the Fortress of Sofala during the first twenty years of the sixteenth century.[92] More often than not, it simply was in the best interests of the state, the recruiting captain, and the individuals concerned to ignore any distinctions between *degredados* and volunteers.

Provided that his or her exile was not for life, a *degredado* was free to return to Portugal once the terms of the sentence were completed. In theory, a *degredado* was required to obtain a certificate attesting to good behavior from local residents and to have these statements certified by the presiding magistrate. In some areas, such as Sri Lanka, the captain-general was responsible for issuing this certificate.[93] In other areas, such as Luanda, it was the *câmara*'s responsibility to register *degredados* upon arrival and generally supervise their presence.[94] Once the conditions of exile had been satisfied, the *degredado* could resume his or her previous life, a *degredado* no longer.

Two examples underline the legal theory of an exile's right to return upon completion of the sentence. In a letter of 1692 to the viceroy of India, the Crown pointed out that those *degredados* sent there who had completed their sentences should be given permission to return to Portugal, if they so desired, stating "only when there is a need for more soldiers there should this permission be denied to those who went with an indefinite period of exile."[95] At the beginning of the eighteenth century, a series of three decrees on regulating the return of Indian *degredados* was exchanged between Goa and Lisbon. In 1706, the viceroy, "wishing to avoid chaos," insisted that "all persons wishing to depart the *Estado da India* can only do so with royal permission." [96] The next year, the Crown passed a similar decree stating that licenses were "the best way to keep that State from becoming empty of the people who could defend it." [97] The Crown the next year, in a transparent effort to extract what service it could from its remaining soldiers in India, reduced the minimum of years of service before repatriation from ten to eight.[98] In the last example of this right of return, in 1777 Queen Maria I wrote to the governor of India informing him that, "not only the disabled soldiers but *degredados* who have completed their exile and who wish to return to this Kingdom [Portugal] should be allowed to do so, since to do otherwise would be an injustice." [99]

The Crown was not always so concerned with injustice, but, on numerous occasions, allowed expediency to rule, particularly in regard to those sentenced to the galleys. There are pieces of evidence that suggest that the system—or at least its main parts—was followed, and that criminal exiles were allowed to return to Portugal upon completion of their time overseas. Aires Teles de Meneses was one such individual allowed to return from Goa after he spent six years in exile. He and his family, as well as their servants, were given permission to return on their own boat in 1676.[100] Sebastião Pires Cardoso was another *degredado* allowed to return. After having served the Crown for eight years in the Alentejo, he was exiled to India for five. By 1697, he had completed those five years and then some. He requested and received a certificate showing completion of exile.[101]

This was how the system was supposed to work. The thrust of this transportation system was to make various officials personally responsible for passing on the exiles under their care to the following stage of the system. Two small additions to this system were added in the 1580s to further refine it. Anyone not producing the necessary documentation at any stage of this process could be jailed; in addition, the finances of individual *degredados* were registered.[102] If the *regimento* had been followed as it was outlined, it would have created masses of documentation, in particular at Limoeiro prison. Judging from the scant evidence uncovered in three years of archival research, it would first appear that the system was not followed or that the documentation was not produced in the quantities required. It is possible that much of the documentation was destroyed in the 1755 earthquake that leveled the main jail of Lisbon and any records that may have been contained there, as well as those in the Ministry of the Marine, which would have contained the galley records. However, the surviving bits and pieces presented here from archives around Portugal as well as a few scattered references to this system indicate that it probably was followed more or less in the manner indicated by King D. Sebastião's 1578 decree. The one jailer's list uncovered certainly shows this system in operation in the late seventeenth century. While that list is perhaps the most convincing single piece of evidence, the remaining pieces of documentation (cited here) make no sense whatsoever when considered individually, outside the system outlined here. In addition, the evidence from the post-1755 period is overwhelming. The various books from the judge of the *degredados* (*juizio dos degredados*) clearly indicate the system being followed as it was outlined by these regimes.

It also becomes obvious, after even quick scrutiny, that the system was riddled with flaws. Where and how they appear can be most revealing; nevertheless, they do not detract from the overall effort made by the early modern Portuguese state. If anything, they provide further evidence of its systematic effort to extract what it could from all of its citizens, including criminals. Supervising prisoners such as these was not only expensive and time-consuming; prisoners caused trouble at every stage of the process. In 1617 in Castelo Branco, for example, disturbances in the city allowed prisoners to escape from jail.[103] Convicts often attempted to escape (and sometimes succeeded) on the way to Lisbon or while in Limoeiro or another jail, such as in Coimbra, where the worried Crown wrote the Câmara in 1660 that "many prisoners have fled from your jails and many more appear to be determined to flee."[104] A chain gang making its way from Porto to Lisbon in 1656 stopped in Santarém where the entire levy escaped.[105] Frequent laws punishing jailers for allowing prisoners to escape give ample testimony to the effectiveness of bribes and the laxity of jailers. One of many of these decrees was an *alvará* of Prince Regent Pedro. In order to prevent additional cases of jailers "in Lisbon and all over the Kingdom allowing prisoners to escape," the Prince decreed that the penalty for this crime would be two years in Castro Marim and a 20$000 *réis* fine for the first offense. In the event of a repeated case, the punishment was twice as long in Castro Marim and the fine doubled.[106] These laws were renewed in 1681, when salaries for the jailers in Porto and Lisbon were set at 60$000 and 80$000 *réis*, respectively.[107] The problem of serious offenders either escaping or simply being released while their trials were pending "because the jail was lacking in comfort" continued throughout the early modern period. Broadsides published in 1754 demanded that those guilty of crimes meriting the death penalty not be allowed to wander around freely.[108]

Long delays the convicted faced in jails thwarted the financial interests of the *misericórdia* and the security concerns of the Crown. Further, prisoners escaped or were held far too long. The Crown was still making complaints in 1754 about these problems.[109] A decree from the Desembargo do Paço in 1624 puts another light on this system and suggests that careful scrutiny of outward-bound passengers was lacking. The Desembargo do Paço reminded lower courts that "Moorish" slaves were not to be allowed within 20 leagues of a port city since "the experience of a few cases . . . has shown the importance of strictly and carefully following this regulation."[110] If Moorish (that is, North African) slaves were escaping from a variety of ports, how many *degredados* (fellow-countrymen who knew the language and customs so much better) would have also managed to elude the system that required licenses for departing ships and lists of those on board? Exiles sentenced by the Goan high court were also occasionally able to escape before their ships left. Such was the case in 1589 when many *degredados* about to leave from Goa for Sri Lanka and the Molucca Islands escaped before their ships left.[111] Prisoners in the Goan jail, like their counterparts in Portugal, had a history of escaping—such as another group that made its way out of the city prison in 1635.[112]

Nor, by any means, were prisoners secure once they left Lisbon. One example of an escape of a large group of *degredados* occurred in 1617. D. João de Almeida was entrusted with a group of criminal exiles, whom he handed over to D. Nuno de Sottomaior, Captain of the ship *Candalaria*. Sixty of the original seventy *degredados* escaped, and the Crown ordered an investigation since this thwarted "the good done to the general welfare by the deportation of these people." The Crown went on to complain that its expenses in collecting and directing this process were considerable.[113] On another occasion, the Crown failed to provide a sufficient number of ships for soldiers and convicts. The fleet leaving in 1643 had a total of 900 soldiers and sailors already on board; there was no room for the convicts. The Crown decided that, given the length of the voyage, it was best not to send them to India on that particular fleet.[114] Supervision on board ship was also lacking, as is evident from the incident of the *Menino Jesus e Nossa Senhora da Piedade* in the 1690s. After their stay in prison and once *degredados* were on board, the cramped quarters and the long voyage combined to spread disease and take life. In both 1687 and 1688, no *degredados* were sent to India, "since experience has shown that it is better not to send prisoners directly from the jails since they prejudice the health of the other passengers. . . . Send them to other places which correspond with India as an exile site."[115]

Another example of the system in operation appeared in Ceuta in 1638. After a chain gang was delivered there, panic and anarchy spread throughout the city. The governor rounded up the parties guilty of causing the disturbance.[116] However, the fact that it occurred in the first place demonstrates both an ordered system to collect and transport exiles as well as an apprehensive familiarity by the public with the immediate effects of the arrival of a levy. Both these factors suggest that this was not the first chain gang of *degredados* ever sent to Ceuta. In line with some of the other incidents already mentioned, this particular case also suggests that supervision of the exile after his or her arrival in the *degredo* locale was minimal. Escape from the exile site was often easy and occurred frequently. Such was the case when the Goan high court noted in 1597 that exiles were not presenting their certificates to captains in Sri Lanka, as they were required to do, and were thus evading the system.[117] Another decree of the Desembargo do Paço in 1625 mentioned that exiles sent to India were not being supervised and were not obtaining certificates showing the successful completion of their *degredo*. In order to remedy this situation, the Crown told the viceroy to compile a secret list of all those completing their exiles so that they could be registered.[118]

What was the annual number of *degredados* who passed through this system? The number of convicts was dependent on the population base as well as a variety of complex economic and social factors. Given the absence of systematic lists that could answer this question with more certainty, any conclusion made here is tenuous. Nevertheless, the data presented here suggest annual shipments from and within Portugal of approximately one hundred *degredados* during the period of this study (1550–1755). This figure is simply an estimate, based on the annual average of roughly seventy-five criminals from the state courts and an additional annual average of twenty-five sinner-exiles generated by the Inquisition. I suspect this annual figure was lower than 100 until around 1600, around 100 for most of the seventeenth century, and probably a bit over 100 for the eighteenth century. Nevertheless, 100 was probably the annual average. Assuming that figure is correct, a total of 20,500 *degredados* were exiled within or from Portugal from 1550 to 1755. Exiles originating from the two high courts in India and Brazil, the lower courts in Africa, and the Goan Tribunal of the Inquisition probably averaged a total of 150 annually. These figures would mean that a grand total of around 50,000 *degredados* were exiled in the Portuguese Empire from 1550 to 1755. This figure is based on the average number of those deported or relocated in Portugal, from the lists cited. In the absence of any hard figures on the number of cases before the Bahian and Goan high courts, the colonial figure is simply an estimate. The caseload before the high court in Salvador from 1690 to 1692 was heavy, totaling some 417 criminal cases, and the number of civil cases was four times that.[119] During the second half of the eighteenth century, these total annual averages of convicts in the Portuguese Empire grew. Those exiled from Portugal increased sharply after the 1750s. For example, in the 1770s, the Lisbon *misericórdia* was feeding around two thousand prisoners yearly. Their records note that around half of these were being released, one hundred or so were being used in public works, and between two and three hundred were being exiled annually.[120] Furthermore, lists of prisoners being held in the presidio of Trafaria from 1795 to 1805 indicate an annual average of more than three hundred *degredados* leaving Portugal. Most of these were sent to Angola, but, following the pattern established in the colonial era, large numbers were also being sent to Maranhão and Pará on the eve of Brazilian independence. Additional Portuguese convicts were directed to Cacheu in West Africa.[121] Internal exile to Castro Marim continued, with the judicial system sending around one hundred minor criminals to Castro Marim until the 1850s.

The theory of this system was straightforward. A relatively serious crime was committed, and the court system eventually convicted the guilty party and exiled him or her to one of the overseas sites in need of population. Midway in this legal process, the criminal was held in the Limoeiro jail to await transportation. This gathering or holding of criminals in Lisbon while they awaited transport illuminates the reality of where and how they were used, particularly at the end of the sixteenth and into the seventeenth century. It would appear that the Crown came to view these *degredados* not as criminals already sentenced by the courts, simply awaiting departure, but as a mobile royal labor force, whose ultimate destination was yet to be determined. The timing and language selected in *alvarás* strongly suggests this attitude. The Crown came to decree that criminal exiles awaiting transportation were to be *applied* to the pressing manpower needs of a specific colony. How this process of servitude and exile began at home and was then extended to newly acquired territories, where criminals were sent, and what they did are the central issues in the next three chapters.

TWO

Penal Servitude, Internal Exile, and the Beginnings of Imperial Exile

Penal exile is a traditional sentence among us.

—FRANCISCO XAVIER SILVA TELLES

The galleys were a form of penal servitude that the Crown found invaluable and that it modified to suit its changing needs throughout the early modern period. A sentence to the galleys was unique in that, unlike all other punishments, it was forced labor rather than banishment, military service, or transportation to a colony. Because of this important difference, the galley system can perhaps be most clearly understood as a quasi-independent, but critical, subcomponent of the entire criminal justice system in early modern Portugal. In addition to the galleys, another early form of punishment was internal asylum: cities of refuge in the European homeland, established during the High Middle Ages. These two punishments were well in place before the Portuguese began their overseas expansion in 1415. Both these systems—forced labor and asylum—were concurrently extended and modified overseas after being tested in the homeland. Criminal-maritime systems using galleys were established in Goa and Salvador; asylum cities also proved useful in various locations throughout the Portuguese Empire.

The Galley System

As with so much of the legal basis of banishment and transportation, penal labor directed to the galleys had its origins in Roman law. Punishment in the form of service in galleys was an important aspect of legal and social control in early modern France, Spain, and Portugal—as well as in other Mediterranean lands such as Malta, Venice, and the Ottoman Empire.[1] The development and use of oar-powered ships from the late Middle Ages until the seventeenth century in Mediterranean Europe required massive inputs of rowers. None of these early modern powers was able to supply the required manpower for galleys through wage labor; during this period, the judicial system became the source of this critical manpower.

Portuguese galleys were similar in design to those used by other Mediterranean powers and developed in Portugal by way of a Genovese connection dating from King D. Dinis (1279–1325).[2] A royal letter to the *câmara* of Lisbon in 1386 referred to a register (*vintenas do mar*) of those men who could serve in the galleys, although maintaining this list would appear to have been an intermediate step in an overall transition to forced labor.[3] Galleys were certainly in full use in Portugal by the end of the fourteenth century when King D. João I leased ten to King Richard II of England for his campaigns in the English Channel in 1389.[4]

The term *galley* is actually something of a misnomer, since work was not exclusively on such ships. Labor began on the galleys themselves and was extended to a variety of naval-related tasks. This was particularly true for the second half of the seventeenth century. During this period, there were increasingly fewer galleys; moreover, the seasonal nature of the work forced the state to adopt other activities for this otherwise idle labor force.[5] Galley prisoners were making rope and filling sand bags for ballast by the late 1600s, for example. By the end of the period under study here, convicts sentenced to the galleys (*forçados*) as well as vagrants were suggested as the logical workforce for chores such as clearing out Lisbon's aqueducts after the 1755 earthquake.[6]

The entire system can perhaps best be understood as one of state-directed labor by convicts and sinners. Sentences to the galleys were reserved for male commoners, who were conveyed to Lisbon in chain gangs together with others exiled overseas. Such levies were not unique to Portugal; similar systems conducted criminals to the galleys in both Spain and France.[7] In the Portuguese case, after their arrival in Lisbon's Limoeiro jail, galley prisoners began their service when they were entrusted to the master of the galleys and his guards. The details of this process, as well as how criminals and "Moorish" slaves were to be treated and what papers were to accompany them, were stipulated in a similar and complementary *regimento* to the broader one governing all *degredados*.

In addition to the state's courts those of the Inquisition directed a large number of convicted sinners (27 percent of the total cases from 1662 to 1699) to forced labor for the state in this system. In the second half of the seventeenth century, the Inquisition sentenced bigamists (in particular) to the galleys. Before this time, those convicted of sodomy had frequently been sent to work in these tasks.[8] The state's courts also provided convicted commoners. Each type of galley had a specific manpower requirement, depending on the number and size of the oars. The number of ships and the other tasks at hand were limited. Therefore, the state required a given, finite number of galley workers. Because of the problems of maintaining security and the expense of providing food and shelter for the men, accepting only the appropriate number was in the best interests of the state. The church and state coordinated their court systems so that the latter received sufficient, but not excessive, manpower. Whenever convenient or necessary, the state either commuted all sentences of colonial exile to the galleys or vice versa—depending on its needs in the docks or overseas in its empire. In other words, the galley system ran parallel to the exile system and alternatively provided emergency manpower (in the form of convicts released from galley service) or absorbed and directed the serious criminal element for the state's labor needs (in the galleys or nearby dockyards).

Legislation directing exile to and from the galleys shows the state's ability to mold the system to fit its own needs. For example, in 1521 those exiled to "The Islands" and to Africa were directed instead to the galleys.[9] Thirty years later, the Crown informed judges that exile to Brazil, in the case of commoners between the ages of eighteen and twenty-five (later extended for men to the age of fifty), should be switched to the galleys for as long as the judge deemed fit. The ratio established by the courts was two years in Brazil to equal one in the galleys; a life sentence in Brazil equaled ten years in the galleys.[10] In 1564, and again in 1567, judges were given the option of sentencing men to the galleys if they had been exiled to Brazil or to Africa, since "most of them do not complete their exile there."[11] Upon five separate occasions during the crisis years of the 1630s and early 1640s, the Crown directed courts to send vagrants and convicts originally sentenced to exile overseas to labor in the galleys instead. The legislation and exile data reveal

that the galley system was forced into a secondary position in royal plan-
ning. The reason was rather simple: Portugal's population base was too low
and the resulting number of convicts was too few to provide sufficient men
for all imperial schemes, much less to staff a small fleet of galleys adequately.
Time and again, when the Crown had to choose between the two, the galleys
would be emptied for an emergency supply of "soldiers" to be sent overseas.

Because of the recurring, and often serious, manpower shortages reflected
in this legislation, providing sufficient labor for the galleys was a constant
challenge to the early modern Portuguese state. As early as 1573 (and probably well before that), Gypsy men had been singled out as a likely labor
source. Laws coupled galley service with their expulsion from Portugal.[12] A
decree of that year (1573) stated that they had thirty days to leave Portugal;
any Gypsy man caught in Portugal after that would face life in the galleys.
Gypsy women would have all their goods taken; half would be given to the
city where they were found and the other half to the *misericórdia*.[13] The
Crown in 1592 stated that "because of the great numbers of Gypsies who
go around committing robberies in the kingdom, . . . [Gypsy] males over
the age of sixteen will be sent to the galleys and women will be punished in
accordance with the law." [14] Twenty years later, "because Gypsies still commit crimes and do not receive the full punishment of the law because they
flee Portugal," penalties directed specifically at Gypsies were increased to
three years in the galleys for the first offense, twice that for the second, and
thrice that for the third.[15] In 1618, the Crown was still being reminded that
there were many Gypsies throughout the kingdom, identifiable by their distinctive dress and language.[16] Further orders to collect Gypsies were issued
in 1639.[17]

The Crown had apparently been somewhat successful in these efforts. In
1647, correspondence between the jailer of Limoeiro and the courts detailed
a problem caused by the presence of Gypsies in jail. Because of these laws,
ten Gypsy men with their wives and families were being held in jail. Unfortunately, they were too old to serve the Crown, and the judicial system did
not know what to do with them. The royal decision determined they should
"live far away from this court and not near the borders." It banished them
to the cities of Torres Vedras, Leiria, Ourem, Alenquer, Montemor-o-Velho,
and Coimbra. They were also prohibited from using or teaching their children Girigonça (Romany), wearing traditional Gypsy clothing, and from remaining idle.[18] Although it may have been novel to apply this relocation to
Gypsies, this shift to internal exile was not new. As early as 1502, courts
were directed that "those sentenced to serve in the galleys, but who were un-

able to do so because of their advanced ages, should be exiled internally, with an increase in the number of years of exile, in accordance with the law."[19]

Two centuries later, the Crown had still not yet been able to deal with the Gypsies to its satisfaction. King D. João V decreed in 1708 that the use of Gypsy dress or speech was forbidden and that no more than two such couples could reside on the same street. The punishment for breaking this law was ten years in the galleys for Gypsy men and an equal period in Brazil for Gypsy women.[20] Another law passed in 1718 ordered that all Gypsies in Portugal be collected and expelled to one of the overseas colonies.[21] Laws expelling Gypsies from Portugal were passed by the Crown as late as 1745.[22]

Throughout the eighteenth century, the Crown become increasingly serious about deporting Gypsies to Brazil and Angola.[23] Once exiled to the colonies, Gypsies did not escape the arm of the law. Upon their arrival in Brazil, the authorities wrote to Lisbon, "Gypsies cause so much trouble stealing horses and slaves" that the Crown in 1760 ordered all Gypsy children to become apprentices and adult males to become soldiers. In addition, they were to be given a fair wage. Gypsies in Brazil were specifically forbidden to trade in cattle or slaves, travel freely, live in neighborhoods of their own, or carry arms. Any Gypsy breaking this law, even on the first instance, was to be exiled to São Tomé or Príncipe for life.[24] Gypsies remained in early modern Portugal in spite of these efforts by the state to deport them; they were mentioned as "living in the wild open spaces between towns and robbing people" in the European homeland as late as 1801.[25]

Gypsies alone could not solve the never-ending manpower shortages of the galleys. That shortage, as well as sentences deemed too brief, caused confusion in the dockyards. In 1606, the Crown was concerned that people exiled to the galleys "should be sent there for a minimum of two years. Many have recently been sentenced for [only] six months and this does not work since they do not have enough time to learn the terminology or their way around galleys."[26]

At the time of the Iberian Union (1580–1640), Portugal had temporarily ceased to maintain galleys. In 1604, prisoners sentenced to service in the galleys were to be handed over to Spanish galleys "since this Kingdom does not have galleys." These prisoners, in turn, "would form part of the service to this Kingdom [Spain]."[27] By 1623, Portugal apparently had at least one galley in service. While it was in the Tejo River next to Lisbon, the Council of State asked for and received a status report on it from the royal quartermaster (Procurador das Armazens). The 198 convicts on board were not in good health; 90 did not have adequate clothing. The prisoners were supervised by what the report called "an absolute minimum of eighteen soldiers and a handful of officers." Commentary made by the Council of State noted that more prisoners were needed and requested that any convicts in Limoeiro or other jails in the country be handed over to serve.[28] The Desembargo do Paço followed one month later by directing that those in the kingdom's jails sentenced to the galleys should be conducted immediately to this ship to begin their sentences.[29] A second decree along these same lines was issued in 1638, which urged that these prisoners be sent "to the usual ports and places where they are collected."[30]

The reverse of this situation—an oversupply of manpower—must have been a factor in Goa in 1597; the Goan high court commuted all *degredados* sent to its galleys.[31] Galleys were used in Portuguese Asia from the early years of the empire's foundation in 1510. However, African slaves probably constituted a good segment of that workforce. As early as 1515, Albuquerque authorized payments for two daily meals of rice for galley slaves, 112 on the *São Vicente* and 120 on the *Santo Espirito*.[32] Galleys and *fustas* (similar but smaller vessels) are much in evidence in the maritime drawings of D. João de Castro from the middle of the sixteenth century.[33] The relative ease of acquiring labor from African slaves for galleys in Asia would have allowed more Portuguese the luxury of exile rather than forced labor at the oar. The Goan high court supervised aspects of this system and wanted to ensure that the system was one of punishment and not strictly labor. In a telling case in 1627, it ordered that a Goan Christian (Canarim) named Jorge, who had presumably been paid to trade places with a convict sentenced to the galleys, be set free at once "since the sentence only applies to those who have committed the crime." The high court ordered the galley officials "not to accept any such future trading [of persons]." The penalty for breaking this law was six years in these same galleys and a fine of 1,000 *xerafins* to be paid to the Goan court.[34]

The penalty of time in the galleys or in public works was also suggested as a source for manpower for the dockyard in Salvador. In a 1692 letter addressed to the king, the colonial government responded to an earlier royal suggestion along these lines stating that this sentence "would not just be for blacks and mulattos, but even for whites whose crimes merited this punishment." The city council of Salvador was to see that prisoners received their allotment of food. "Galleys," it was noted, "would be useful to guard the Brazilian coastline."[35] The next year, an official was named to receive and supervise convicts sentenced to the galleys, a punishment that would "place terror in the hearts of delinquents thereby stopping the repeated excesses which have occurred here." Six chains were immediately available in Salvador for a dozen men, since "there are no prisons available for them." When additional chains were needed, the Crown would be informed.[36] Fourteen years later, the Crown was seriously concerned that there should be a galley to protect the Brazilian coast and ordered criminals sentenced to the galleys from the high court in Porto to Salvador to work the oars. In the event that more men were needed still, the Crown authorized the governor-general to purchase up to thirty slaves, using money from the royal treasury.[37] Apparently, many of these prisoners, who should have been kept in the city's jail, were allowed to roam freely around the city, an item the king brought to the attention of the governor in 1689.[38]

The *regimento* for those sentenced to galley service in Lisbon (and that was undoubtedly used as a model for the galleys in Goa and Salvador) required that prisoners be given a daily biscuit ration and paid 10 *réis* daily "to purchase meat or fish." [39] This ration and salary were to be distributed to galley prisoners every fifteen days. However, the reality of that salary—even if it were paid on time—was starvation. In 1630, the Council of State noted that convicts on the galleys were starving and that serious supply problems made helping them difficult.[40] Once they had completed their sentences in the galleys, the *regimento* also stipulated that convicts were to be issued certificates of completion, along the same lines as those issued to exiles.[41]

Prisoners in the galleys did occasionally get a lucky break when manpower in the colonies reached a critically low point and was coupled with a lack of inmates in the Limoeiro prison. One such juncture occurred at the Fortress of Cacheu in 1644. Soldiers were badly needed; the Overseas Council turned to the galleys for its source. In early September of that year, eight galley prisoners had their sentences commuted to military service in Cacheu; six more were added to this list in the following month. Given the severity of galley service, it is not surprising that, in the cases where the crime is stated, their offenses were murder and two of the four most serious in the land: theft and counterfeiting. The time remaining (in some cases as many as nine years of a ten-year sentence) was commuted to military service in West Africa.[42] Other convicts, such as João Lopes from Torres Vedras, were pardoned after serving a number of years in the galleys. In 1652, he was pardoned from his remaining time in the galleys because of the many years he had already served.[43]

What was life like for those who worked in the galleys? Those in the galleys were typically commoners convicted of serious crimes or (frequently) bigamists convicted by the Inquisition. Fortunately an eye-witness account exists on life in the Lisbon galleys written by an atypical, literate prisoner. Dr. Charles Dellon, a French doctor working in the Estado da India, was falsely accused by powerful enemies and denounced before the Goan Inquisition. In 1675–1676, he was deported from Portuguese Asia and sentenced to ten years in the Lisbon galleys. This sentence was carried out regardless of the Lisbon court's ruling that the Goan court should not send them their *degredados*, but rather use them on the galleys in Goa.[44] He arrived in Lisbon in December 1676 and joined other prisoners sentenced to work in the royal dockyards. Fortunately for the doctor, his efforts to be released were successful, and he was set free only a few months after his return to Europe. His published account is understandably much more concerned with the greater injustice done to him by the Inquisition, rather than the details of his time in the Lisbon galleys. Nevertheless, his short passage on life in the galleys of Lisbon in 1676 is revealing and strongly reenforces several key points suggested by the legislation. The two justice systems of church and state did converge here in the galleys. By 1676, labor was not actually on a ship, but on related tasks in the dockyards. The biscuit ration and other foods mandated in the *regimento* were being given to convicts, but, like those in the Limoeiro and other jails, prisoners with money were able to acquire better food. One source of manpower—the "fugitive and intractable slaves," mentioned by Dellon—were purchased by the state.[45] Condemned slaves, as early as 1521, could be sold to the state at a price agreed to by two men.[46] The galleys were also a judicial sentence of last resort for *degredados* who left their original exile. Escapees from colonial exile were typically sent to the galleys; those who fled would be returned for extended sentences or could theoretically be killed.[47]

At some point in the mid-seventeenth century, the various Mediterranean powers turned from galleys to faster and more modern ship designs, which did not require manpower at the oar. Most maritime authorities agree that galleys became obsolete after the Battle of Matapan in 1717.[48] During this transition process (that is, roughly 1650 to 1720) the state merely redirected this labor to other endeavors. The Portuguese, during much of the first half of the seventeenth century, alternated between maintaining and abandoning galleys. This necessitated shifts in criminal sentencing. By the mid-eighteenth century, prisoners sentenced to galleys (or public works, as this sentence came to be known) were instead exiled to Portuguese India.[49] Records from 1755 to the 1830s indicate that the judicial system abandoned the sentence of public works and was sending convicts to all regions of the empire, especially its African holdings and Maranhão and Pará in Brazil.

Exile Within Portugal: Asylum Cities (coutos do reino)

During the early fourteenth century, the Portuguese Crown began to use a system of asylum cities (*coutos*) to populate border regions that had remained sparsely populated after the *reconquista* or that were devastated during the wars with Castile during the second half of the fourteenth century. Critical cities and towns were designated as legal havens for criminals other than those guilty of fraud or treason.[50] This system was initiated by King D. Dinis in 1308 and continued, with some important changes, throughout the early modern period until 1691–1692.[51] Actually, internal exile was only suspended in 1691 and reestablished in 1703 in order to curb "the great number of murderers who have left Portugal and roam Castile." Guards at the frontier were directed by the Crown to ensure that these criminals resided in the border areas the guards deemed most convenient "which will serve as asylums . . . in the same way that the *coutos* did until they were abolished in 1692." [52]

In spite of the need for population in the overseas empire after 1415, some of these internal *coutos* would continue. A small but important step in the overall process of forced or state-sponsored colonization was the transformation of asylums into *degredo* sites. This is what occurred after the beginning of the sixteenth century. Some of the more important sites are shown on Map 2 and include: Noudar (made a refuge in 1308), Sabugal (1369), Miranda do Douro, Freixo d'Espada à Cinta, Caminhã (1406), Monforte do Rio Livre (1420), Segura (literally, "safe," 1421), Celorico de Basto (1441), Chaves (1454), Marvão (1483), and Sesimbra (1492).[53] Typically, a ceiling was placed on the number of criminals who could claim asylum in each locale. For example, only thirty individuals would be pardoned by moving to Celorico de Basto; fifty was the limit placed on Monforte de Rio Livre.[54] This form of pardon was specifically directed at male criminals, but females were also pardoned by moving to one of these towns—with the additional proviso that they could not be guilty of adultery. A further clause allowed male residents to leave the safety of their homes and transact business within 10 leagues of their homes without fear of capture. Three months of the year, these pardoned men could move freely around the kingdom as long as they maintained their homes in asylum cities and traveled with letters of authorization issued by the local judges.

Asylum could be, and was, withdrawn from any individual city once the Crown felt that its population had reached a satisfactory level or another city

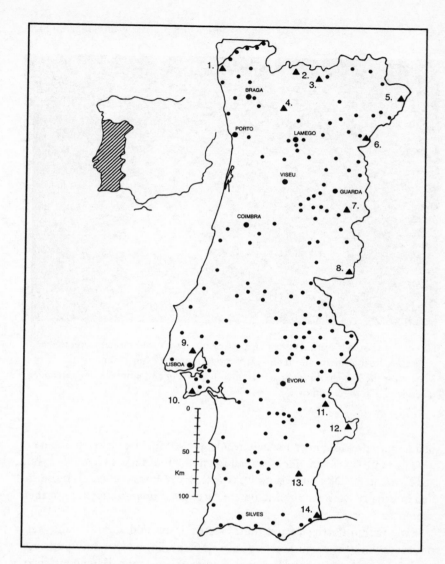

Map 2. Principal Population Centers of Portugal in the Fourteenth and Fifteenth Centuries, with Sites of Internal Exile. Adapted with permission from A. H. de Oliveira Marques, *Portugal na crise dos séculos XIV e XV*, vol. 4 of *Nova História de Portugal* (Lisbon: Editorial Presença, 1987), 185.

Sites of internal exile are numbered:
1. Caminha; 2. Monforte do Rio Livre; 3. Chaves; 4. Celorico de Basto; 5. Miranda do Douro; 6. Freixo de Espada à Cinta; 7. Sabugal; 8. Segura; 9. Alhandra; 10. Sesimbra; 11. Marvão; 12. Noudar; 13. Mértola; 14. Castro Marim.

Figure 4.   Castro Marim. While many cities and towns in Portugal were used as exile sites during the medieval and early modern periods, none could rival Castro Marim for the length of time it served this function or the numbers of *degredados* it received. Photo by author, 1996.

had a more pressing need for new residents. Mértola lost its status as a *degredo* site in 1535; Alhandra (a small town north of Lisbon) lost its asylum status in 1586.[55] Not surprisingly (as with other forms of exile), those exiled internally were required to obtain certificates upon completion of their sentences.[56]

Exile within Portugal from the 1520s until the mid 1800s became synonymous with the small town of Castro Marim, in the extreme southeastern corner of the Algarve. However, in spite of legislation designed to channel minor criminals there, other towns within Portugal were occasionally used as exile locales as well, such as Miranda do Douro or Marvão. However, none approached Castro Marim in terms of the number of convicts exiled or the span of years the town was singled out as an exile site. Castro Marim began as an exile locale in 1524 and temporarily lost this status with the other internal asylums in 1691.[57] Female convicts were sent there in the 1740s and 1750s. For example, female transvestites were sentenced to three years in

Castro Marim, and men who dressed in women's clothing faced two years in Africa.[58] In response to a riot in Porto in 1757, 478 people were given sentences ranging from death to temporary banishment from town. Of these, three men and nine women were sent to Castro Marim.[59] Not just the state's courts but also those of the Inquisition used Castro Marim as the primary site for internal exile. The latter used it for a total of 14 percent of all cases (107 individuals) involving exile from 1662–1699. Sins that merited exile to Castro Marim included: interfering with the work of the Holy Office, profanity, practicing Judaism, and witchcraft. By the end of the seventeenth century, this little town had grown to a population of approximately 600. Much of this growth was no doubt due to the economic activities generated by this constant influx of free labor provided by the church and state.[60]

Asylum cities such as Castro Marim were a feature of a number of southern European societies and were not unique to Portugal, but they would fade with the rise of the absolutist state. In his highly influential essay *On Crimes and Punishments*, first published in 1764, Beccaria discusses the asylum city and concludes that the power of the state should extend to every part of its territory. Therefore, asylum cities should not be tolerated.[61]

Internal exile within Portugal did become increasingly associated with Castro Marim during the period under study in this work. After the rise to power of the Marquês de Pombal and the 1755 earthquake that destroyed much of the Algarve, Pombal would try a new strategy with forced labor and colonization in Portugal: create a new city, 4 kilometers to the south of Castro Marim, and force people to live in it. In 1774 he created the Vila Real de Santo António and sentences of forced labor to Castro Marim began to taper off slowly around 1800 and ended by the middle of the nineteenth century.

This system, along with some of its details, would be taken overseas and modified. In 1493, convicts sent to São Tomé were allowed to return to Portugal for a limited period (not to exceed four months) to transact business. The four-month limit started at the time of the required registration with a judge in Lisbon.[62] Three years later in 1496, *degredados* on São Tomé were given virtual carte blanche to import goods from Portugal and to conduct slave raids in the Mina area.[63] Within twenty years, the right to leave the island was revoked. By 1560, any *degredado* found off the island of São Tomé had the length of his exile doubled.[64] Presumably, too many *degredados* were not returning to São Tomé; this aspect of the system was discarded.

The case of asylum in Portuguese America is even more striking. In a mid-sixteenth-century effort to increase the Portuguese population, all the

Figure 5. The Fortress of Aguada, Goa. This fortress was constructed at considerable expense by King D. Filipe III in the early 1600s to protect the main maritime entrance into the city of Goa at the mouth of the Mandovi River. At the bottom of the fort is the Central Prison of Goa, constructed in the early twentieth century. Photo by author, 1991.

capitanias (captaincies) were considered *coutos* for those fleeing Portugal.[65] Asylum cities in later colonial times, with one notable exception, were absent in Brazil. In 1625, the Vila de Nossa Senhora da Conceição was made a legal haven for any and all criminals, if they appeared armed and ready to fight the Dutch.[66]

In the Estado da India, both Cannanore and Damão were referred to by King D. Sebastião in 1567 as "[preexisting] havens [*coutos*] where adulterous women can relocate if necessary."[67] In an effort to solve manpower shortages, the two critical forts of Mormugão and Aguada were declared *coutos* for *degredados* or murderers in 1624. These two fortresses controlled all maritime movement in the critical central region of Goa. Those who sought asylum in these two places had to register twice a month in special books that "would be kept at each locale specifically for this purpose."[68] Ten years later, the villages next to the fort of Mormugão were added as asylums for those guilty of all crimes, except the usual unforgivable four (including falsifying papers) as well as injuring someone with a sword.[69] This seems to have had some effect, at least for Mormugão; population figures compiled in 1719 show sixty-three "white" (that is, Portuguese or *castiço*) men there, although this same list also notes many deserters. The next year, Mormugão had thirty-two Portuguese or *castiço* soldiers and sixty-two Goans. Fort Aguada only had twelve "white" men on the same rolls.[70]

In an effort to prevent criminals from going over to "the lands of the heathens," Damão, Quilon, and Guala in 1610 were declared asylums, with the usual provision that this status did not apply to those guilty of unpardonable crimes. At the same time, the asylum status of Cranganor and Columbo was terminated; anyone still in these cites who required it could relocate to one of the new *coutos*.[71]

Of the places on this list, Fort Aguada was singled out as an asylum by two concurrent conditions: its isolation and constant need for additional manpower. These two factors made it one of Goa's de facto prisons. In 1620, only a few years after its construction in 1603, Francisco de Sousa was held prisoner there.[72] Another *degredado* was sent to Fort Aguada in chains in 1667.[73] A third prisoner, Jerónimo de Mendonça, arrived in India in 1682 with a letter placing him in a special category of prisoner-exile. The Crown offered to pay all costs involved and wanted him placed in a "fort or other secure place." Viceroy Francisco de Távora put him in Fort Aguada under the care of Captain D. António Sotto Mayor, who promised to keep a close eye on him and "not allow him to leave."[74]

Fort Aguada was actually somewhat precocious in this aspect; by the midnineteenth century, the area directly below it became the site of Goa's central prison.[75] After all, the change from a haven (where criminals are pardoned) to an exile location (where criminals are encouraged or forced to relocate) is a relatively small one. The last step in this process is to transform the location into a prison: a place where criminals are not allowed to leave. This last phase separates early modern and modern punishment in Europe. During early modern times, prisons were places where criminals were temporarily held until their sentences were determined. By the beginning of the nineteenth century, extended sentences in prison itself became the punishment in most European countries. In the Portuguese case, *degredo* continued to be the principal punishment until the 1950s.

It would appear that internal exile, while remaining important, would also take a backseat to exile overseas. In the Ordenações of D. Manuel I, any male exiled within Portugal was given the option of having his sentence cut in half if he agreed to serve in one of the North African presidios (see below). If the original sentence had only been banishment from town or district, a *degredado* or *degredada* could reduce his or her sentence by half by residing in Castro Marim. Those who escaped would have their sentences doubled.[76]

An example of the systematic use of internal exile as punishment appears from an incident that occurred in 1726. A group of thirty-eight nobles insulted and attacked a Crown judge, a *corregedor*, in the Rossio of Lisbon.[77] As punishment for this affront to royal authority, they were exiled for three years, each to one of the cities and towns within Portugal. D. Luís Cezar, the man whose name heads the list, was sentenced to three years in Mazagão, changed to the Tower of Belém. Because of the reduction in sentences given for those sent to North Africa, it was obviously considered much more difficult (and pressing) than any internal Portuguese site; the fact that D. Luís's sentence was changed to the Tower of Belém tends to reinforce the idea that he was the ringleader. A total of thirty-eight individuals were exiled as a result of this incident. Of these, three were noted as having been reprimanded and have no exile locale stated. Of the remaining thirty-five, three have no site listed, and two were given mild sentences of banishment of 40 leagues out of Lisbon. D. Luís, as noted, was put in jail. The remaining twenty-nine people were sent to variety of exile locations in Portugal. None of these new exile locations were as remote as the asylums used earlier. The Crown was continuing to use exile, but it had also taken into account the nature of the crime committed. In addition, the fact that this was a group of nobles may also help to account for their more attractive exile locations. Had a ragtag group of commoners insulted this judge, their exile might very well have been to North Africa, as the law outlined, or even to places more distant, such as Angola.

The North African Presidios, Madeira, the Azores, Cape Verde, and São Tomé

The beginnings of Portuguese overseas expansion in North and West Africa during the fifteenth century have been discussed from a variety of viewpoints and with emphasis placed on distinct, but related, aspects. Blake as well as Diffie and Winius tend to view this as a commercial dispute between Portugal and Spain as well as between the Iberians and the Ottomans and their allies. Oliveira Marques and Magalhães Godinho have suggested the quest for wheat and gold as the motivation for Portuguese interest in this region. Boxer and other maritime historians such as Armando Cortesão and Damião Peres have outlined the Portuguese experience in this region charting the African coastline and becoming familiar with navigation using the southern stars and new wind and ocean currents.[78] Teixeira da Mota deals with those same issues as well as the social interaction of the Portuguese with the peoples of West Africa, particularly in Guinea Bissau. Verlinden concentrates on feudal and newly emerging forms of land grants that developed as a result of Portuguese occupation of the Atlantic Islands. Saunders discusses one aspect at the core of this early immigration, both forced and free: replacing lost manpower with African slaves.[79] Criminals exiled to this region are yet another aspect of the process of the Portuguese maritime venture.

At the beginning of the fifteenth century, the Portuguese began to cast a covetous eye on the grain-rich cities along the coast of (present-day) Morocco. Cities such as Ceuta, Tangier, Salé, and Azamour were well connected to the northern, interior, wheat-producing areas of Morocco and were termini, not only for trade in grain but also West African gold.[80] Ceuta fell to the Portuguese in 1415 (a date often used to mark the beginning of European overseas expansion) and remained part of the empire until 1640. The fact that it was a city of fabled riches (including wheat in abundance) can only have added to any religious spirit of conquest.[81]

A "shell game" in which the Portuguese eagerly participated but were guaranteed to lose followed the conquest of Ceuta in North Africa. In their attempt to establish control over North African wheat and West African gold, they established a military presence at the perceived terminus of the trade—only to discover that the North Africans would then redirect this trade to a city under their control. All these would shortly become targets for Portuguese military expansion. These *lugares de Africa* (places in Africa), the *Algarve de além* (Algarve on the other side, sometimes simply referred to as *Africa*), were the chain of garrison forts that the Portuguese Crown maintained along the Atlantic coastline of extreme northwestern Africa (modern Morocco).

After the conquest of Ceuta, an attempt was made to capture Tangier in 1437, but it failed. The next target was Alcácar Ceguir (Al-Qasr al-Sagir), captured in 1458 and under Portuguese control until 1550. Tangier and Arzila were occupied by the Portuguese in 1471. Tangier remained a Portuguese territory until it was given to the British as part of the dowry of Catherine of Bragança in 1662. Arzila's (Asila) imperial role was smaller and limited to the periods from 1471 to 1550 and 1577 to 1589. Azamour (Mulai Bu Saib) came under the Portuguese rule from 1513 to 1541. Mogador (Essauira, Portuguese from 1504 to 1510) and Santa Cruz do Cabo de Gué (Agadir, 1505–1541) were followed by the capture of Safim (Safi, 1508–1541) and Mazagão (El-Jadida, 1514–1769).[82]

The North African enclaves were eventually recognized as imperial liabilities: they were strong consumers of wheat and other goods, constantly in need of additional personnel, yet producers of very little. They offered no control over the countryside around them and required constant expenses for the army to defend them from frequent attacks and blockades. This reality was formally recognized by King D. João III in 1542 when he abandoned Safi and Azamour, Alcácar-Ceguir in 1549, and Arzila in 1550.

Of the cities on this list of presidios, Tangier and Mazagão were the most significant *degredo* sites during the period of this study. Because of the many different cities needing men, the Crown required flexibility in sentencing exiles to this region and in 1519 informed judges "not to sentence [*degredados*] to a specific place but, when the sentence is made, to make it to one of the places on the other side [of the Straits of Gibraltar]."[83] Many *degredados* escaped by persuading or bribing captains to issue premature certificates of completion. Specific laws were passed in the early seventeenth century to prevent this practice. *Degredados* found with such certificates were to be treated as what they were—convicts who had left their exile sites before completing their sentences.[84]

These garrisons were usually undermanned and were favored exile locations for males committing serious, sometimes unpardonable, crimes throughout much of the early modern period. Each of these garrison cities under Portuguese rule has been the subject of study; unfortunately, *degredados* or soldiers, in spite of their relative importance, were not central subjects in these works.[85] However, in his authoritative study of Portuguese Mazagão, Dias Farinha estimated that the population of the city was between 1,500 and 2,000 from the late sixteenth until the mid-seventeenth century. Around half of these were single men in the cavalry, artillery, and navy.[86] In a *consulta* of 1624, it was suggested to King D. Filipe IV that the solution to shortages in the army sent to fight the Dutch in Salvador could be remedied by removing the "hardy and experienced men from the garrisons in Ceuta, Tangier, and Mazagão which now surpass the numbers required by Your Majesty."[87] However, any surplus that existed must have either been a temporary aberration or a surplus on paper only.

Supplying manpower is one problem, the use of exile locations another. How quickly did these North African garrisons become incorporated in the judicial system as exile locations? The answer appears with the arrival of the first Portuguese soldiers. A general pardon was issued in 1415 for those criminals who had served in the army conquering Ceuta in that year and who would agree to remain there for brief periods of up to one year.[88] A similar pardon for military service in the assault on Tangier was issued in 1437.[89] Two years later, one Gomes Esteves had his ten years of exile to Setúbal reduced by half for serving in this battle.[90] The first pardon with a condition of required service in Ceuta appeared in 1439, only twenty-four years after its conquest.

During the period of 1415 to 1456, at least 455 criminals were exiled to Ceuta; the vast majority (383) were deported in the six years between 1450 and 1456.[91] In those same six years, only one criminal was sent to Tangier. Crimes, when listed, were murder, forgery, counterfeiting, and blasphemy. These figures do not count the people already sentenced there, approximately 200 total. In the eleven years between 1481 and 1492, numerous criminals were either exiled to or avoided serving in these garrisons. In the latter case, payment of a fine exempted the criminal from going overseas. The cities and number of cases were as follows: Arzila, 113; Ceuta, 63; Tangier, 62; Africa or the Algarve de Além, 32; Alcáçar-Ceguir, 11; and Safi, 1. The crimes committed ranged widely from murder, escaping from jail, adultery, smuggling, to insulting a judge, and other serious crimes.

The shifting of exile locales among the European homeland, the Atlantic Islands, and North African garrisons during much of the fifteenth century demonstrates that the punishment of *degredo* was quickly interwoven into a new fabric that blended the internal with the overseas. A review of the major sets of published documents for the period reveals that eleven criminals originally sentenced to internal exile in Portugal were commuted to the North African outposts. Around fifty-eight cases were commuted in the opposite direction, from North Africa to Portugal. Between the Atlantic Islands (that is, the Azores, Madeira, Cape Verde) and North Africa, five cases were commuted in each direction.[92]

As in the case of all materials with criminal exiles in early modern times, bits and pieces relating to them can be seen in much larger statements. For example, an author in the early eighteenth century writing on manpower shortages in the North African presidios noted, "In the time of King D. João III [1521–1557], in a battle in Safim, when it was surrounded by over 100,000 men, the captain-general was forced, because of the lack of men, to order that the women take up arms."[93] Not many Portuguese women were exiled to these rough frontier towns. In fact, by the late sixteenth century,

Portuguese women were not allowed to be exiled to these presidios. Instead of North Africa, they were to be sent to one of the internal asylum cities, Brazil, São Tomé, or Príncipe, according to the severity of the crime committed.[94] Nevertheless, more women were present than the documents might suggest. Several women with Portuguese names were present in Arzila in 1561, including one D. Isabel who was specifically mentioned as being Portuguese.[95] At Alcácar-Ceguir, archaeological evidence indicates that the females formed 28 percent of the almost two hundred graves examined from the Portuguese period; however, few women over the age of forty appear to have been present.[96] In Mazagão in the early seventeenth century, Matias Valente had his daughter with him in what must have been a rough frontier society. Her residence there is indicated in Valente's petition to the Desembargo do Paço for justice after D. Jorge Manuel de Albuquerque entered his house and "dishonored" her.[97]

At the same time as these North African adventures, or perhaps as a result of them, the Portuguese continued to press farther down the western coast of Africa and to explore the mid-Atlantic region. They landed on the islands of Porto Santo and Madeira in 1418–1419, and colonization began in 1425. They arrived at the eastern and central Azores in 1427 (and Flores and Corvo in the western Azores in 1452), and colonization began there in 1439. Both Madeira and the Azores were (relatively) quickly colonized after their initial discoveries and a similar future was envisioned for both island groups: they were to be granaries to grow and export wheat to the *metropole*. In the case of Madeira, wheat was being grown (and exported to Portugal) in 1455 —only twenty-five years after colonization had begun.[98] However, it was quickly discovered that sugar would thrive on Madeira; wheat was abandoned for this much more valuable crop. By 1500, Madeira "had become the world's greatest producer of sugar . . . a prototype of that momentous and tragic social and economic system of sugar and slavery that was to be repeated, on a far larger scale in the West Indies and Brazil."[99]

In addition to these imperial agricultural plans, in both cases, *degredados* were first envisioned as possible colonizers. For example, the Crown first planned in 1453 to populate the island of São Miguel in the Azores with criminals and began to do so the next year.[100] There were a few cases of exiles sent to Madeira during the first thirty years after its initial colonization. However, the fertility of both Madeira and the Azores made both island groups attractive and forced colonization unnecessary. Madeira was populated in the 1420s by farmers from lands "belonging to Prince Henry or to the Order of Christ, the majority coming from the Algarve."[101] The Azores were colonized later in the 1460s and 1470s and included families brought from Flanders.[102] In both cases, *degredados* were first considered, but the islands were able to attract a sufficient number of free colonizers.[103]

Where, then, were *degredados* sentenced overseas during the fifteenth century, if not to the Azores or Madeira? Both the presidios of North Africa and internal exile remained in use throughout this period. In addition, the islands of Cape Verde were used as exile sites as early as six years after the first arrival of the Portuguese in 1460. A published collection of documents from this period shows fourteen exiles sentenced to the Cape Verde Islands from 1466–1513.[104] When the Portuguese first arrived, they considered the islands to be virtually uninhabitable. In the words of Orlando Ribeiro, "In such a land so unfavorable to agriculture, the type of colonization which was characteristic of the Azores and Madeira was not possible."[105] That is to say, *free* colonization was not possible, and the use of *degredados* was one answer that was attempted. By 1515, after the early phase of Portuguese colonization, *degredo* to the Cape Verdes became infrequent. Guiné (modern Guinea-Bissau) was also used as a *degredo* site during the first phases of Portuguese expansion. A recent study has outlined nineteen cases of *degredados* guilty of a wide range of crimes exiled to Guiné between 1463 and 1500.[106]

It was not Cape Verde, but the islands of São Tomé and Príncipe (see Map 3) that rapidly became associated with *degredo* by the end of the fifteenth century. São Tomé was discovered in 1471 or 1472. By the time of the publication of the *Ordenações Manuelinas* in the early sixteenth century, this island was identified as the ideal exile location for the most serious of criminal exiles. The label stuck throughout the early modern period and well into the nineteenth century; of all Portugal's overseas colonies, São Tomé should be the one most closely identified with forced exile. The island was the destination of one of the more horrific deportations that took place in early modern Portugal: two thousand children under the age of eight were taken from their Jewish parents in Portugal in the 1490s, forcibly baptized, and deported to São Tomé.[107] Much of the continual problem in maintaining a stable European population base was undoubtedly caused by malaria, as in other tropical areas such as coastal Angola and Mozambique. Nevertheless, the Crown never ceased in its efforts to populate the island with *degredados*. It could be argued that São Tomé, with its slavery and sugar cultivation, was, in some ways, a model for what was to follow in Brazil. It could also be stressed that São Tomé was also another type of model: an early modern island penal colony with two distinct and parallel forms of forced labor. White, European criminals conducted a slave trade and supervised black African

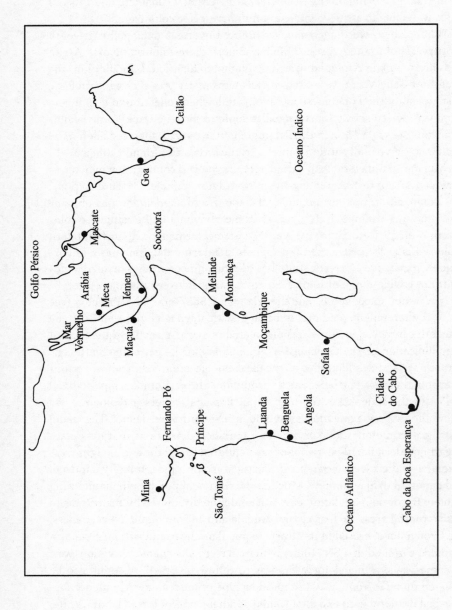

Map 3. The Portuguese Coastal Presence from Mina to Sri Lanka. Adapted with permission from Duncan Haws and Alex A. Hurst, *The Maritime History of the World* (Brighton, U.K.: Teredo Books, 1985), 1:187.

Golfo Pérsico

Ceilão

Goa

Mascate

Socotorá

Arábia

Meca

Iémen

Melinde

Mombaça

Mar Vermelho

Maçuá

Moçambique

Oceano Índico

Sofala

Fernando Pó

Luanda

Benguela

Angola

Cidade do Cabo

Príncipe

Mina

São Tomé

Oceano Atlântico

Cabo da Boa Esperança

slaves producing refined sugar on the island.[108] For this reason Teixeira da Mota called the island a "human laboratory. . . . The settlement [being] novel and quite different from Mediterranean-type colonization."[109]

The Crown certainly went out of its way to ensure that *degredados* sent to São Tomé would be made as comfortable as possible, under the circumstances. By 1506, the Crown counted "around 1,000 residents on the Island, the majority of them exiles living from slave raids (*resgates*) on the mainland." Each exile was to be given a male or female slave for his personal service; the cost would be paid by the state, from royal taxes.[110] A few years later, the Crown required that anyone being sent to São Tomé should go for at least five years.[111] The nearby island of Príncipe was used for exiles until it lost that status in 1549. After that date, all exiles who would have been sent to Príncipe were to be sent to Brazil.[112]

Another aspect of this mixture of internal Portuguese and North African-Atlantic islands exile sites was its flexibility. The ratio of sentences in these distinct locales (one year overseas for two years of internal exile) was apparently in practice well before it became law in the Ordenações of D. Manuel I. It was put into practice in the case of Gil Eanes, who in 1451 had the site of his exile shifted from Ceuta to Ouguela and the length doubled from three to six years for his murder conviction.[113] Another case of a two-year sentence being doubled when shifted to Portugal occurred in 1452 when a convict was sent from Ceuta to Marvão.[114] In addition, the system was sufficiently lenient to allow someone such as Fernão Ribeiro, exiled to Ceuta for murder for three years, to have his site shifted to Freixo de Espada à Cinta in 1451 (for the same length of time) because he had no money.[115] Poverty also allowed Constança Fernandes to have her exile shifted from Ceuta to Miranda.[116] João Freire had his locale shifted from Ceuta because he was a fisherman.[117]

The Crown was both flexible in sentencing and generous in pardoning those forced into royal service in these presidios. In 1617, Jerónimo de Figueiredo petitioned for a pardon from his sentence of six years to one of the *lugares da Africa*, and Rui Fernandes did the same for his four years for judicial contempt in Elvas. Rui asked for this because he had already served time there and was a breadwinner, having a wife and children.[118] Ten years later, Gaspar de Brito asked for and received a pardon from his five years of exile to Africa for his fight with D. Álvaro Coutinho.[119]

The use of newly acquired or discovered areas is another aspect of the Portuguese process of colonization. Among their other cultural traits, the Portuguese took their judicial system with them overseas and readily converted new territories into an older system of exile. Several aspects of this system of exile were first applied to the Portuguese presidios of North Africa and the islands during the late fifteenth and early sixteenth centuries and would eventually define their global penal system during the following three centuries. The entire imperial *degredo* system became notable for ratios to equalize sentences between and among sites; payment of fines, often combined with internal exile to replace service overseas (at least in minor crimes); and a relative leniency on the part of the Crown to grant pardons, especially in recognition of royal service. All these aspects, at work in North Africa and the Atlantic Islands, contributed to a flexibility that made the system responsive to both individual desires and imperial needs. This system grew hand in hand with the empire and came to include Portuguese lands in Asia, South America, and elsewhere in Africa.

Convicts and the Imperial Reality of Exile

Degredados also assist in the colonies, particularly where illness
discourages volunteers from settling. . . . When they escape from the
chain gangs before departure and roam freely in Portugal, the country
becomes full of perverted criminals, thieves, and [people with] other
vices. The colonies, where these people are less bothersome, remain
without them.

— *Overseas Council, 22 February 1656*

Well before the *degredado* left Portugal, the Crown began to refer to him as
a soldier rather than the more accurate exile, criminal, or convict. Occasionally the term *degredado* was avoided by the use of phrases such as "those
in the Limoeiro jail" or "those in irons." This terminology reflected the
Crown's desire that these people, former threats to society and its stability,
become useful in the empire.[1] In the words of King D. Filipe III, the transformation from *degredado* to soldier was based on a "wish to empty my
Kingdoms of scandalous men with bad habits and whose evil lives are prejudicial and provide bad examples where they live. . . . Becoming occupied
with war will improve them in their habits."[2]

Because of the frequent interplay between these terms in the documents,
it is difficult to determine whether a group leaving Portugal was composed
of volunteer soldiers or *degredados*. The city of Évora used this blurring of
categories to its advantage in early 1640: after a twenty-year series of royal
decrees setting quotas of men to serve in India and Brazil, the city was either
unable or unwilling to send more volunteers and emptied its jail to achieve

its municipal quota.[3] In another example ten years later, King D. João IV noted, "All persons currently in Limoeiro because they failed to leave with their captains, I now order released with the understanding that from here on, those who fail to leave on the [appointed] day with their captains will be rigorously punished." Soldiers and *degredados*, jail and military service were often interchangeable terms in early modern Portugal.

In fact, the Crown often deliberately confused these terms. Males selected first for military service would have been the poor and single—those who either had no families or whose social position made them vulnerable to impressment. Given the quota system, there would have been considerable pressure from the community to offer these men to spare others. In short, these were the marginal figures in the community. The Crown and town councils were quick to point out how well suited these figures, particularly vagrants, were for military service. The *câmara* of Lisbon suggested "the lazy and idle be rounded up and sent to Brazil to serve. Since, for the most part, they are young single men, they are best suited to become soldiers."[4]

Single men serving as soldiers contrasted most sharply with *casados* (married men) and occasionally with the term *voluntários*—those who served freely. Two extended examples of *degredados* that specify ages and marital status tend to support the thesis that *degredado* soldiers were the younger, single males in society. A list of one hundred convicts exiled from Portugal in 1755 reveals that seventy-two were single (the marital status of another thirteen was not stated).[5] In addition, the average age of these unmarried men was twenty-one, seven years younger than the average married male.

The recruitment process also ignored the very young ages of some, such as the child Bernardo Tavira de Sousa who left northern Portugal for India in the 1680s at the tender age of nine.[6] Repeatedly, the Crown reminded captains and others that boys under thirteen were not to be allowed to serve abroad.[7] However, the Crown ignored its own best intentions in this regard when, in 1619, it decided that the solution to the numerous poor boys who roamed the streets of Goa was to round them up and "put them into my royal service on my ships, so that they may be of use."[8] Almost forty years later, Frei João de Cristo petitioned the Overseas Council to be allowed to place all the young boys who reached India on ships in the Colegio dos Reis Magos in Goa.[9]

At times when manpower was critical, the sick were not immune from impressment, although individuals were sometimes encouraged to change captains. The *misericórdia* of Goa ordered in 1576 that those sailors and criminals in the hospital were not to serve or to be forced by others to do so.[10] In an effort to prevent sailors from changing ships without permission from their captains, those who did so were to be exiled to the Molucca Islands for ten years. Captains who allowed these sailors on board were to receive the same punishment as well as loss of credit for any years of service.[11] Simple dereliction of duty was punished by exile to places such as Anjadiva Island, just off Goa's southern coast.[12] Gangs of young boys also roamed the streets of Lisbon in what the Crown and city council felt were alarming numbers. In 1625, the *câmara* suggested that they be rounded up, placed in a vacant building used as a hospital during epidemics, and trained as sailors.[13]

By 1670, the Crown went so far as to admit that the administrative structure it designed to supervise *degredados* overseas was not working. Agencies of the Crown were not aware who was a volunteer serving overseas and who was a criminal exile since "many *degredados* go overseas and after serving [as soldiers] ask for [and are awarded] posts in the same manner as volunteers. In order to stop this practice, the Secretary of Exiles must send a list of exiles to the Secretary of State, who will then know not to reward these people."[14] Later reminders along these same lines, such as that made by the Crown in 1703, point out the impossibility faced by the Crown in sorting out the convicted soldier from the volunteer.[15]

The link connecting soldiers and criminals would only be broken by the creation of a professional military after the middle of the eighteenth century. Until that point, the Crown extracted whatever military service it could from convicts; it rewarded such service when rendered, and pardoned runaway soldiers in an effort to obtain from them whatever cooperation it could.

Transportation Connecting the Empire

The *carreira da India* was more than the maritime voyage from Lisbon to Goa; it was one of the great voyages of its day—only rivaled by the Spanish route connecting Manila and Acapulco. Like the judicial system itself, it linked Lisbon with the empire. The ships making this voyage were the immediate destination for many of those sentenced to locations overseas.

The ideal departure dates for the *carreira* were well known and, in theory, well established. The summer storms near the Cape of Good Hope and the monsoon winds in the Indian Ocean were the two natural phenomena to be considered. A Lisbon departure in March or April meant a September arrival in Goa, with the end of the summer monsoon. For the return voyage, departure from India in late December or early January would have meant an arrival in Lisbon in August.[16] In practice, this system was often delayed, with the resulting hardships of a longer and more violent passage. The exact course of the ship of fleet was "in the *regimento* or sailing instructions, outlined by the authorities in Portugal or India."[17] In it, the authorities might allow or mandate a stop at Luanda or any of the other locations along the route. Once out of sight of Lisbon, it was the captain's responsibility to see that the rules were followed. Boxer's work, as well as other studies, has shown that such *regimentos* were frequently ignored. For example, the outward bound voyage in 1616 included a number of *degredados* from the Limoeiro prison and stopped in Luanda, although their *regimento* did not call for them to do so.[18] In 1635, another fifteen men were sent to India as soldiers.[19] The Crown went to great efforts to coordinate the arrival in Lisbon and sentencing of *degredados* with the departure of these annual fleets, with mixed results.

Tremendous nautical distances separated the various parts of the empire. The *carreira* from Lisbon to Goa was more than 12,000 miles and was a difficult and frequently dangerous journey. Such was the case on the outward-bound voyage in 1562. At one point on that trip when it appeared that the ship would sink, a Jesuit priest aboard was called to hear panicked confessions, first from sailors on one side of the boat and then the other, back and forth. Fortunately, the storm passed and the ship was able to complete its voyage. Writing later from Cochin about this experience and the people on board and their deeds, the priest said "there were many evil and wicked things of which I was very afraid before I left Lisbon. The cause of some of these, as is well known to His Majesty's officers, whose jobs it is to know, is the type of people there are who leave on these ships."[20] Another Jesuit making the same voyage two years later described it as "a type of probation to prove who are the true sons of the Company [of Jesus] . . . and for one to truly come to know oneself." This same priest stated that, of the "650 people on board, over 500 were in extreme poverty and had only the 'King's law.' Of these, many died of hunger."[21] The mortality rate, under the best circumstances, is estimated to have been between 30 and 50 percent.[22] Rates as high as 50 percent were common and would appear to have been caused by scurvy and other forms of malnutrition. "Diogo do Couto tells us that in the fleet in which he returned to India in 1571 nearly 2,000 men died out of a total of

4,000 who left Lisbon. In the six year period 1629–34, out of 5,228 soldiers who left Lisbon for India, only 2,495 reached Goa alive."[23] The voyage was made even more dangerous by the practice of everyone wanting candles next to his bed that, the Jesuits noted, "causes many fires."[24]

A typical voyage would have tried to leave before March or April from Lisbon and might have stopped in Mozambique—a strategically located but unhealthy port, a place where "between 1528 and 1558 over 30,000 men died . . . , mainly from malaria and bilious fevers."[25] Typically, the fleet arrived in Goa in September.[26] Thus the *Fugger Newsletters* reports of an agent who left Lisbon in April and arrived in Goa in early October. His voyage was becalmed for forty-seven days near the equator and he "had to suffer great heat and torment . . . severe cold . . . and several great storms."[27]

The voyage from Lisbon to Angola, while much shorter, could also be dangerous. In 1630, forty *soldados* and six priests were about to leave Lisbon for Angola, but the twenty *pipas* of water that had been placed on board were insufficient. Many broke on the voyage, and it sometimes took five to six months, not the expected four, to reach Luanda.[28]

Degredados *and the Estado da India:*
Problems in the System

Many people died en route, of this there can be little doubt. Much of the official correspondence, however, stresses that too few soldiers were being sent by Lisbon for the far-flung needs of Portugal's Asian empire. In a telling outline of the flaws of the system, Viceroy Miguel de Noronha in 1630 stated, "If 300 men are organized at the Casa da India in Lisbon, only 250 will embark for India. In the end, your Majesty will have less than 100 soldiers."[29] How close to the truth was the viceroy's statement? In 1633, King D. Filipe IV ordered 1,400 soldiers sent to India, partly because of the decreasing numbers of such soldiers as well as the fact that "many people once they arrive there, take another road."[30] The number of soldiers who actually left Lisbon or arrived in India that year is unknown. Given that the records from the Casa da India were destroyed in the 1755 Lisbon earthquake, fundamental questions such as the number of Portuguese in Asia will remain a mystery. Nevertheless, a rare detailed list of those sent in 1685 shows four ships with a total of 922 officers and soldiers leaving Lisbon. A different list of 880 names shows who was supposed to arrive in Goa. However, of these, only 569 people were actually present; 311 (163 soldiers) were missing or dead on the outward voyage.[31] The figures for 1690 show 160 soldiers leaving Lisbon, but the ship's secretary listed 164 (144 soldiers and 20 passengers). Of these soldiers, 115 arrived in Goa.[32]

The *carreira* illustrates several problems in arriving at a solid figure of how many *degredados* were sent to Portuguese Asia or elsewhere. Boxer, in his numerous works, and Magalhães Godinho both report that the mortality rate was high; they also indicate how many ships left. However, the number of soldiers on board is unknown. Therefore, whatever number left Lisbon, some percentage (perhaps as high as thirty) would have to be subtracted to determine how many actually disembarked in Goa. A second percentage would have to be subtracted for those who never recovered in the hospital—a frequent resting place for new arrivals. For example, in 1607 the Crown wrote to the governor of India, "We have been informed that each year in the Hospital [of Goa] three or four hundred Portuguese between the ages of eighteen to thirty die."[33] This was at a comparatively good time; the mortality rates on the voyage and in this hospital only increased during the seventeenth century.[34]

An additional problem that drained manpower (from the state's viewpoint) is mentioned in the 1630 complaint made by the Viceroy D. Miguel de Noronha. Once a soldier arrived in India, one of the easiest and quickest methods to evade service was to join a religious order. By 1588, the Jesuits noted that murderers were not to be allowed to join the Society of Jesus, as stated in their statutes.[35] If the distinction between *degredado* and soldier were often vague, by 1635 there was also some overlap between soldier and brother. In a joint *parecer*, the Mesa da Consciência e Ordens and Conselho do Estado commented on the many soldiers in India. When they attempted to enter Goan monasteries, these two administrative bodies urged "they should be examined to determine if they are moved by the Holy Spirit or by necessity."[36] The city of Goa was well known for the number and wealth of its churches and monasteries. The Crown and church passed a series of laws to prevent additional soldiers from entering, but by 1672 Viceroy Luís de Mendoça Furtado e Albuquerque wrote to Lisbon, "I feel that I must inform Your Majesty that the religious orders here are filled with soldiers, despite the many laws which the prelates have passed. . . . I understand that they have over two hundred soldiers in all the monasteries."[37] Not just *degredados* from Portugal but also local convicts in Goa escaped punishment in this manner. This was the case with António da Cunha de Melo—sentenced to exile by the Goan high court—who entered the monastery of Santo Agostinho and became a brother.[38] Entering these monasteries was but one of several strategies used by *degredado*-soldiers to evade service.

Fidalgos sometimes took their independence too seriously and had their power checked by the Crown; in a sense, these companies became private armies. The loyalty of the individual soldier was interwoven with his economic dependence on the *fidalgo* during the rainy season. One example of this conflict appeared in 1615 when the Crown instructed the viceroy to deal "with rigor against all soldiers who, after being paid, flee battles and stay behind on land [for example, in Goa] and become involved in the private affairs of fidalgos."[39] Much of the legislation mentioned was also motivated by the squabbles of these captains rather than by larger social problems in Goan society. In fact, a *relação* of 1569 went so far as to say that "punitive justice is only given out to poor soldiers, local Christians, and people with little . . . ; captains, fidalgos, and the powerful escape any punishment."[40] During the seventeenth century, law and order in the city of Goa deteriorated. For example, in 1616 twenty to thirty murders per year were noted in Goa, and *fidalgos* were fingered as sheltering the guilty.[41] *Fidalgos* and their special interests were frequently blamed for thwarting justice and causing much of the legal anarchy common at the time.[42]

The single Portuguese men in Goa (*soldados*) were the basis for the military presence, yet "there were never at any single time during the seventeenth century more than a few hundreds."[43] Pearson suggests what seems like a contrary view when he says, "Up to 5,000 footloose and idle soldiers could be resident in Goa," until he adds "in the rainy season."[44] The rainy season was the off-duty time for the *soldados* and many remained in Goa during the heavy rains from June through August. The number of residents was probably much closer to the "few hundreds." During the monsoon season, soldiers had little to do but kill time in Goa or one of the other coastal cities to the north.[45] *Soldados* who remained in Goa took one of two routes during these annual off-duty periods, either banding together in clubs or living with an unmarried Goan woman.[46]

François Pyrard de Laval, a French resident in Goa from 1608 to 1610 who made the above observations, also left little to the imagination as to how the *soldados* made ends meet: they "live a knavish life. . . . By night they murder and rob, and make no scruple about killing a man for his money."[47] "They [*soldados*] wander around sacrificing themselves to Venus and Bacchus."[48] Pyrard de Laval also left a good description of *soldados* and their general state, specifically noting that these were peasants, exiled to India for a variety of crimes, who could not return before the end of their sentences.[49]

The City of Goa

The city of Goa itself was located a few kilometers inland, at the edge of the Mandovi River in the district of Tiswadi (see Map 1, page 15). The Portuguese often referred to the city as an island, since the neighboring swamps virtually made it one. Goa was a large and cosmopolitan city, the economic, cultural, religious, and administrative center of the Estado da India. One of the expressions common at the time demonstrated this magnificence: "If you have seen Goa, you need not go to Lisbon."[50] It was described in 1548 as being "three leagues around and, as everyone knows, there are at least 40,000 Hindus residing here."[51] "The city is very large and has more than twelve or fifteen thousand hearths or homes, counting the Portuguese and the Canarims [Goan Christians]."[52] "Many of the Portuguese men who live here are married in Portugal and marry again here."[53] Fifty years later, Pyrard de Laval described in glowing terms the general order of the place. "I have often been astonished . . . how the Portuguese have managed to construct so many superb buildings . . . and at the good order, regulation, and police they have established, and the power they have acquired, everything being as well maintained and observed as it is in Lisbon itself."[54]

Marriage was of more than passing importance. As the general economic decline of Goa continued throughout the seventeenth century, marriage provided something the state could not: security. In the words of the Goan high court, when the justice Luis de Mergulhão Borges was singled out for royal criticism when he married without royal approval, "without marriage, there is nothing to eat."[55] The Crown promoted the status of married men (*casados*) at the expense of *soldados* in several ways. *Casados* were exempted from military duty and from several municipal taxes.[56] Only *casados* were allowed to hold municipal offices. The most obvious distinction between the two was that the *casados* were allowed to wear a mantle or cloak, something forbidden to *soldados*.[57] In his recent study of Portuguese Asia, Boyajian has also commented on the importance placed on marriage for merchants in Asia.[58] (The entire issue of marriage, particularly in the Estado da India, is the underlying theme of the second half of this study.) Marriage provided *soldados* with immediate and practical means of sustaining themselves and yet another respectable method of escaping their *soldado* status.

This particular method by which *degredados* could escape or improve their status becomes all the more interesting in light of the practice among Goan Christians known as *ghorzanvoim*, or "son-in-law of the house." "In a family having only one daughter or more and no sons, the son-in-law marrying one of them is virtually adopted into the family of the bride."[59] This custom is common in parts of southern India and prevents the loss of the daughter's dowry and other familial wealth: "Her riches and wealth are therefore owned jointly by them all [that is, the wife, her family and new husband]. In Kerala, this system is called Dath."[60] The question then becomes *how long* the Goans have practiced it. If the custom dates from early modern times, it would have provided soldiers with a respected and well-established method of escaping military service.[61]

The annual correspondence between Lisbon and Goa has several recurring themes, one of which was the lack of manpower. Usually this was expressed as the need for additional soldiers, but sometimes the authorities in Goa were more specific. In 1653, for example, the Viceroy D. Vasco Mascarenhas complained to the authorities in Lisbon that the greatest need in the Estado da India was leadership. Specifically, he mentioned the critical need for captains-general for Sri Lanka and the Straits of Hormuz.[62] Another pressing requirement was for (military) engineers, which the viceroy pointed out "were sent to the hinterlands of Brazil, but not here in spite of the very great need for men practiced in that art."[63]

The lack of a military architect in Goa did not prevent the Lisbon authorities from insisting that a new fort be built for the protection of women and children. The Council of Government answered that this plan was simply beyond the capabilities of the city and, even if it were not, there was no one who could direct such work.[64] This small example demonstrates another theme in the annual exchange of correspondence: Lisbon tended toward long-distance micromanagement of the Estado da India, in spite of the lengthy delays in correspondence. Lisbon had its own priorities, which frequently did not match Asian realities.

Lisbon also tried to provide good examples for the common people in Goa to emulate. In this list of criminals sent here and there, it is revealing that at one isolated point in 1613, D. Pedro de Castilho, the viceroy of Portugal, wrote the viceroy of India a letter to accompany several young noblemen going to India. In an obvious effort to play up their positive potential for the *degredo* rabble in Goa (as well as a tacit recognition of the morality common there), he cautioned the viceroy to "counsel them and encourage them to live up to the virtue of their [families'] pasts."[65] Another member of the nobility, Francisco Trancoso da Fonseca, left for India with his wife and children in 1623. The Crown directed the viceroy to give him one or two villages in Sri Lanka, a position in Diu, or a vacant post of equal value.[66]

The Goan Relação *and the Inquisition*

In two parallel judicial efforts, based on metropolitan models, a *relação* was established in Goa in 1544 by King D. João III "because the increase in the number of Christians requires more ministers of justice."[67] In addition, a tribunal of the Inquisition was formally established in Goa in 1560, but several autos-da-fé took place there between 1543 and that date.[68] These two courts functioned in a manner parallel to those in the European homeland, creating their own *degredados*. Unfortunately, the documentation from most of the cases heard before these two courts appears to be lost. As a result, what is known appears in correspondence with Lisbon and in the four or five summary books in the Goan archives.

Until its loss to the Dutch, Sri Lanka was a favored exile of the Goan high court. In a rough parallel, Sri Lanka in the 1600s was to the Goan *relação* what the North African presidios were to European courts in the 1500s. Both regions had pressing requirements for soldiers, and both areas were deemed critical—for very different reasons. As in the case of North Africa, supervision of soldiers in Sri Lanka was frequently lax. For example, the court noted in 1597 that *degredados* sent there had not been presenting themselves to the captain [for military service] and must start doing so.[69] As with other areas of the empire, soldiers' payments were tardy, the infrequency of which "put the security of the entire island at risk."[70] Also parallel to exile in the North African presidios, during the late sixteenth and early seventeenth centuries, *degredo* to Sri Lanka was normally reserved for those guilty of minor or middle-range crimes. For example, the captain of the *Salvação*, D. Luis de Sousa, was held responsible for its loss and in May 1618 was exiled to Sri Lanka for an indefinite period. The Goan high court further stipulated that he could not hold office while there and was not to leave the island without royal permission.[71] Manuel de Sousa was another individual sent there for two years in 1623 for defrauding the state.[72] The nature of the crimes committed by *degredados* sent to Sri Lanka only changed once the military situation became desperate. Before that happened, the viceroy had even attempted or at least seriously considered populating the island with Goans. In 1633, the Crown reminded the viceroy that the island of Sri Lanka could and should be populated with Goan volunteers and not by forcing them to move there.[73] By the next year (1634), military events on the island had shifted against the Portuguese to the point that Luis Murzelo could petition Lisbon to be pardoned from his life exile to the Molucca Islands to life in Sri Lanka.[74]

The Molucca Islands (in modern-day eastern Indonesia) were a favored exile locale of the Goan high court for a variety of serious criminals while this region was under Portuguese control. Documentation on this area from the sixteenth century is rare, but some social aspects of the resident Portuguese is evident in Jesuit letters. For example, in one of his letters to King D. João III in 1546, St. Francis Xavier complained about the pagan life the Portuguese led in India as a whole and also on these islands, needing the Inquisition since they were "following Moorish and Jewish ways."[75] The Portuguese, St. Francis wrote, set a bad example for the conversion of heathens to Christianity.[76] Without preachers, they tended to stray from the faith.[77] Father Lourenço Pires noted in 1566 that "many Portuguese [in the Molucca Islands] have run off and are now hiding in the wild." With some satisfaction, he noted that "God's justice is served since many die of fevers or of hunger."[78] Many Portuguese who settled in these islands came for two or three years and took up local wives.[79]

Although Portuguese political control was slight in this region, some cultural influences were more durable and tended to transcend administration. The Portuguese language, for example continued to be the lingua franca in Southeast Asia well into the seventeenth and even the eighteenth century, a fact that irritated the Dutch governor of Batavia, Van Dieman. "In June 1641, he took sweeping measures to protect and spread the Dutch language because the use of Portuguese was found to be increasing in Batavia and in the other trading posts of the Dutch East India Company."[80] "Both the Sultan of Macassar and his son who succeeded him in 1638 were able to speak, read, and write Portuguese."[81] On the island of Ambon, Portuguese was used "far into the eighteenth century."[82] In addition to the Portuguese language, another legacy was their faith. Pockets of Catholicism remained (and remain) in Southeast Asia long after Portuguese political control ended; sometimes this was combined with Portuguese-speaking peoples, such as those the Dutch encountered in Malacca after 1641.[83] Forms of Portuguese were spoken in Malabar, Malacca, and Sri Lanka "until well into the nineteenth century."[84]

The Portuguese, of course, lost most of their holdings in this region with the appearance of the Dutch in the early years of the seventeenth century. The Moluccas passed to Dutch control in 1605.[85] By 1661, the Estado da India had shrunk to Goa, Damão, Diu, and Macau. Also within the judicial orbit of the Goan high court, the eastern half of Timor remained in Portuguese hands and was used as an exile site for criminals from Mozambique throughout the nineteenth century.[86]

Exile from Goa to Southeast Africa was reserved for the most serious criminals; specifically, *degredados* were sent to man the presidios on Mozambique Island or at Sofala or Quelimane, as well as to the interior region of Monomotapa (in modern Mozambique and Zimbabwe).[87] These locations were used throughout the early modern period for the most serious criminal exiles from Goa, including a number of murderers. One *degredado* sent there in 1649, guilty of embezzlement from the state's share of the annual ship to Mecca and escape from the Goan jail, was Diogo Mendes de Brito. His sentence was exile for life plus a fine.[88] Based on similar sentences, Ruy Lourenço de Távora was probably guilty of murder when in 1622 the Goan high court sentenced him to ten years in Angola, a locale eventually abandoned by the Goan *relação* and reserved for the most serious criminals from Europe. His case also demonstrates the relative flexibility of sentencing, particularly during the crisis years of the Luso-Dutch struggle in Asia. He was fortunate to have the king commute his sentence to an equal period in Malacca.[89] However, he had not left for his exile by 1623 and volunteered for service in the fleet leaving for Muscat.[90]

As part of the overall Portuguese military effort against the Dutch, pardons in exchange for military service were issued with great frequency during the early and mid-seventeenth century. In one such case, the Crown ordered all sentences of exile to the Molucca Islands to be shifted to Malacca in 1622.[91] Eventually, the Goan high court would follow practices used by other courts in the empire and would attempt to turn criminal punishments into fines.[92] In an internal court memorandum from 1777, the Goan Court defined a sliding scale of fines in *milréis* by site of *degredo*. For each year of exile: out of town 4$000; to Anjadiva Island 6$000; to Diu or Damão 8$000; Timor or Mozambique 10$000; and to Sofala 20$000.[93] In this last case (Sofala), the sentence could only commuted with Royal approval.[94] This scale of fines continued in Goa at least until 1827.[95]

Degredados *in West and Southern Africa*

In West Africa, excluding for a moment the island of São Tomé, Portuguese use of the region as an exile locale appears to have diminished after the initial phase of exploration in the second half of the fifteenth century. Cacheu and Bissau (in modern Guinea-Bissau) only reappear in the documentation in the second half of the seventeenth century and then only in the specific context of supplying soldiers to the fort in Cacheu. This military response was needed to support Portuguese claims to the region in response to increased threats made by other Europeans, mostly the French in the Senegal region.[96] The Cape Verde Islands were occasionally used for *degredo,* but not with great frequency. Two revealing cases from the middle and late seventeenth century show the Crown beginning to use the mainland of West Africa for exiles from Cape Verde and vice versa. In 1652 two African men were exiled from Cacheu to Cabo Verde.[97] In the 1690s, the governor and the bishop of Cabo Verde exiled the lover of Nicolau de Araujo, the captain of the calvary, out of town and off the island because of their scandalous and illicit affair. Both the Overseas Council and the king concurred with this punishment.[98]

Like West Africa, Angola was not a common exile site during the sixteenth century.[99] However, both São Tomé and Angola developed into primary *degredado*-receiving regions during the seventeenth century. In the case of São Tomé, the use of criminal exiles as soldiers was in direct response to Dutch threats to the island throughout the first sixty years of the 1600s. Although this was partially true in the Angolan case, more long-term colonization plans were coupled with greater military requirements.[100] *Degredados* and *degredado*-soldiers were perceived in Lisbon as the solutions. The first governors-general of Angola in the late 1500s and early 1600s brought large numbers of soldiers with them; many (if not most) of these were *degredados*.[101] One such soldier was Thomas Fernandes, in jail in Évora for the murder of António Luis. In 1636, he was given a sentence of exile for life to Angola.[102] Fifty years later, a large group of up to two hundred *degredados* left Portugal for Angola, but stopped in Madeira, where another one hundred were added to the group. A total of around three hundred arrived in Luanda.[103] Just two years earlier, a group arrived from Portugal on São Tomé.[104]

In this context, Madeira itself had now become an exporter of *degredados* not only to Africa but also to Brazil. In the month of March 1697, authorities there were able to quickly find one hundred soldiers to send to Maranhão and another two hundred for Angola.[105]

Members of the clergy, such as João da Mota, were also exiled to Angola for punishment. In 1671, he was exiled to Portugal from Goa by Viceroy Luís de Mendonça Furtado e Albuquerque so that the Portuguese authorities could send him to Angola, São Tomé, or elsewhere. This was something the Goan courts could not do, given his clerical status.[106] In a similar case of limited authority in dealing with punishments for the clergy, Padre José da Silva Maciel was exiled to Brazil by the Goan archbishop for murder in 1695, but he was still living in Goa two years later.[107] The archbishop of Lisbon was requested to look into the matter and force him to leave.[108] Father Diogo So-tomaior was another cleric first detained in a monastery and then exiled to Angola for two years. At the end of these two years, he was to be expelled from his order because he was "incorrigible."[109] These priests and other *degredados* were guilty of serious sins and crimes; given the status of Angola among the various *degredo* sites during this period, they were punished with exile to one of the most difficult and demanding places in the Portuguese world, as their unpardonable crimes merited.

Degredados *in Brazil and Maranhão*

In accordance with the policy of depositing exiles along newly charted coasts in West and South Africa, Brazil was used as an exile site with the arrival of the Portuguese in 1500. Pedro Álvares Cabral left two *degredados* on the Brazilian shore, near Porto Seguro.[110] The first indication of Brazil's being incorporated into the legal system of *degredo*, to be used in place of another colony, was in 1535, when Portuguese America was substituted for São Tomé.[111] Obviously, this situation did not endure; São Tomé's involvement with exile in the Portuguese world was extensive. It was in 1549, at the time of the arrival of the first governor-general of Brazil, Tomé de Sousa, that large shipments of *degredados* arrived in Brazil. More than six hundred *degredados* were supposedly on the ships that brought the governor to Brazil.[112] While this figure appears in much of the literature on sixteenth-century Brazil, its accuracy is difficult to accept in light of the numbers of exiles carried in other shipments during this period and afterward. When one of the donataries, Martim Afonso, arrived with his settlers, they totaled some four hundred, with no comment made as to how many may have been *degredados*.[113] When the first sixty European settlers arrived in Espirito Santo, they included "several" *degredados*. There can be little doubt that exiled criminals formed a large segment of the European population in Brazil during the sixteenth century. Pero Borges, the *ouvidor-geral* (superior court magistrate), on an inspection tour of the South in 1549 noted many *degredados* holding offices, including positions in the judiciary, in spite of restrictions to the contrary.

Consider the sources for these numbers. Much of the twentieth-century literature on colonial Brazil notes that Tomé de Sousa's expedition was composed of four hundred soldiers and six hundred *degredados*. The source is

Capistrano de Abreu. A few individuals such as Vianna and Varnhagen note that it was actually six hundred soldiers and four hundred *degredados*.[114] Neither states his source for this critical piece of the *degredado* puzzle, but Vianna suggests his to be the letters of Father Nóbrega, who also was on that voyage with the new governor. Varnhagen suggests his source as the official correspondence between the governor and Lisbon. Nevertheless, a close reading of both the early Jesuit letters and that official correspondence reveals that neither mentions *degredados* nor the number of people who formed that expedition. The actual source is Gabriel Soares de Sousa.[115] Several have even interpreted these numbers to be French criminal exiles, sent in 1555 to establish a French colony in Brazil, although Villegagnon, the head of the French expedition, took with him only some "honorable persons . . . sailors and artisans.[116]

It was also just at this time (the late 1530s and the 1540s) that the Inquisition was founded in Portugal. Given the timing, is it not then probable that the majority of these four hundred *degredados* came from the courts of the Holy Office? In the Évora tribunal, for example, at least 284 prisoners were sentenced by that court in the decade of the 1540s.[117] An additional 101 cases (minimum) were conducted in Coimbra from 1541 to 1546.[118] The number from the Lisbon court in this same decade was probably higher than either of these other two tribunals. Although many exiles in Brazil were undoubtedly sinners exiled by the Inquisition, others would have been criminals sentenced by the civil courts. Hundreds of *degredados* in one shipment to Brazil in the 1540s appears unlikely, unless it represented a major, coordinated effort by both the church and state to populate Portuguese America.[119]

Forced exile to the state of Brazil (that is, the southern two-thirds of the modern country) reached its peak in the sixteenth century, while the colony was still an imperial backwater when compared to Goa and Portuguese Asia. *Degredados* quickly appear in Portuguese America; their debauched and scandalous relations with the Indians, as well as the poor example they set for other colonists, were subjects raised in much of the early colonial correspondence.[120] The first Jesuits arrived in Brazil in 1549; in the years immediately following, they noted "Indians who live along this coast [of Brazil] are untamed and wild, and to this land only *degredados* have come and they are of the most vile and perverse sort from Portugal."[121] Others felt that Brazil was wasted on *degredados*, and they should be put to work and not allowed to roam freely: "only married people should come to this land because it is wasted on *degredados*, who do a lot of damage here. Those who are here should be chained and put to work on royal works."[122]

The colonial government apparently did just that; in 1549 it made a lump-sum payment of 55$713 *réis* to sixty-two people for *resgates* (raiding parties) for exiles and *forçados* who had escaped from their assigned municipal tasks in the city of Salvador.[123] Another *degredado* working in the capital of the colony was the official stonemason, Nuno Garcia, a "young lad, exiled here for eleven years for his part in killing a mulatto man."[124] Several Jesuits in the city took pity on him and petitioned Lisbon on his behalf. Nuno had completed one year of his exile; when he had completed five, the Jesuits asked that the remainder be pardoned. In the event the Crown did not agree, they mentioned the possibility of selling some cows they owned to give him money.[125] Other *degredados* and "homens de mal viver" (men living by dishonest means) lived as slave-raiders on an island near Salvador in the mid-sixteenth century.[126]

It was during this period also that the Goan high court, as well as European courts, used exile to Brazil for some of its most serious criminals. In something of a local scandal in Goa in 1559, several Portuguese men were caught in the act and pleaded guilty to sodomy. A few were burned at the stake, including an adult responsible for teaching reading and writing. Those considered too young for such punishment were deported to Brazil for ten years, a sentence often given to murderers and comparatively lenient, particularly considering the perception of the crime.[127] *Degredados* were also sent to Brazil from Angola—with some frequency in the sixteenth century and in special cases in the 1600s.[128] The length of such exile was usually set at a minimum of five years. Crimes that merited a shorter period were punished with exile to North Africa, one of the *coutos* in Portugal or outside the kingdom, to the galleys, or São Tomé or Príncipe, depending on the individual and crime committed.[129]

In the same manner as courts in the Estado da India, Brazil not only received *degredados*, but its own judicial system exiled colonial criminals. In the first few years of the colony, captains under the donatary regime were given nearly complete judicial authority. They had the authority to appoint *ouvidores* who could hear civil and criminal cases. In the case of the former, the judge could fine criminals up to a maximum of 100 *milréis*. In criminal cases involving "people of higher quality," judges could sentence individuals to ten years in exile and fines of 100 *cruzados*. Death sentences could be issued for others. The usual unpardonable crimes were exempted from this list: heresy, treason, counterfeiting, and sodomy.[130]

Local attitudes toward the acceptance of *degredados* in Brazil say much as to how desperately the community wanted to increase the European element of its population. São Paulo, a true fringe area in the mid-sixteenth century, saw *degredados* as the colonizers they needed and requested that they be sent there, "provided that they are not thieves, so that they can help populate this town, since there are many local *mestiça* women here with whom they can marry and populate this region." [131] In other more central regions, *degredados* were not always welcome. For example, in the 1590s, the city council of Olinda complained that the city, "already had enough people and *degredados* exiled to Brazil should be sent to the captaincies in the south or to Paraíba." [132] The high court of Bahia, which began functioning in 1609 (suppressed from 1626 to 1652), suggested in 1610 that "the *Capitania* of Rio Grande does not have very many people. If someone is to be sentenced to exile here, send him there." [133]

The courts in Europe were ordered to be specific as to the exact exile location in Brazil by the late seventeenth century.[134] Well before that, the *relação* of Salvador had already reinterpreted exile sites in light of its own colonial reality. In a short memorandum to this effect the high court of Salvador stated that crimes in Portugal meriting internal exile would be punished by exile to Pernambuco or Rio Grande [do Norte]; crimes in Portugal punished with exile to Africa would be to Rio de Janeiro or the other captaincies in the South; exile to Brazil from Portugal would mean being sent to Angola, Ceará, or Maranhão; those in Portugal sent to Angola, São Tomé, and Príncipe would face the same punishment in Brazil.[135]

Not just the high court but also more local institutions, such as the city council of Salvador, used *degredo* for a range of infractions of municipal regulations—such as selling wine, olive oil, or cod at inflated prices. In the mid-seventeenth century, sentences of exile ranged from six months out of town to two years in Angola, depending on the quantity of goods sold.[136] Civilians who supplied spoiled wine to the soldiers in the Morro Fort faced the possibility of being exiled there for one year.[137] The Inquisition, although not as established in Brazil as it was in Goa and the homeland, made periodic visits and used exile as one of its punishments.[138]

By 1662, some prisoners sentenced to Angola, São Tomé, and other colonies were being sent to Brazil only because of basic logistical difficulties within the empire. In a letter to the Crown, the Casa da Suplicação complained, "There are no ships going to those places [Angola and São Tomé] so the *misericórdia* is spending a lot of money on [feeding and clothing] these prisoners. Ships for Brazil are leaving and from there the prisoners could continue on to their *degredo* sites." The Crown agreed to this new routing of its prisoners and stipulated that a *carta de guia* be drafted for this group to clarify the Crown's intentions.[139] A few issues come to mind as a result of this complaint. First, it is rather telling of Brazil's centrality in the empire in 1662 that it appears to be more of a transportation hub rather than Lisbon. Second, concern over the expenses of the *misericórdia* are the underlying motivation for speed. Third, there was, of course, a strong possibility that these *degredados* never reached African ports and remained in Brazil, particularly if they could make their way to the fringe regions of Portuguese America.

After the crisis period with the Dutch had passed, in the 1670s Brazilian courts were encouraged to use Angola and only Angola for sentences of exile, "to increase the manpower there in the presidios." Angola was to be used in lieu of all other sites, with the appropriate reduction in sentence to correspond with the crime committed.[140] As early as 1664, *vadios* in Salvador were a problem, and in 1682 a group was sent to Angola for royal service.[141] Judges in Pernambuco, for example, exiled criminals and vagrants to Angola during the first half of the eighteenth century.[142]

Although the high court of Porto was still using selected regions of Brazil for exile as late as 1706, the discovery of gold in the Brazilian interior brought a quick halt to forced colonization in most of Portuguese America.[143] The Brazilian reality had quickly come full circle from European *degredados* being forced to move there. The Crown passed three *alvarás* beginning in 1709 designed to prevent "the depopulation of Portugal" by the free flow of people to Brazil. From 1709, the Crown ordered that only sailors, missionaries, or those who had land or positions in Brazil would be allowed to emigrate there. Those who obtained the required licenses for departure would not be allowed to take servants with them. All were required to depart from Porto or Viana with their passports issued by the high court of Porto. Those caught attempting to evade this procedure were to be put in jail for six months, fined 100 *milréis*, and exiled for three years to Africa. In addition, no foreigners were to be allowed to go to Brazil.[144]

Exile to Brazil proper, including the New Colony of Sacramento, was suspended in a fourth decree of 1722, requiring judges to banish exiles to Maranhão, Cape Verde, Ceará, Angola, India, or Castro Marim—but not to Brazil.[145] However, as Alden has pointed out, forced exile within Brazil to the New Colony of Sacramento continued until the 1770s.[146] Furthermore, the authorities were again reminded that no one was allowed to depart for Brazil without a passport.[147]

Other evidence of Brazil's demographic maturity at roughly this same time comes from a 1690 *consulta* from the Overseas Council, considering

Brazil as the possible source of manpower to fortify India. Ships filled with Brazilian soldiers sent to India "could return to Brazil with the cloth and spices of India. The local people here [in Asia], seeing our power at sea and our manpower, would have cause to fear us." By late colonial times, Brazil appears to have been largely self-sufficient in soldiers. The place of origin of a company formed in the late 1700s in southern Brazil showed only 32 percent to be from Portugal, with the remainder from a variety of regions in Portuguese America.[148]

Although the system of rule by donataries in the sixteenth century eventually gave way to a royal governor in Salvador, for most of the seventeenth and eighteenth centuries (from 1621 to 1774) Portuguese America was divided into two separate states: Brazil and Maranhão (see Map 4). This region of Brazil's North, Maranhão and Pará, was a fringe area of the empire during early modern times. This vast area, "the breath of its coast being 400 leagues and the interior *sertão* (grasslands) almost without end," is an important one for the study of forced colonization.[149] In spite of a number of glowing accounts designed to encourage immigration, in the seventeenth century Maranhão came to depend upon forced and state-sponsored colonization, while the remainder of Portuguese America moved away from it. This region had been ignored by the authorities in Lisbon during the sixteenth century; its only two cities were both established in the early seventeenth century: São Luís do Maranhão, first founded by the French in 1612 and Nossa Senhora de Belém do Pará, founded four years later in 1616.[150] Significantly, both cities began next to forts, and the European element present in the seventeenth century was largely composed of *degredados* and soldiers from Europe, as well as from other regions of Portuguese America.[151] In a typical example of dispatching a group of *degredados* to Maranhão, Bento Maciel Parente, the newly appointed governor, was about to depart for his post in August 1636. The Desembargo do Paço ordered him to take with him "up to two hundred men of a suitable age . . . from those whose crimes do not merit a different [that is, more harsh] punishment . . . as we have done on a past occasion."[152] Soldier-*degredados* such as these mutinied from time to time, especially when they were not paid. This forced captains and even the governor to bankroll soldiers from time to time.[153]

During the seventeenth century Maranhão and Pará came to be linked with the Azores, through both free and forced colonization. Overpopulation and a series of earthquakes on the Azores in the seventeenth century spurred emigration. In 1619, 1622, 1649, 1667, and again in 1673, 1674, and 1677 the Crown organized and paid for the transportation of couples from the Azores

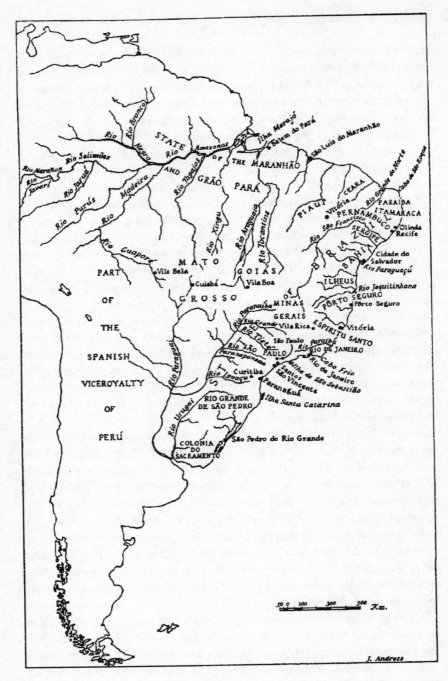

Map 4. Colonial Brazil and the Maranhão in 1750. Reprinted with permission from C. R. Boxer, *The Golden Age of Brazil: Pains of a Growing Society* (Berkeley and Los Angeles: University of California Press, 1969), 276.

to Maranhão.[154] By the early eighteenth century, the high courts in Salvador and Portugal were methodically sending *degredados* to Ceará.[155]

The Crown was aware from a very early date that Portuguese America was ripe for colonization. Since women born in Portugal married quickly, it became a favored exile location for most *degredadas* (that is, female criminals) as well as any other women who "may have erred in their pasts."[156]

At least in terms of Maranhão and other fringe regions, the Crown attempted colonization using marginal figures, both male and female. In 1618, when Simão Estaço da Silveira left Lisbon for Maranhão, he took with him "some 300 people, some [of these] . . . young women, who all married after we arrived and had a life there that would have been impossible here [in Portugal] and they received land."[157] In this account, Silveira goes to some length to present Maranhão in its best possible light with the stated goal of encouraging Portuguese to move there.

Women were specifically banned from exile to North Africa; a few isolated cases exist of women sent to São Tomé and Angola. Although many may have been sent to India during earlier times, it appears that female criminals were increasingly deported to Brazil throughout the seventeenth century. For example, in 1638 Serafina de Jesus was exiled for five years to Brazil for murdering her husband.[158] Had she been a man, the sentence would probably have been ten years to Angola or São Tomé.

In the second half of the seventeenth century, the Inquisition in Portugal turned to Brazil as its primary destination for female sinners.[159] During this period, European tribunals of the Holy Office sent 158 of a total 253 (62 percent) female sinners to Brazil. Only a handful were sent to other overseas colonies, while the remainder were exiled within Portugal, either to Castro Marim (16 percent) or banished from town (9 percent). The most common sins that merited Brazilian exile were giving false testimony to the Holy Office, heresy, Judaism, witchcraft, and bigamy. Male sinners in Portugal at this same time were sent to work in the galleys (41 percent), internal exile (24 percent), Brazil (23 percent), Angola (7 percent), and other overseas destinations (5 percent).[160]

By this time, the central regions of Brazil were viewed as prime regions for colonization, requiring a stronger female component that could be supplied by the Inquisition. The Crown had different methods it would apply to its holdings in Africa and Asia.

FOUR

Convicts, Renegades, and the Military

It is not these people, Your Majesty, who defend the little honor we
retain in India.

— *HAG. MR34 f. 206, 25 January 1670 (1671?)*

Renegades in West Africa, known as *lançados*, were an important feature of
early modern Portuguese relations with the peoples of that region. *Degredados* were deliberately left along the shores of newly charted coasts, while
native peoples were captured and brought to Portugal. In both cases, the objective was to create agents who would develop the linguistic and cultural
skills to act as interpreters.[1] *Lançados* left on the shores of West Africa were
usually convicts guilty of serious crimes, such as murder. João Barreto, in his
study of Portuguese West Africa, defined them as "generally, people of little
moral fiber who served as intermediaries between the indigenous people and
merchants. They lived in native straw huts, allied with one or more indigenous women whose customs and lifestyle they easily adopted."[2]

The Crown at first encouraged the policy of having *lançados* in this region
to facilitate commerce. *Degredados* sailed on the voyages of both Vasco da
Gama and Pedro Álvares Cabral. Da Gama took twelve *degredados* with him
and probably left several in Southeast Africa.[3] Once in place, it became clear
that the Portuguese Crown was unable to control them. In an effort to keep
these regions free of non-Portuguese commercial activities, in 1518 the

Crown reversed the policy of creating *lançados* and attempted to round them up.[4] According to Meintel, these *lançados* and their descendants developed into a distinctive group that regarded itself as both Portuguese and African and continued to play an important role as intermediaries in West Africa, notably in the spread of Cape Verde Creole as the language of commerce.[5]

What quickly developed from this experiment? The state abandoned the policy of deliberately creating runaways and replaced it with the controlled, directed use of *degredados*—as had been done previously in North Africa and in the colonization of Madeira and other islands. Exploration of the route to India was complete; people were now needed to provide logistical and other support for the *carreira da India* and were relocated in a wide variety of strategic locations between Lisbon and Goa. This would explain why *degredados* and *degredadas*, clearly labeled as such in the documents, reappear in Sofala (Mozambique) in the early years of the sixteenth century.[6]

By the late seventeenth century, the Overseas Council was beginning to note runaway soldiers living in the interior of Angola. However, these individuals were not mentioned as frequently in official correspondence as *lançados* in West Africa or *renegados* in Asia, or even Portuguese pirates in the West Indies.[7] Other Portuguese had settled in Spanish America earlier, principally in the great silver city of Potosí and along the coast of northern South America.[8]

Renegados mark the final phase of exile when *degredados* or others left the Portuguese military and cultural sphere and crossed over to "the other side." The basis for this term (at least as it was used in South Asia) was the underlying belief that these soldiers abandoned Christian society, often to serve a foreign (especially the Mogul) army. A priest writing in 1630 contemplated this process and concluded that although soldiers may not have left the Christian Portuguese orbit with the intention of dropping their faith, the result of years of living among heathens caused the Portuguese to adopt other religions.[9]

By definition, runaways such as these are beyond the law and at the edge of the sources, but they do appear from time to time in legal records. *Renegados* crop up early in the history of Portuguese Asia—as early as 1512 when Albuquerque wrote to the king, informing him that he would be pardoning "men who have gone over to the Moors [that is, Moslems]."[10] Albuquerque appears to have had some success in this effort, since two years later he wrote Lisbon to say he had "rounded up several escapees who went over to [serve] Idalcão" [Ismail Adil Khan, Sultan of Bijapur].[11]

Albuquerque continued looking for *renegados*. In 1515, he ordered payment of 14 *xerafins* to Jerónimo de Sousa, captain of the galley *São Vicente*, and 2 *xerafins* to Pero de Vargas for "searching for men who went over to the Moors."[12] Albuquerque also used foreign bounty hunters. In that same year (1515), he ordered the factor in Hormuz to pay "forty *xerafins* and other goods to Raiz Gaexer, a Moor, for capturing Diogo d'Alvito along the Persian Coast and six other Portuguese men who had gone over to the Moors."[13] At the same time, Albuquerque ordered several additional payments to the king of Ormuz for his assistance in helping to capture runaway Portuguese men.[14] Several other examples of early *renegados* are offered by Subrahmanyam in his recent overview of the Portuguese in Asia.[15]

By the end of the sixteenth century, Jesuits were writing that "many Christians [from the Bassein area] have left our Holy faith for the lands of the Moors."[16] As early as 1596, viceroys began a series of general pardons aimed at bringing these individuals back to the fold.[17] One of the major goals of pardons was to make it possible for *renegados* such as these to return. The Crown in Lisbon did not always agree with these plans. At first, much of the legal documentation suggests a series of pardons issued by the viceroys in Goa, followed by cancellations from Lisbon.[18] By 1596, viceroys were given the right to issue limited pardons, with the aim of enticing criminals to return to the empire.[19] In 1606, the Crown began the first of its own general pardons. Two cases from 1621 are examples of this trend: Manuel Veloso Peixote was pardoned for the murder of Francisco Lemos and for wounding António Carneiro (*homen da terra*, that is, Goan); and Bartolomeu Luis, resident of Chaul, was pardoned for killing Paulo Ruiz. Both were noted as being "absent and now in Moslem lands."[20]

Perhaps it is worth pausing to question the exact relationship between criminal exiles and renegades. In theory, all or almost all *degredados* sent to one of the colonies went overseas to serve the Crown as soldiers. Soldiers, by definition, were not married and frequently served in what the Portuguese perceived as remote locations, such as the interior of Angola, Muscat, or Diu. Soldiers were also frequently underpaid, paid late, given promises in lieu of salaries, or simply not paid at all. Under these circumstances, it was in the best interests of soldiers not to depend exclusively on the Portuguese state to provide income. Instead, their interests were better served by generating additional funds through independent economic activity (such as trade or smuggling) or establishing independent support, such as with indigenous peoples through marriage. This interaction could easily reenforce any desire to desert, which from these remote posts was frequent and effortless. Nor was it necessary that the location be removed from the center of Portuguese

Figure 6.   Ruins of a Church in Bassein, near Bombay. Bassein was one of the richest cities and areas of Portuguese Asia. Today the city is in ruins and is surrounded by the northern Bombay suburb of Vassai. Photo by author, 1991.

activities. The city of Goa itself was at the edge of Portuguese territorial control; slipping over to Ponda or other areas under the control of Bijapur was an easy avenue of escape and was frequently taken.

Desertion would have been an attractive alternative for soldiers who lacked the connections to obtain a position in the bureaucracy or who did not have the initial investment to become traders. Desertion also offered a new life to those who had a skill in demand, such as casting or using cannon or to those, such as Luís de Fonseca, guilty of one of the four unpardonable crimes. In 1618 he was burned in effigy by the Goan Inquisition, convicted of sodomy. Presumably, he knew the penalty awaiting him since directly after committing it, he "changed his faith by running away to Moorish lands." [21] All *renegados* were not necessarily soldiers, and all soldiers were not *degredados*. Nevertheless, the evidence indicates that many, if not most, *renegados* were those who had little to keep them in the Portuguese world and the most to gain by leaving it. *Degredados* from Portugal, and many of those convicted in the colonial courts, fell into that category.

Renegades in Asia became synonymous with service to the Moguls, and a Portuguese community was definitely established in Agra in the sixteenth century.[22] However, before its collapse in 1565, the Hindu kingdom of Vija-yanagar tolerated Portuguese *renegados* in its territories, including a quasi-Portuguese colony in São Tomé of Meliapur, near Madras (Map 1).[23] In the 1530s, the town had a population of some fifty to one hundred households.[24] While on a visit there in 1567, a Jesuit priest noted many resident Por-tuguese; several were punished for their sins with exile to Diu.[25] Another quasi-Portuguese colony existed in Bengal, centered in Hugli. Rodrigues da Silveira claimed there were two thousand Portuguese from Bengal serving the Moguls around 1600.[26] Almost a century later, a Portuguese report on Christian missionary activity in Bengal mentioned "three hundred sons of the [local] Portuguese [there who] went to serve the Moors." This report continues at some length and mentions additional Portuguese who married and settled in other regions of Bengal.[27] Subrahmanyam has also shown the existence of Portuguese or quasi-Portuguese communities in the late seven-teenth century on the Coromandel coast, south of Madras.[28] The importance of these communities should not be underestimated; they offered *degreda-dos* a new life in a tangible destination—where fellow countrymen spoke their language, practiced their religion, and generally led profitable lives. Boyajian suggests that the persecution of New Christian merchants in Goa resulted in an additional Lusitanian element seeking such refuge.[29] In both cases, the course of action took these individuals out of the political and ju-dicial control of the Portuguese Crown to nearby Luso-Indian communities.

Portuguese runaways did not serve only South Asian powers. A few later cases show *renegados* who had gone to live or work for other Europeans in Asia. For example, in 1704, forty-five officers and sailors from the ships *São Caetano* and the *Nossa Senhora da Piedade e Santo António* went over to the French (*passaram pellos franceses*). The official report on this incident listed their names (thirty from the *São Caetano* and fifteen from *Nossa Sen-hora da Piedade e Santo António*) and indicated their ages; many were quite young. Some sixteen sailors were under the age of twenty—two of these, Manuel de Almeida de Novaes and one other—were only fourteen.[30] By 1780, the British in Bombay had formed a regiment composed exclusively of Portuguese renegades. Although not mentioned with any frequency in his-torical accounts, their existence is known because three soldiers from this regiment were captured by the Portuguese; the British turned the affair into an international incident, claimed they were British subjects, and demanded their immediate return.[31]

The continual manpower shortage caused by the departure of renegades

Figure 7.   The Chapel of Our Lady of Light, São Tomé, near Madras. São Tomé was the main Luso-Indian population center outside the empire. Photo by author, 1991.

forced the Portuguese state to use both the carrot and the stick. The Crown in 1605 decreed that deserters caught fleeing the scene of battle were to be killed.[32] By contrast, the viceroy of India even went so far in 1627 as to pardon all renegades who killed another renegade, but that decree was invalidated by Lisbon a year later.[33]

This situation remained unchanged a century later when the viceroy complained to the king that soldiers arrived and either immediately joined a religious order or fled to work in the interior of India.[34]

It would appear that women as well as men became renegades, since a decree issued by King D. Sebastião in 1567 specifically mentioned this problem. Women guilty of adultery were "going over to the Moors after hiding from their husbands in the asylum of churches. This causes great harm to their souls and their honor." To alleviate this problem, it was suggested that they be transferred to the *coutos* of Damão or Cannanore.[35]

Renegade men and women appeared in several unlikely places. Fernão Mendes Pinto, in his well-known *Travels*, mentioned meeting two Portuguese renegades: one unnamed woman encountered in (modern-day) Laos in 1545; and another, Nuno Rodrigues Taborda, encountered near Malacca around this same time.[36] Father Pedro Pais, S. J., after four years in a Yemeni jail, wrote in 1593 that he had been able to conduct mass for the other Christian prisoners "with a small copper crucifix brought by a renegade [Portuguese] woman."[37]

General pardons aimed at Asian *renegados* (although most did not include those guilty of any of the four unpardonable crimes) continued throughout the seventeenth century. There is evidence to suggest that these pardons, if not successful, were at least awarded in some cases. D. Manuel de Azevedo was one such lucky fellow. After killing João de Abreu, he fled to "heathen lands where he cannot confess or hear mass." In light of his twenty-five years service to the Crown, he was pardoned. The Goan high court commented that these persons, in addition to satisfying their consciences, would solve shortages felt in the ranks of soldiers.[38]

Although rare in the sixteenth century, pardons became common in Portuguese Asia during the seventeenth century and were issued by the Goan high court with increasing frequency after 1650. It is not a coincidence that these were years of true crisis in Portuguese Asia. In 1660, the Overseas Council stated, "The lack of people in India is caused by deaths by natural causes and by constant fighting with the Dutch." The council suggested giving governors or viceroys the authority to issue pardons (with the usual crimes excepted). Doing this, they felt "would bring back many guilty of murder."[39] Several conditional royal pardons were issued using language such as, "I have been informed that there are many Portuguese soldiers who serve the Moors and heathens, some to get better pay and others to escape punishment."[40] Further clarification of this pardon showed that it was not intended for anyone guilty of the usual unpardonable crimes.[41] Typical of these is that issued in 1677, which reaffirmed an earlier general pardon for "all [Portuguese] criminals who are now absent from Portuguese control and in Moorish lands." Exempted, as always, were those who had committed counterfeiting, sodomy, heresy, or treason.[42] One problem, and indeed one of the major reasons the Crown was reluctant to issue more pardons of an even wider scope, was that they sometimes backfired. Renegades offered the possibility of returning to the fold would accept, and then take advantage of the opportunity to "commit graver crimes" when they evened an old score.[43]

Foreign renegades who joined the ranks of the Portuguese should not be ignored, although cases of them were rare. The few non-Christians who adopted the Portuguese were greeted with open arms. In 1512, Albuquerque welcomed João Machado (original name not stated), "a man who was a Turk [that is, Moslem], became a Christian, and married a local woman [*mulher* da terra]." Albuquerque provided four *milréis* for his wedding.⁴⁴ Five women on the island of Hormuz converted to Christianity in May 1515 and were each given some cotton cloth and half a *xerafin*.⁴⁵ Albuquerque, in a highly symbolic gesture that same year, gave two converts, Nicolau and João Fernandes, suits of Portuguese-style clothes.⁴⁶ Joining the Portuguese could provide a new name, life, and faith. In the case of a certain Dona Joana, joining the Portuguese and conversion to Christianity also gave her the opportunity to select a new husband. In 1601 she abandoned her former husband and Hindu faith and was rewarded with a lump-sum payment and the position of *feitor* (head of a factory) of Damão as a dowry for her future husband.⁴⁷

The Military, Soldiers, and Renegades

The Portuguese military was widely noted for its lack of discipline at home, in India, and elsewhere. In the late 1570s, an Italian traveler in Portugal made the rather scathing comment, "This nation was not born for war nor for order because here one does not find the discipline, the honest rigor, and the obedience demanded by the military." ⁴⁸ The rank and file, as with other early modern European armies, was largely composed of single men. In the Portuguese case, few of these soldiers were volunteers; most were impressed in one of the periodic sweeps of the country or forced into royal service through *degredo*. This would explain the overlap in the meanings of single man, soldier, and *degredado* that has permeated much of this discussion. As a result of its constant manpower shortages, the early modern military was closely linked to criminals and their punishment; these two seemingly unrelated systems were actually interdependent. In fact, the organization most immediately concerned with renegades was the military, not the judiciary.

Francisco Rodrigues Silveira, a soldier in India in the late sixteenth century, felt the decline in military discipline in Portuguese Asia had three causes. The first was the maritime manner in which the Portuguese dominated much of the trade in Asian waters and the great distance at which they operated from their bases in Lisbon and Goa. Included in this first cause was also the unnecessary pomp and splendor with which the viceroys governed in Goa. The second cause was Portugal's lack of a tradition of military training "as done in the other nations of Europe." The third cause, according to Rodrigues Silveira, was that the Portuguese were influenced by the climate and stars in South Asia, which blinded them to their errors and made them "easily adopt the dress and ceremonies of the local peoples." [49] Soldiers, "so far from home, were responsible for feeding and clothing themselves, renting their own houses and buying their own firearms, and being ready to leave on a campaign, all this and only being paid once a year—if at all." Rodrigues Silveira discussed the general misery of ordinary soldiers in the Estado da India and concluded that the large number of *renegados* who served foreign princes and soldiers and who married local women could be directly attributed to this lack of steady salaries. According to Rodrigues Silveira, Portuguese men in Asia were numerous; they simply fled to places like Bengal and were not available for service. Hence the viceroy and other nobles constantly needed new recruits from Portugal, not for imperial defense or other plans made in Lisbon but for their own schemes. [50]

The minimum number of years of required service before repatriation was another obvious motivation for soldiers to desert. The Crown and viceroys made several attempts to shorten the ten years of mandatory service under specific conditions, such as marriage to one of the orphan girls from the Recolhimento da Nossa Senhora da Serra in Goa, or the reduction in this minimum from ten to eight years in 1708. By the middle of the eighteenth century, volunteer soldiers were only required to provide six years of military service in India and could not be forced to reenlist or otherwise be prevented from returning to Portugal. [51] Given their obvious mobility, desertion by sailors was a special problem. By 1718, the viceroy thought it best to simply let them serve as they wished, since regulations designed by the Crown to ensure a minimum of three years of service only "pushed them to *terra firme* to serve other Kings. It would be better," said the viceroy, "to allow them to return to their homes when they wished." [52]

By 1705, the situation in the Estado da India had become desperate enough that the Crown suggested the viceroy seriously consider creating regiments of local Goans to solve the chronic manpower shortages, since "so many [Portuguese soldiers] flee in all directions." Lisbon went on to request the names and descriptions of those who had fled royal service. [53] The first list, compiled for the intervening years of 1705 and 1706, listed fifty-eight soldiers and sailors who had deserted in those two years. [54]

The viceroy was still wrestling with these same issues in his correspondence with Lisbon in 1727 when he complained that this exodus of convicts was an expensive process that weakened Portuguese resources while supporting its enemies. He urged that no more convicts be sent and in their places, the Crown would be well served to send three hundred disciplined men annually. The same viceroy continued his analysis to suggest why soldiers initially deserted. Some did "because they come from Lisbon with that idea. Others desert because they arrive with nothing," and still others deserted because the captains gave them very little to eat; what they did receive was "poorly prepared and rotten." [55]

The solution to this problem, and that of *renegados*, the Crown replied, was not to place soldiers exclusively in the frontier forts suggested by the viceroy, since this would "only hasten the process of their desertion." Rather, the Crown instructed that they should be placed in a variety of forts around Goa to aid in its defense." Regarding the "manner in which the captains sustained them, choose your captains [more] carefully and make sure they do what they are required. If they do not, punish them in accordance with military law." [56]

How many soldiers were there at any given time in the Estado da India? This question is tied to the basic demography of Portugal, the number of exiled criminals, and other single men present in Portuguese Asia. The truth is that no one knows, although documentation survives that offers some impressions. A *relação* of 1568 stated that there were between two and four thousand soldiers listed on a padded *matrícula geral*, while a similar account from the next year put that figure at fourteen or fifteen thousand men.[57] This second account of 1569 describes at some length the fraud surrounding the *matrícula*, or "viceroy's garden," so-called because it was through it that the viceroy "gathered all manner of fruit" from payments made to his family and friends.[58] Diogo do Couto, in his well-known *O Soldado Prático* (ca. 1600) commented on this abuse, stating that in most forts it would be a miracle to actually find half the total number of soldiers listed on the *matrícula*.[59]

In 1627, the Estado da India had an estimated four to five thousand soldiers total in all locations.[60] In terms of specific locations, Macau in 1635 had 850 married Portuguese men. "In this city [Macau], there are many Portuguese sailors, pilots, and mestres. Most of them are married in Portugal and some of them are single." [61] In the same year, Diu had fifty-nine married Portuguese men living outside the fortress, "but there used to be many more. . . . There are around 100 married black Christians." [62] Inside the fortress, 350 soldiers were present and listed on the *matrícula*.[63] In 1639, when Malacca was about to fall to the Dutch, a report made to the Council of Seventeen stated that Portuguese soldiers in Malacca totaled fifty, with three thousand *casados*.[64] A list of the *soldados* present in Chaul in March 1677 shows that nineteen of them were classified as "white," thirty-two were black (*pretos*), and the race of one was not stated. Many of those listed

Figure 8.   Gateway into the city of Diu. Diu was an isolated outpost in Portuguese India, remote from Goa and the central regions around Bombay. The entire city of Diu is surrounded by a wall, shown above, and is located at the east end of the island of the same name. Photo by author, 1991.

were not qualified for duty because they could not shoot. A company roster shows six whites, sixteen blacks, two *mestiços,* and eleven whose race is not stated and also mentions many who have fled.[65] By 1688, the governor of India had at his command some twenty-two companies of soldiers, each with a captain. The total manpower of these companies was just under 1,000: 63 officers and 859 soldiers. The size of a company ranged from 64 to 13, with most around 40.[66]

While the documentation linking *degredados* with soldiers in Portuguese Asia is particularly rich, a few cases from other regions demonstrate that

Figure 9. The main square of Macau. Founded in the 1550s, Macau was the second city of Portuguese Asia and an important funnel for southern Chinese trade and the South China Sea. Macau was well connected with Canton and southern China, Japan, Timor, Malacca, and ultimately Goa. Photo by author, 1997.

these men were present throughout the empire. *Degredado* soldiers were specifically mentioned as being discipline problems in Brazil, where in the 1630s they were reminded to register with the authorities to obtain their service papers.[67] São Tomé, while threatened by the Dutch in 1653, was in dire need of anyone from the jails who could be useful. A memorandum from the Overseas Council listed three or four likely candidates, including João Alvares, a widower in jail in Lisbon for hitting a woman. He had a small daughter, but "was a friend of drink." Another possible recruit was a Frenchman, also married, in jail for trying to sail to Brazil.[68] João Carvalho Moutinho, the captain of the Fortress in Cacheu, wrote the Crown in 1666 suggesting that *degredados* be sent there to serve as soldiers.[69] Five years later in 1671, the governor of Angola asked for fifty men annually to staff his forts. In a tacit acknowledgment of this military-*degredado* link, he continued "if no others are available, then men from Limoeiro [jail] should be sent."[70] Salvador Correia de Sá singled out runaways in the Brazilian interior near São Paulo as a logical source for soldiers to confront the Dutch. He issued a pardon to this effect in 1640, extended to those near São Vicente, urging them to form companies under captains and join him in the North.[71]

In 1692 alone, the supply of *degredados* from the homeland was being drained much faster than it could be replenished. In February of that year, José Pinheiro requested that thirty of the youngest *degredados* be made a part of his company about to depart for Cacheu, where "they could marry with the local women and multiply." This example from Portuguese West Africa was a particularly misfortunate exercise. Of these thirty, eight died on the way and the remaining twenty-two, some in ill health, arrived in Cacheu. Many of these attempted to escape.[72] On the other side of the Atlantic, in November the governor of Maranhão asked all the cities under his administration to draw up lists of possible soldiers for each town. He was given lists of those unable to serve because they were too young, old, or infirm. The Overseas Council responded by asking that up to twenty criminals from the Lisbon jail be sent to Maranhão.[73] A much larger shipment of 120 *degredado*-soldiers arrived in Ceará in 1720.[74]

Restrictions placed on mobility, at times, made soldiers appear suspiciously similar to *degredados*, even if they were not criminals. These limitations further blurred any remaining distinctions between military outpost and jail and appeared throughout the empire—not just in its Asian sectors. In the captaincy of Pernambuco in 1617, for example, the governor, D. Luís de Sousa, directed the master sergeant of the presidio, Pedro de Castro, to conduct a house-to-house search to find several runaway soldiers, escort them to the presidio, and turn them over to the captain. Doing this, the governor stated, "would be for His Majesty's service, and they should not be freed until I order it." This was accomplished in one day, and five prisoners were turned over to the captain of the fort.[75] In that same year, two *degredados* escaped from the harbor in Belém do Pará, and the captain responsible wrote the Council of State to protest his innocence in the matter.[76]

In spite of the best efforts of royal officials, *degredados* and others managed to elude restrictions placed on the movement of people within the empire. Notably, those in Africa were apparently able to reach Brazil without attracting attention. The master sergeant of Santiago (Cape Verde) did just this in 1648.[77] *Degredados* and women from the Casa Pia (that is, prostitutes), destined for Benguela, were mentioned as loitering in Luanda, where they, as well as Gypsies, boarded ships and escaped to Brazil in the 1660s.[78] *Degredados* sent to Brazil in the late 1600s returned to Portugal before completing their sentences; many sent to Angola from Brazil around this same time also returned home before completing their sentences.[79]

In an example from 1708, the Crown ordered increased inspections of ships in Brazil coming from the Estado da India, because many soldiers had been leaving Portuguese Asia without authority. Any soldiers apprehended were to be sent to Portugal and an inquiry was to be held there as to what sort of help they received, "since it is well-known that they could never make these trips without assistance from officials on the boats." In his response, the governor noted that, although four ships from India were in the harbor, it was fruitless to inspect them since they had been there for many months. Although there had been such fugitive soldiers on board, they had long since disappeared. The Crown was concerned enough about this loss from Portuguese Asia to reissue this law the next year.[80] Restrictions placed on those wishing to depart the Estado da India were not new. Similar laws had been passed by viceroys since the 1630s.[81]

In regard to Angola, the Crown felt that the reason so few soldiers volunteered for service was that once they had arrived, they were locked in the presidios and felt as if they would be there forever and would never be able to return to their homes in Portugal. From now on, the Crown directed, these soldiers would only have to serve six years in Angola before being allowed to return, unless they married while there, in which case they could only return with royal permission.[82] The Crown was also concerned that soldiers sent to Angola from Madeira died like flies and those who remained alive were useless. It requested that only men from the hottest places—the Alentejo, the Algarve, the interior of Bahia, and Pernambuco—be sent to Angola.[83]

In addition to Luanda, soldiers were constantly needed along the chain of presidios the Portuguese maintained along the Cuanza River, southeast of Luanda. Forts were established in Massangano, Muxima, Cambambe, and Ambaca.[84] A document from 1624 noted that these four forts had "around 250 soldiers, more or less, and more should be sent there to ensure that we retain what has cost us so much in work and people [to conquer]."[85] By the mid-seventeenth century, Massanango had become large and important enough to warrant its becoming a *vila* in 1654. By the early 1660s, the town had a chapter of the Santa Casa da Misericórdia that administered a hospital for soldiers stricken with tropical illnesses, in spite of the complaints from the Luanda chapter that it had no right to do so.[86]

By the end of the period under scrutiny, the viceroy of Goa, D. Luis de Meneses, Conde de Ericeira, authored a reformist tract on military discipline that validates much of this earlier criticism. In the penalties suggested, it is possible to see common problems faced by the military and the use of exile

as one of their proposed solutions. For example, it was obvious that failure
to respect and obey sergeants (in particular) and officers was a sore point and
one that went to the heart of military command. D. Luis de Meneses suggested that the penalty for failure to obey an officer be two years exile to
Chaul; offending him should be punished by three. Offending a sergeant, he
proposed, should result in three years to Chaul, followed by an additional
five to Diu. He further suggested that deserters be executed; those who sheltered them should be fined 200 *xerafins*.[87]

This period of military reform was indicative of the second half of the
eighteenth century. Soldiers were given a number of special rights, such as
in 1760 when those age fourteen or older, "in light of the service they render," were allowed to make wills and otherwise direct their estates. Soldiers
on the battlefield could make their wills, orally or by writing with their
swords on the ground. These were important concessions in view of the age
of majority (twenty-five) and the legalistic mentality of the society that required written, notarized wills.[88] The training, diet, and daily regime of ordinary soldiers were scrutinized in a new, more rational manner. This new
concern was responsible for the appearance of texts such as the 1748 *Exame
de Bombeiros*, a practical and theoretical handbook on how to be an effective
sapper.[89] In 1797 a small, slender handbook was published for distribution to
the rank and file. In it, the main causes of soldiers' illnesses and their pre-
vention are outlined in detail, as are a number of pointed suggestions on how
to keep troops well fed and happy.[90] Around this same time, a practical man-
ual on being an effective commander was published in *O Capitão de Infantaria Portuguez*, and places were reserved in each company for cadets.

Far-reaching military reform did much to assist in the creation of a professional military in Portugal, a military no longer dependent on convicts to
fill its ranks. In turn, the judicial system had to find another penalty, once
the military-*degredado* link was severed. A number of European powers
were able to make a definitive break in this connection by the late eighteenth
or early nineteenth century. The Portuguese case was not as clear-cut and
occurred somewhat later, in spite of the best efforts of military men such as
the Conde de Shaumburg-Lippe, who attempted an early professionalization
of the Portuguese army in the second half of the eighteenth century.

Much of the historical writing, especially in the nineteenth and early
twentieth centuries, presented the decline of the Estado da India as a parallel
to the decadent morality of its Portuguese inhabitants.[91] In particular, the
nature of *soldados* was presented as having changed since the early sixteenth
century, when they were "heroic Lusitanian conquerors of the East," the

figures immortalized in Camões's epic poem of Portuguese global discovery, *The Lusíadas. Degredados* did not begin to arrive with the decline of the Estado da India. Quite the contrary, they were present from its very foundation, as noted by Albuquerque's own letters and their presence at the fort in Sofala in 1515. It is true that both their numbers and relative percentage of the Portuguese population increased during the course of the seventeenth and eighteenth centuries.

In a rather wistful remark made in 1669, the Overseas Council noted that "experience has shown us how poorly we are served by criminals and vagrants from Limoeiro, who only run away to the land of the Moors and come to no good in those parts."[92] Nevertheless, the Overseas Council and other agencies of the state only increased the flow of *degredados* to India during the course of the seventeenth and eighteenth centuries. Numerous decrees throughout the seventeenth century mandated groups of *degredados* to board the annual departing fleets. This process appears to have only accelerated in the eighteenth century. In 1731, some 382 *degredados* came from Lisbon to Goa and another 228 arrived six years later.[93] Many *presos* (prisoners) arrived in Goa in the post-1750 period.[94] One extended example of a levy in 1755 contains 100 criminals listed by name, place of birth, age, marital status, and length of exile. This list concludes with the statement that "in addition to these . . . many more [*degredados*] will be sent there after they arrive here in the levies." In both 1789 and 1790, large shipments of *degredados* arrived in Goa. The group of 1789 was composed of 113 *degredados* from Portugal and 8 from Salvador. The group the next year was even larger—233 to India and 11 to Mozambique.[95] It becomes clear after reviewing these examples that during the seventeenth century the Estado da India was only one of many locales used for exiles. During the first half of the eighteenth century, Portuguese India and Maranhão (in that order) were the two principal destinations for penal exiles from Portugal. After 1755, internal exile continued to Castro Marim and exiles were sent throughout the empire. Sentences of public works, such as the galleys, were eliminated.

The process of judicial sentencing was complex; exile sites shifted. Nevertheless, the basic pattern was the familiar tripartite division of crime (minor, serious, and unpardonable), and the more serious the crime, the greater the distance of the place of exile. As the empire expanded, new sites of exile were quickly incorporated into this judicial framework. In the early period from 1415 to 1500, minor crimes were punished by internal exile, serious crimes by removal to North Africa, and unpardonable by either galley duty or sentences to São Tomé. In the next century (1501–1600) courts in Porto and Lisbon sent minor criminals to internal sites as well as to North Africa; serious offenders went to the galleys or Portuguese Asia; and unpardonable criminals were sent to the galleys, São Tomé, or Brazil. The high court in Goa sent offenders to Bassein and other *praças do norte* (the string of Portuguese port cities extending from Diu to Chaul in northern India); to Sri Lanka, and the galleys; for unpardonable crimes, to the Molucca Islands or Mozambique. In the period from 1600 to 1700, European courts favored internal exile, especially to the town of Castro Marim, for minor criminals; Brazil, North Africa, or galley service for serious offenders; and São Tomé, Angola, or Maranhão for unpardonable offenses. The Goan court used the *praças do norte*; galley service or Diu; and Mozambique for its sentencing. The high court in Salvador followed this pattern with minor criminals being sent to Pernambuco or Rio Grande [do Norte]; serious offenders to Rio de Janeiro or Maranhão; and its unpardonable cases to São Tomé or Angola. By the eighteenth century, the European and Asian courts had not altered their sites, while the court in Salvador had shifted to using the New Colony of Sacramento for minor offenders; the galleys, Maranhão, or Ceará for serious criminals; and Angola and São Tomé for unpardonable crimes.

In the early years of the nineteenth century, one report suggested that Portugal was deporting around 160 *degredados* annually, to all of its colonies, but, by the later years of that century, Portugal would follow the pattern used by England in Australia and select Angola as the primary destination for penal exile.[96] In 1883, a *deposito geral de degredados* was established in Angola, and Portugal briefly flirted with agricultural penal colonies in the highlands of its largest and most promising African colony.[97]

However, before that occurred, penal exile was molded by the judiciary to respond to the series of crises that defined the greater seventeenth century in the Portuguese world. Although much of that flexibility has already been suggested by the cases mentioned here, it becomes most obvious when, in the next chapter, I examine the coordinated pattern of individual and collective pardons issued by a variety of royal agents.

FIVE

The System Responds to Change

It is in the multiplication of laws, decrees, and resolutions that confusion is born.

—*Resolution of the Mesa da Conciência e Ordens, c. 1750*

We ask Your Majesty for a pardon . . . since this is a new land, so lacking in the basics, it is appropriate that many pardons and favors be given in order to help it develop.

—D. DUARTE DA COSTA, *Governor of Brazil,*
to KING D. JOÃO III, *3 April 1555*

Flexibility in sentencing its criminals was one of the defining characteristics of the penal exile system established by the early modern Portuguese state. This flexibility operated at both the individual and collective levels and was defined in terms of adjustments in lengths and locations of sentences. Individual examples of this process appear in the records as appeals, pardons, or commutations of sentences from one locale to another—after a successful appeal to one of the high courts or the Desembargo do Paço.

Collective commutations of sentences during the seventeenth century were frequently in response to a crisis. The overall pattern of these shifts is not easily discerned because of the piecemeal manner in which they appear in the documentation; any rationale behind these pardons only appears after they have been organized in a coherent, chronological format.

After organizing shifts in sentencing in just such a manner, it becomes clear that the concept of the penalty of exile itself was transformed during early modern times. During the fifteenth and sixteenth centuries, *degredo* was a straightforward sentence in response to the crime or sin committed, in accordance with the law. In the seventeenth century, exile quickly developed into royal service wherever manpower was required at that particular moment, *in spite of any laws that countermanded that particular application*. After the crisis years of the seventeenth century had passed and galley service was eliminated, exile reemerged as a colonizing tool for the empire, particularly for areas such as Portuguese Asia or Africa, which were unable to attract sufficient free immigration.

Individual Pardons and Appeals

Pardons appear with the first documentation from the Estado da India, such as that issued by Albuquerque in 1512, removing the penalty of exile imposed on António Fernandes.[1] The next year, Albuquerque pardoned Duarte Pereira, in light of his services to the Crown, from his sentence of exile for the murder of his wife.[2] As exhibited in cases in North and West Africa, Albuquerque's actions did not demonstrate any departure from the evolving legal traditions that characterized *degredo* in the Portuguese world.

Appeals and pardons fill the books of the Desembargo do Paço as well as lower courts and are even the subject of some royal correspondence between Lisbon and colonial governors. Over the course of the seventeenth century, the Desembargo do Paço had a check placed on its authority to commute exiles sent to the galleys, Angola, or Brazil. These, of course, would have been locations reserved for criminals guilty of one of the four unpardonable crimes. In 1612, it was noted that this body "did not usually commute" the sentences of criminals sent to those exile sites.[3] Fifteen years later (1627), this body was specifically told that they did not have the authority to commute death sentences—only the king had that power.[4] Nevertheless, the Desembargo do Paço was allowed to commute other sentences.[5]

Appeals by members of the nobility were to be expected, since they had the knowledge and means to exploit the legal system. Cases involving commoners, such as those sent to the galleys and elsewhere, who could and did appeal their cases are perhaps more interesting. Several examples will illustrate this complex appeals process in action. The appeals of eight men and one woman, all convicted of murder, were successful and yielded mixed results. In 1616, Luís Mendes Lobo's sentence of ten years in Angola was reduced by half by the Desembargo do Paço.[6] The Goan high court in 1621 pardoned Manuel Correa (from a sentence of three years in Damão) and reduced the seven-year sentence of António Fragoso de Azevedo to five years.[7]

Domingos João and Beatris Fernandes both petitioned the Desembargo do Paço for pardons in 1629. Domingos asked that his sentence of life in the galleys be commuted to life in Brazil; Beatris (petitioning for her husband, the convicted murderer) asked that the time remaining from his sentence of exile to the Cape Verde Islands be commuted.[8] Other convicted murderers during the course of the seventeenth century asked for, and received, pardons, reductions in the duration of their sentences, or changes in exile locations.[9] Still others, such as Baltasar Teixeira, either explicitly requested military service or asked to be sent to places where such service was unavoidable.[10] Alexandre, Manuel, and Francisco de Mello were such soldiers. Sentenced to life in the galleys, the Desembargo do Paço showed great clemency when it commuted their sentences to life in Maranhão.[11]

On other occasions, criminals left their original exile sites and appealed to the courts to legitimatize their departure after the fact. In this process one can see the criminal readily adopting the rationale used by the Crown. That is, the *degredado* was obviously aware of general commutations of sentences and applied the commutation to his own case, with the assumption that the courts would agree—and they frequently did. José Pereira was one such case. He avoided his original *degredo* site (location not stated) and went to Maranhão in 1623. When he petitioned the Desembargo do Paço to authorize this shift in his exile, they did so with the stipulation that, "if [he were] caught outside [Maranhão] he would face the full consequences of his [original] sentence, without appeal."[12] Francisco de Carvalho Candeiro requested and received a change of site for his exile from Angola to Maranhão in this same year.[13] Rui Lourenço de Távora did not even bother for an appeal and was simply noted by the Goan Viceroy D. Francisco da Gama as "now going to [fight in] Muscat rather than to his sentence of exile in Angola."[14]

Pardons once given could also be withdrawn. D. António Telo de Meneses discovered this in 1622 when his case was reviewed by the Desembargo do Paço. His original sentence of four years of exile to Angola was pardoned and then for reasons not stated his pardon was revoked.[15]

These examples demonstrate the flexibility of the courts in sentencing and pardoning, particularly when one reviews the legislation in effect at the time. That is, it is clear that by 1628—only twenty-six years after its publication—the courts no longer felt bound by the strict guidelines on the punishment of exile as outlined in the *Ordenações Filipinas*. Rather, these examples show a remarkable ability and interest on the part of the courts and other royal agents to coordinate the interests of the state with punishments for crimes committed and individual preferences in exile locations.

Other Individual Adjustments in Sentencing

Clemency was not unknown and numerous examples demonstrate the mercy, gratitude, or even greed of the state. When money was scarce, one quick method to obtain it was to allow courts to suspend normal criminal sentencing and substitute civil penalties. In an early example of this process, the Crown allowed the city of Évora in 1524 to commute all sentences of exile of six months or less to fines, since at that particular moment the city faced a number of heavy expenses.[16] The highest judicial body in the land—the Desembargo do Paço—provided another example of the Crown's willingness to at least seriously consider commuting all criminal cases into civil law, punished by fines "which would total 200,000 *ducados*." By their calculations, the "10,000 convicts who roam the interior of Brazil," would have provided enough money to both fortify the colony and remit an excess to Europe during the crisis years of the 1620s and 1630s. In 1629, the Desembargo do Paço suggested to the Crown that this sum could be raised by commuting all criminal sentences into fines on a scale "conforming to the nature of the crimes committed as well as the person who committed them." The only exceptions to these fines were to be for those guilty of unpardonable crimes. In a related suggestion, if this were applied to Brazil, the Desembargo do Paço suggested, then it would have an impact on more than 10,000 convicts who roamed around that country freely, not living in the towns.[17]

In previous cases, the courts in Porto, Lisbon, and Goa, at times when their financial needs were great, converted the criminal case into a civil matter, settled by a fine.

On a personal level, exile could sometimes be avoided by the payment of a fine to institutions other than the courts. D. Duarte da Costa, governor of Brazil, writing from Salvador to King D. João III on 3 April 1555, suggested that the Crown would be well served to send the governors provisions that outlined the use of one *capitania* or another as an exile site, the use of galleys, and the granting of pardons for those sent there. In addition, he suggested fines that would support the local hospital.[18]

In another example in 1628, Julião Francisco was pardoned from his six years of exile to Brazil after he agreed to pay the Hospital de Santo António 8 *milréis*.[19] Eight years later, Matheus Fernandes Camilo paid the same hospital 40 *milréis* to receive a full pardon from a life sentence to the galleys.[20] On the island of São Tomé, Lourenço Pires de Távora was pardoned for killing the dean of the cathedral of that island. He had been sentenced to three years in exile to one of the garrisons in North Africa, but he was pardoned after paying sixty *milréis* to the Mesa da Consciência e Ordens. The Crown further noted that this pardon was granted because of his advanced age.[21]

Pedro Manoel, one of the jailers in Santarém, was shown great clemency by the Crown. Sentenced to two years of exile to Africa for allowing prisoners to escape, he asked for and received a pardon because of his wife and five children; exiling him "would leave them destitute."[22] Fernão Cabral was also shown the mercy of the Crown after he cut off the ears of Francisco de Mello. His death sentence was commuted to an indefinite period of exile in North Africa.[23] Gaspar Cardoso, a jailer in Limoeiro prison in Lisbon, was sentenced to two years in exile in one of these same presidios and received a pardon.[24] Luis Nunes, a ship's pilot, was held responsible for the loss of the *Conceição* and sentenced to the galleys, only to also receive a pardon.[25]

The Crown was not only merciful but also quick to acknowledge services rendered to it. Although the place of residence could and did diminish the length of an exile's sentence, the Crown also showed clemency through the courts to reward soldiers for their services. In other cases, the Crown extended pardons as transparent bribes to encourage military service. In an example of the latter, in Angola in 1591 any exile condemned to five years or less for "a nonscandalous crime" was offered a pardon if he agreed to fight in the current battles in the interior (*guerra da mata*).[26] In other cases, both Ascento de Siqueira de Vasconcelos (sentenced to exile to Africa in 1627) and Domingos de Oliveira were pardoned to allow them to raise companies of soldiers and find ships.[27]

Henrique Correia da Silva was an additional example of such recognition by the Crown. He was captured and jailed in Lisbon's Limoeiro prison after leaving his exile in Tangier. However, since he had originally left to take part in the struggle to expel the Dutch from Brazil (probably in 1625), his service to the Crown was recognized, and he was only required to return to Tangier to complete the remaining term of his original sentence.[28] Manuel Fragoso was pardoned from a death penalty and D. Jorge Manuel de Albuquerque had his exile shifted from Angola to Brazil since they both agreed to "help with [the recapture of] Pernambuco in 1630.[29] Other *degredados* who had served on the coast of Mombassa under Captain Pedro Ruiz Botelho or Captain André de Vasconcelos (but not under the others) were singled out for their exemplary service, and their sentences of exile were forgiven if the lengths were one year or less.[30]

Those *degredados* who served with distinction with the governor of Angola, Salvador de Sá e Benavides, in battles against the Dutch were selected for conditional pardons. The Crown asked for a list of their names and of the crimes committed.[31] Manuel da Cunha was one such soldier. He had originally been thrown in jail in Elvas for a crime "of very low moral quality." He was first sentenced to death, then to the galleys, then to Angola where he served well as a soldier. Given the language describing it and the original death sentence, his crime was probably sodomy. Nevertheless, he was granted a pardon by the Crown in 1649.[32]

General Pardons

General pardons run parallel to the series of crises that punctuated the decline of the Estado da India and westward shift of the focus of the Portuguese Empire in the seventeenth century. In response to a long list of emergencies, a general pardon for all *degredados* willing to enlist was the normal procedure implemented by governors and the courts. This process started with the first campaigns in North Africa and was extended to the Estado da India in the late sixteenth century; the Goan high court continued to issue a series of general pardons throughout the entire seventeen century. The first three examples were those issued in 1596, 1601, and 1606. The first of these allowed the viceroy or governor to issue a limited pardon to criminals who were "*lançados* in various areas"; the second (1601) allowed him to commute death sentences, including those issued by the Goan high court.[33] The pardon of 1606 forgave five years of exile if the *degredado* presented himself before the viceroy for military service within six months. It further promised that any remaining time would be "reconsidered in light of services rendered."[34] Typically, these last two pardons omitted those guilty of any of the four major offenses.

In later correspondence with Lisbon, the governor was forbidden from pardoning exiles who were members of the military orders, but his right to pardon others was confirmed.[35] A broader general pardon was issued in 1615 to any and all Portuguese, even murderers, in "light of that which pleases God and my service and offers remedy to those Portuguese who have gone off to live with the Moors and the heathens."[36] Three years later, another pardon was issued, the second one specifically directed at *lançados* in Bengal. Bringing them back into the fold, the document stated, "would increase both the number and quality of people in the *Estado da India*."[37] In response to the crisis in Hormuz in 1621–1622, the governor of India issued a special pardon for anyone agreeing to sail at once to supply the city with soldiers.[38]

Two interconnected military struggles dominated the Portuguese world in the seventeenth century. It is not surprising, therefore, that they also dominate the series of pardons. These were the Wars of the Restoration of Independence (1640–1668, fought largely in the Alentejo) and (to use Boxer's phrase) the global struggle with the Dutch (1604–ca. 1662). In a desperate bid for manpower for the former, the Crown even went so far as to offer citizenship to any Gypsies who enlisted.[39] Responses to the latter include many of the commutations listed during this period, such as those pardons associated with the defense of Malacca in 1604 and 1622, Brazil in 1626 and 1650, and São Tomé in 1639 and the 1650s.

In 1653, in response to the Dutch threat, the Goan Conselho do Estado (Council of State) issued a general pardon in the name of King D. João IV for all those involved in any disturbances in the recent infighting on Sri Lanka at the time of the Dutch occupation of the island.[40] The next year (1654), in response to the crisis in Muscat, the Goan high court approved a general pardon, issued by António de Sousa Coutinho, for all those willing to fight there.[41] These general pardons, with the same crimes exempted, were repeated "for those who are in Moorish Lands" in 1657, 1660, and 1677.[42]

As eager as all the authorities may have been to bring *lançados* back to the fold and to make *degredados* useful, the Goan high court eventually questioned the governor's authority to pardon those it had sentenced. In a 1669 test case, António de Almeida de Sampaio was sentenced to two years in exile in Chaul and fined 400 *xerafins*. The council of government pardoned him. When the Goan high court complained to Lisbon, the Overseas Council sided with the governor, stating in March of that year that such pardons were valid.[43]

Premature Departure from Exile

The last stage of this legal process of penal exile concerned the punishment given to those criminals or sinners who violated the terms of their sentences. In spite of the Crown's intentions, before completing their sentences, *degredados* left their assigned sites without permission and returned to Lisbon or their usual places of residence. This problem was addressed in the *Ordenações de D. Manuel I*, which specifically prohibited *degredados* from leaving the sites of their exiles to return home or to come to court. They were required to remain in exile until they were eligible for certificates of completion of sentences.[44] In fact, the main function of these certificates was to mark the end of punishment and allow the individual to return home if he or she so desired.

In 1607, decrees were reissued specifically prohibiting escapees from jails or convicted *degredados* to appear in the same city as the king, the court, or the Council of Portugal. Anyone who did this would be returned to the site of his or her original exile.[45] Obviously, these individuals were making their way to court to request a pardon. The fact that laws were repeated would indicate that officials at the sites of exile often did not restrict the movement of criminals in the manner in which the state and the legal system had envisioned. The premature departures of criminals from North African presidios and other regions by hiding on ships were recurring incidents mentioned in much of the correspondence.[46] *Degredadas* who left one of the internal Portuguese *coutos* (either for the first or second time) were frequently sent to Brazil for a length of time to be determined by a judge.[47]

In some cases, *degredados* went to great lengths to avoid exile overseas. In one case, João de Pareja de Siqueira first claimed sanctuary in the monastery of Vila Longa in an effort to evade his ten-year sentence of exile to Mazagão. The Crown was well aware that criminals attempted to avoid exile by hiding in monasteries.[48] In this case, João then left the monastery and established himself in São Miguel in the Azores. In spite of his reported illness, he was sentenced to one of the other garrison cities in North Africa. In the event that he fled his site, he would be sent to India.[49] Convents and monasteries apparently were havens for such criminals on a number of occasions. For example, one day in July 1697 during the hours of the afternoon, seven escaped prisoners arrived at the convent of São Bento in Monção, where they requested and received shelter from those pursuing them. Late that night, they fled over the border into Galicia.[50]

Ratio of Sentences

An additional characteristic of this system of *degredo*—the ratio of the lengths of sentences among differing exile locales in the empire—was developed and constantly modified by the courts during the sixteenth and seventeenth centuries. These ratios were important since they offered judicial guidelines for resentencing *degredados* who escaped from their original sites or for modifying an original sentence to fit a new locale. These ratios, when viewed over the broad scope of the period under study here, offer an imperial "pecking order" or a strong indicator of the relative desirability of one colony in relation to another.

Generally, those guilty of leaving the site of their exile before the mandated time could have their sentences doubled. In the early sixteenth century, the length of banishment from one's town or region, the least serious level of *degredo*, could be cut in half if the *degredado* relocated to Castro Marim. In turn, internal exile to Castro Marim could be reduced by half by service in the North African presidios. In other words, fours years of banishment from town equaled two years in Castro Marim or one year in North Africa. If the original sentence had been to Africa and the *degredado* fled to Brazil, in the early seventeenth century, the proper length was to double it. "Those sentenced to the galleys, Angola or Brazil who escaped would face the death penalty." [51] A little later, a more elaborate equation was devised: those who escaped their original exile would serve twice their sentences if to Brazil; their original time (only) if sentenced to Africa; and sent to Africa if from Castro Marim.[52] If the original sentence had been banishment from the court and the conditions of the exile were violated, the new site was Castro Marim. If the sentence had been for life and it was disregarded, the new penalty could be life in the galleys or even death.[53]

Leaving the site of the original exile could frequently result in being sent to the galleys. For example, this was applied to anyone who escaped exile from Brazil in the sixteenth century. If he escaped the galleys, the *degredado* faced returning or possibly death.[54] This was the case for any priest or monk from the Mosteiro da Santa Cruz. Any individual who broke a house rule would be exiled to Brazil; if he left Brazil, he would be sent to the galleys.[55]

New Crimes

The sentencing for new crimes committed before exile began remained a murky area in this otherwise complex, but reasonably clear, legal picture. At first, the Crown attempted to punish *degredados* for the new crimes first, and then to have them complete the terms of their original sentences. In cases when convicts were unable to pay required fines, the courts experimented with substituting sentences in Brazil or Africa in lieu of fines (at the same ratio of two years in Brazil to equal one in Africa).[56] In an example that falls midway in this legal process, João Caro Sardinha, in jail in 1652 and about to leave from Lisbon for India to complete his exile, was sentenced for his earlier crimes before departure.[57] Eventually, the Crown concluded that the more prudent course of action would be to exile criminals first and have them sentenced by the judge in the new locale for any crimes committed in the interim or at a later date. The injured party was directed to address his case to the judge of the new site where the *degredado* would be put on trial.[58]

Punishing a convict who was already in exile proved to be more difficult than this law would suggest, particularly when exile to a new site was indicated by the courts. This became a problem for *degredados* in São Tomé and Angola. Where could the courts send someone who was already living in one of the two least desirable colonial locations? The court in Luanda posed this question and was instructed by the Overseas Council that convicts should be sent to Benguela, if the sentence was five years or less. Those whose sentences were longer should be sent to São Tomé.[59] Judges on São Tomé could reverse this process and send their *degredados* to Angola or elsewhere in Portuguese Africa. This was a problem also faced by other European powers using exile as a colonial tool, and none had a satisfactory solution. Van Dieman's Land (modern-day Tasmania) and later Norfolk Island were used by the British and Australian authorities, while the French sent some of their most problematic criminals to their holdings in the South Pacific.

A related problem centered on where to detain convicts in these exile locations while they awaited sentencing. Cabo Verde had a jail in good working order in 1651, since several citizens of Cacheu were locked up in it and asked to be released.[60] In Luanda, by 1674 both the jail and the pillory had fallen into disrepair and needed fixing.[61] Two years later in Goa, the city council was having difficulty keeping its jail in a usable state and was forced to temporarily transfer its prisoners to the Casa da Polvora (gunpowder factory).[62] The entire island of São Tomé was a virtual penal colony—so much so that there was apparently no jail there—at least not in 1683. In that year, after committing a one-man crime wave, Fernão Soares de Noronha escaped from the island because there was no secure place to detain him.[63]

The entire system of exile and punishment for new crimes created (or perhaps recognized) a strict order of desirability of locales, starting closest to home (banishment, internal exile in Castro Marim) and ending with those spots considered most remote and unhealthy. During early modern times, the galleys, São Tomé, and Angola occupied this latter position for most criminals sentenced from Europe and America. Mozambique fulfilled this role for Portuguese Asia. The most remote site of all (but certainly not unhealthy) was the island of Saint Helena. Although mentioned in several texts as a possible exile location, there are few references to demonstrate that it was ever used as such. In 1535, for example, five years of exile in Brazil could be reduced by one year if exile were shifted to this island.[64] Until its capture by the Dutch, however, the Crown did flirt with the idea and considered fortifying it in 1608.[65]

Perpetual Banishment and Death Sentences

The final and most severe form of exile was perpetual banishment with concurrent loss of nationality. By all indications, the early modern Portuguese state frequently threatened to use this but, in fact, only did so as a last resort. Far more typical were the numerous clemencies and general pardons discussed above. The Crown did occasionally use this most severe form of banishment. However, these instances are rare enough that the few examples virtually leap from the documents. In 1649, two church officials from the cathedral of Lisbon refused to follow orders given to them by a justice and were exiled to Monção and Miranda. The question was posed as to why they should not also be denaturalized.[66] Another such case occurred in Goa in 1693 when Father Pedro dos Anjos was denaturalized as a result of disobedience, in all likelihood breaking the terms of his original banishment.[67] Another rare example was the case of Luís Francisco de Assis Sanches de Baena, who abandoned his assigned exile in Miranda and moved across the Spanish border to Zamora for the purpose of contracting a marriage. It is noteworthy that he apparently decided to remain there before his case came before the Crown attorney (*procurador da coroa*) in August 1744. He was stripped of his nationality, as well as any honors, income, interest, and pensions. Furthermore, he was forbidden to contract any further business in Portugal.[68]

The ultimate weapon at the disposal of the state was, of course, capital punishment. Numerous sentences, as well as individual laws, indicate that the penalty of breaking exile would be death. For example, in 1603, King D. Filipe III, in a decree to the judge of the *comarca* in Portalegre, stated that death was the penalty for those fleeing their sentences of life in the galleys or to Brazil.[69] "So natural is the love of liberty and so excessive these decrees," stated later royal decrees in 1607 and 1614, the death penalty was modified by these rulings.[70] Nevertheless, the Crown did occasionally use the death penalty, such as in two cases from the Estado da India. A "rich New Christian" was exiled from Cochin in 1559 for the crime of sodomy. He returned anyway (to Cochin) and "continued sinning." He was caught, sent to

Goa, and either drowned or burned.[71] In the case of the convicted murderer Fernão de Miranda, the Goan high court noted that he was the leader of a "scandalous gang" of murderers in Basseim, and agreed on the death penalty in 1618, since "delaying would allow him time to escape from prison since he has many relatives there as well as in Chaul."[72] Sailors who left their ships without permission faced a death sentence.[73] In a similar manner, anyone resisting or impeding a minister or court official faced the death penalty.[74] Every indicator encountered highlights the reluctance of authorities to carry out such a sentence. More typical was the *threat* to carry it out rather than its actual implementation, such as the sentence given to Luís Afonso de Mesquita in 1654. In that year, he was exiled to Brazil with the understanding that if he were to leave his assigned locale he would be executed.[75] Several criminals in Lisbon's jail in 1690 were sentenced to exile with the notation that they faced death if they attempted to return to Portugal.

The frequency of these dire threats and the number of people who returned do not correspond with the paucity of death sentences carried out. As a result, one can only assume that the Crown found it more useful to extract some service out of a *degredado*, however limited that might have been, rather than carry out its own threats. Because of its limited population and global requirements, people (even serious criminals) were simply too few to waste. In some ways, the situation in Portugal has a parallel in similar cases in which the legal structure did not have the luxury of carrying out its own death sentences, such as colonial North Carolina, where "even when the death penalty was required, few people were actually ordered to hang for their crimes."[76] This general thesis is further supported by recent evidence uncovered by Hespanha. In a sample of 294 criminals in Lisbon's jail in the 1690s, he found only three cases of capital punishment.[77] Furthermore, all three were guilty of murder; others guilty of the four most serious crimes, instead of facing death, were sent to Africa, India, or the galleys. In analyzing additional data from Lisbon's civil courts from 1601 to 1800, Hespanha found a staggeringly low average of around two death sentences annually.[78]

These indicators point out that capital punishment, although existing in much of the legal theory of both the state and the church, was rarely carried out in early modern Portugal. This was not the case in other European powers at the same time and demands an explanation. Why did the Portuguese authorities avoid using capital punishment? Part of the answer would appear to be in the country's low demographic base. This lack of people, coupled with extensive global requirements, forced the courts to transcend death sentences based on legal texts. To put it another way, Portugal had too few people and too many needs for the Crown to afford the luxury of not using each and every one of its citizens, including these criminals and sinners. Individual citizens were simply too valuable and the state's needs too great to afford the exercise of additional social control through capital punishment.

It would appear that the state used the death penalty infrequently. But, infrequent when compared to what? These few cases of capital punishment cast another light on the role played by the Inquisition. Studies of the Holy Office in Portugal have concluded that, after its initial phase in the mid-1500s, the number actually sentenced to death by that institution dropped sharply. Although these totals were modest, the fact that the state's courts were even less prone to use capital punishment would partially explain the public perception linking the Holy Office with death sentences.

Collective Shifts in Sentencing and Imperial Policies

What then is the larger significance of this pattern of shifting exile locations in the seventeenth century? Boxer has subdivided the Luso-Dutch struggle into three periods, each with its own central concern: 1641–1644 centered on Sri Lanka and Asia in general; 1645–1654 centered on Pernambuco and Angola; and 1655–1663 on renewed Dutch activities in Asia.[79] When the shifting of *degredado* locales is examined against this framework, a total of three general decrees issued during the first period are relevant: one each to Mazagão, São Tomé, and India. In Boxer's "middle period," seven decrees were issued: three to Maranhão; one to Brazil, Maranhão, and São Tomé; two to São Tomé alone; and only one to India. The third period had a total of five decrees, one each to Mazagão, Cape Verde, Cacheu, São Tomé, and Maranhão. It would appear that Boxer's tripartite division does not apply to the Crown's use of *degredados* as soldiers.

By contrast, Winius has argued that 1656 marked the turning point of the Luso-Dutch struggle because of the Portuguese loss of Sri Lanka. Furthermore, this reflected a calculated strategy of the Overseas Council, to use the limited resources of the Crown to save Portuguese America and Africa, even if this was at the expense of most of Portuguese Asia.[80]

Two other historians who have dealt, to some extent, with this issue are Magalhães Godinho and Oliveira Marques. Magalhães Godinho, unfortunately, has tended to skirt a direct statement on this issue but in his concise survey of the empire in two articles for the *New Cambridge Modern History*, he reaches the conclusion that "from 1675 onwards . . . the [Portuguese] Empire became essentially an Atlantic one, based on Africa and Brazil."[81] Oliveira Marques first points out in his *História de Portugal* the great increases in royal income obtained from Brazil from 1588 to 1640: "26,400 *cruzados* in 1588, 84,000 in 1607, 108,000 in 1619 and almost twice that last figure in 1640—still less than India but growing much faster."[82] Later, he says that Brazil was the empire after the 1690s.[83]

Caio Prado Junior comes to a rather perfunctory conclusion on this issue, agreeing with Azevedo and Peres that immediately after the 1640 restoration, Brazil was the center of the empire.[84]

Winius suggests that this concern for Brazil over India is clearly reflected in the number of *consultas* of the Overseas Council that discussed men and supplies for each region: eighty-seven for Brazil and nineteen for India.[85] This same concern is reflected in the Crown's use of the emergency manpower available in the form of *degredado-soldados*. On at least eighteen separate occasions between 1600 and 1656, agencies of the Crown shifted exile sites between Portuguese America and Asia. Of these, thirteen were to various regions of Portuguese America, and five were to India. In addition, four internal decrees from the Goan high court relocated *degredados* within the Estado da India. The seven remaining decrees from this period provide additional evidence that Winius's evidence may be correct; four shipments were directed to São Tomé alone, one was directed to Cape Verde and São Tomé, and only one relocation each was made to Mazagão and Cacheu.

The majority of the wholesale shifts noted were after the peace treaty concluded with the Dutch in 1661 and the Spanish in 1668. As a result, it is obvious that the Crown made several transitions along the way, in addition to straightforward military needs. First, up to 1600, *degredados* were sent to predetermined exile sites. Second, during the crisis years (1620–1668) when military manpower was needed globally, a more flexible method determined *degredados'* ultimate destinations by matching availability with current need. The last turn of this system in the seventeenth century used exile as a straightforward tool for colonization, to provide manpower where free immigration could not. In addition to Angola and São Tomé, another example of this process can be seen in legislation directing *degredados* to the forts of Cacheu and Bissau and the island of Príncipe during the last half of the seventeenth century. The case of India is even more striking; five decrees sent *degredados'* there before 1656, but sixteen were passed from 1656 to 1701. The Maranhão, Pará, and other regions in Brazil's North were also used as exile sites during the first half of the seventeenth century. These areas were joined with Ceará and fringe regions of Brazil's interior, such as Mato Grosso, by the end of that century.

This overall pattern relates to two additional distinct arguments in the literature. In the case of Portuguese India, Ames has argued that, contrary to the common perception that the Luso-Dutch wars drained it of all vitality, the late seventeenth century saw important economic activity in Portuguese Asia.[86] The series of decrees (above) was the Crown's method of providing some of the manpower needed to ensure that. In regard to the overall pattern of Portuguese emigration, Sousa Ferreira states that until approximately 1650, *colonos* (state-directed emigrants) were the norm. After the 1650s, an additional stream of individuals developed—those who emigrated (mostly to Brazil) for personal motivation, independent of the state.[87] The overall shift of *degredado* sites away from Brazil and to Portuguese Africa (especially Angola) and India during this period confirms Sousa Ferreira's "unofficial" shift of immigration to Brazil. In other words, by the 1650s, Brazil was able to attract enough free immigration that the use of *degredados* was simply not required, at least not to the central regions of Portuguese America.

Defining Characteristics of the System and Its Utility to the State

In spite of the warning to judges (noted at the beginning of Chapter 1), penal exile proved to be one of the most popular punishments in early modern Portugal. In the end, what functions did this system provide for the early modern Portuguese state and what were its defining characteristics?

One of the more complex and intriguing components of this system was its overall flexibility. During the course of the seventeenth century, this *degredado* system proved to be multifunctional for the state and capable of providing alternatives for the convicted. It was notable for its flexibility at a variety of levels.

The length and locale of the sentence became mutable. This flexibility appeared in the early stages of the empire during the fifteenth century in North Africa. It not only continued throughout the period under study here but also became the rule rather than the exception during the second half of the 1600s. *Degredados* were forwarded to Lisbon in a rational and systematic manner. The Crown increasingly came to view them not as convicted criminals simply awaiting transport to sites predetermined by the courts. Rather, the agencies of the Crown, the Overseas Council in particular, came to view *degredados* as a pool of potential labor that could supply critical manpower wherever it was most urgently required at home or overseas. This is particularly evident from the data; sixteenth-century dates are few, and the seventeenth century dominates—particularly the second half of that century.

The system provided an emergency labor pool as needed for crises or for special projects. Examples of this can be found in the Crown's reaction to the battles in the War of the Restoration of Independence. Repeatedly, convicts and runaway soldiers were directed to the Alentejo for military service. Other examples have been demonstrated in the Crown's response to crises in Hormuz, Malacca, and Sri Lanka in the Estado da India and in Brazil.

This system of exile was a colonization tool for the state both at home and overseas. During the fourteenth and fifteenth centuries, much of this effort was channeled to the border towns in Portugal. By the beginning of the sixteenth century, the Crown embarked on a long-term effort lasting 250 years to secure its southeastern border region by transforming the village of Castro Marim into a town. Convicts and sinners sentenced to Castro Marim had little recourse other than to participate in the principal economic activities available to them. For men, this would have been military duty or fishing. For women, prostitution was one of their few options. Both men and women could act as smugglers or work in the salt pans. Overseas, São Tomé, Maranhão, Angola, and Mozambique were all centers for *degredados*. In spite of the numerous problems that have been discussed here, the Crown only dropped a region from this list when free colonizers made forced colonization obsolete. After an interlude using Portuguese India, it then only further intensified its efforts in the remaining African colonies, Angola and Brazil's North and Northeast in particular. An important subcomponent of the entire system was the workforce assigned to the galleys. The galleys were concurrently staffed by the lay courts as well as those of the Inquisition and could absorb or discharge men as required.

This system of exile offered alternatives to the convicted in terms of length and location of exile. This has been shown at some length through the convicts' use of appeals. In addition, numerous opportunities were available for the convicted to escape the system by entering a monastery, arranging a marriage, or deserting.

The two most severe steps in the *degredado* system—loss of nationality or death—were rarely used. Rather, the Crown tried offering pardons with increased frequency during the second half of the seventeenth century (at least in the Estado da India) in a (largely futile) effort to bring *renegados* back into the army and navy.

Finally, this system of penal exile ran on a parallel course with three others: the galleys, the courts of the Inquisition, and the Santa Casa de Misericórdia and its interaction with the state in these colonizing efforts. Until now, I have been largely concerned with the latter two systems and with men. *Degredadas* (female penal exiles) did exist and have been mentioned in a few cases, notably from the Inquisition. Generally, women were not sent to the North African garrisons or elsewhere in Africa, except for those guilty of the most serious crimes. In the place of Africa, most *degredadas* were confined to internal exile or to Brazil, unless they were married and their husbands were guilty of the same crime. In that case, by the end of the eighteenth century, they were supposed to be exiled together overseas.[88] If only the man was guilty, he was allowed to take his wife with him, preferably to one of the least populated regions of the empire.[89] In the third parallel system, directed by these same agencies of the Crown as well as the *misericórdia*, the early modern Portuguese state came to direct the lives of an important segment of single women and the critical colonial roles they occupied.

SIX

Single Women and the Early Modern State: Metropolitan Models

I am just an orphan, an eighty-five-year-old orphan in this world.

— *Conversation with a neighborhood woman, Lisbon, 1990*

In 1524, the viceroy of India discovered three women aboard one of the ships arriving from Lisbon and decreed that any woman who attempted to reach the Estado da India in such a manner, without royal approval, would be banished to one of the *coutos* in Portuguese Asia, even if she was married. Her husband would be returned to Portugal in chains. If the woman was a slave, she would be sold to raise funds for captives. Captains who failed to turn over such women would lose their salaries.

The concern that caused such drastic measures was the "abomination . . . that these men should depart with women in the ships, at the obviously great risk to the women's souls."[1] Nevertheless, Portuguese women did arrive in India, such as when Bishop D. Fernando complained to the king that on his ship during the outward voyage (1532), women were on board and sailors played cards.[2] A number of captains either turned a blind eye or allowed women on board. Women are mentioned with surprising frequency in much of the official correspondence.[3]

In spite of regulations to the contrary, Portuguese women made their way into the empire and, in the Asian case, did so relatively early after 1510.

Their presence, unfortunately, can usually only be discovered when something went terribly wrong; they suddenly appear in official documentation. The one great exception to this overall pattern is a select group of orphan girls authorized to make the trip to India as early as 1545; D. João de Castro himself took several on his voyage in 1547, and still other orphans arrived in 1561.[4] In 1548, one Jesuit father noted, "Many women have come to India on the ships this year. In the middle of a storm, there was one who, although I made every effort, would not make her confession and separate herself from her evil ways."[5] Another woman of "ill-repute" was discovered on the fleet of 1555.[6] More so than any other source, these Jesuit letters provide an eye-opening record of day-to-day experiences on the *carreira da India* and frequently mention women aboard ships.

On what must have been a much duller voyage seven years later (1562), the captain had the priests encourage orphans and other women on board to undertake spiritual exercises. This same captain apparently ran a tight ship; anyone who swore was forced to pay 100 *maravedis* to the *misericórdia*.[7] On this same outward-bound trip, events at one point looked quite grim when the ship was caught in a violent storm. A priest on board was overwhelmed with men and women wanting to confess.[8] Either on that same voyage or the one directly before it, two women were married before the ships reached Mozambique.[9] Another priest on the 1565 voyage reported nine or ten women present.[10] In the next century D. Maria de Noronha, wife of D. Fernando Mascarenhas, and D. Maria de Meneses returned on the boats from India.[11] Women such as these, who did have permission to make the journey, could be accompanied by two female slaves.[12]

Although entire Portuguese *reinol* (born in Portugal) families residing in Asia or Africa were rare, they do appear in the documentation from time to time. For example, Manuel Paez da Vega died on the outward-bound voyage to Goa, in the company of his wife and two children.[13] Both José and Jaque Couto had their families with them in India and were given permission to return to Portugal with them in 1627.[14] Natália de Sá, a Portuguese woman, was reportedly captured in East Africa by the forces of the Ottoman Sultan in 1630 and became a martyr when she refused to renounce her faith and become a *renegada*.[15]

All of this incidental evidence would indicate that Portuguese women were present in the Asian empire from its early years and were generally far more evident than much of the literature might have one believe. Most of these women had little to keep them in Portugal and left Europe for better opportunities overseas, as did most men. These women reflect a number of complex social issues, as do orphans and prostitutes who became state-sponsored colonizers. The state came to view them as colonizers, while it linked the empire with the charitable institutions that supported them. Specifically, both male and female orphans and reformed prostitutes played important roles; and they, too, were colonizers. In fact, from the Crown's perspective, these women were the ideal brides for *reinol* men, a category that included *degredados*. Before examining the experiences of orphans, a few words are in order about their legal rights and the framework in which the state supervised them.

The Juiz dos Órfãos

The position of probate judge (*juiz dos órfãos*) was of central importance to the figures in this study since, as the title indicates, his duties extended to supervising orphans, as well as administering the estates of the deceased. For example, this process surfaces in the written exchanges in 1586 between the *juizes dos órfãs* of Espírito Santo (Brazil) and the town of Aveiro regarding the estate of António Manuel, who died on the way to Portugal to receive his inheritance from his deceased parents. The *juiz dos órfões* of Espírito Santo wrote his counterpart in Aveiro to attempt to collect this inheritance for the three surviving daughters. Miguel de Azeredo, an owner of a sugar mill in Espírito Santo, was appointed their guardian.[16] The duties of this position were outlined in the Manueline Ordinances (1505) and included the general supervision of minors and their estates. Any locale with a population of four hundred or more was required to have a separate probate judge; in smaller towns, the *juiz ordinário* was allowed to preside in these cases. The probate judge had to be over the age of thirty and maintain a book listing the names and goods of all orphans in his jurisdiction.[17] He was also required to appoint a tutor or guardian for a two-year period for orphan boys under fourteen and girls under the age of twelve. This tutor had to be older than twenty-five and under seventy. Twenty-five, in fact, was the age a male could initiate the legal process of petitioning for emancipation; orphans below that age could only marry with the judge's permission. The judge also had to be over thirty and had to supervise a secretary who maintained registers of all orphans in his jurisdiction, along with their goods and the names of their guardians.[18] Actually, male orphans could come of age at twenty-five, and females could marry at eighteen without parental consent.[19] Minors whose fathers were *degredados* with life sentences were considered orphans and could reach the age of majority at twenty-four or twenty-five, via the same legal process as above.[20]

In smaller towns, the position of *juiz dos órfãos* was generally outside the professional judiciary and more or less perceived as a civic duty, a position with few rewards but that absorbed a great deal of time and energy. Several such judges petitioned the Desembargo do Paço in the 1590s with complaints along these lines, stating that the position required a lot of time and paid little.[21]

Posts in larger towns and cities were filled by the professional judiciary. The careful selection process and the training and experience of the various candidates confirm the professionalization of this aspect of the judiciary. For example, in 1590 the post of *juiz dos órfãos* of the city of Évora became vacant, and six people were considered for it. Among these, António Carvalho had been a judge in Sintra; Francisco Veloso had been a *juiz dos órfãos* in Santarém and a *juiz da fora* in Torres Vedras; Agostinho Cardoso was a civil justice (*ouvidor do crime civil*); and one candidate named Baltesar had been the *juiz da fora* in Avis.[22]

In a similar selection process made at the same time, three people were considered for the post in Beja, and four were considered for the town of Silves.[23] Three *letrados* (university graduates) were considered for the position in Santarém: Simão Ferreira, the *juiz da fora* of Trancoso; Agostinho Cardoso, the *juiz da fora* of Óbidos; and Mendes Rodrigues, the *juiz da fora* of Marvão.[24] In Porto in 1593 and 1594, two *juizes dos órfãos* were selected from long lists of candidates drawn up for the occasion. The list from 1593 included Pedro Barreto, a judge in Viseu; Pedro Godinho, previously a justice in Faro, Silves, Loulé, and Mértola; Francisco de Teive, who had presided over cases in Silves and Fronteira; an additional judge who had served in Olivença and Avis; and Simão de Figueiredo, a judge in Castelo de Vide. They all received favorable reviews of their work, but Simão de Figueiredo was selected for the position.[25]

The next year, four married *letrados* were being considered for an additional post in the same city, and favorable reports had been received about all of them, as well. Diogo Ferreira do Carvalho had been the *juiz da fora* of Viseu for six months. Miguel Rebelo, the justice in Guimarães for two years, had also served in Ponte de Lima. Baltasar Jacome do Lago, a criminal justice in Lisbon for the past six months, had previously served as a judge in Alenquer and Castelo de Vide. The fourth and final candidate, João Freire, had been a judge in Viana for more than three years and had previously served in Loulé, Campo Mayor, and Serpa.[26] In an example from a much smaller

town, Inácio Arnaus de Queirós wanted to continue being the *juiz dos órfãos*
in Pedrógão, but, in his petition, stated that if that was not possible, his office should be awarded to his sister-in-law because she "is an orphan and really needs this help [that is, dowry] in order to marry."[27]

The ideal situation had the *juiz dos órfãos* and *da fora* in residence and not
holding the post longer than three years. Nevertheless, as can be seen from
the examples above, it was not always possible to limit the term of each justice to three years in one city. In 1594, the Crown noted that the judges in
Elvas and Estremoz had already served six years in these positions.[28]

Overseas, probate judges were also appointed once every three years. In
a letter to the viceroy of Portugal, Bishop D. Pedro de Castilho, King D. Filipe III reminded him to appoint these *juizes dos órfões* every three years in
Brazil.[29] In 1603, the *câmara* of Macau was awarded the right to elect a *juiz*
and secretary of *órfãos* each three years, who would serve "in the same way
as granted to the city of Goa."[30]

Minor positions associated with these judicial offices were awarded to the
deserving in recognition of royal service. In 1590, the post of secretary of the
probate court (*escrivão dos órfãos*) in the town of Coruche became vacant
on the death of the officeholder, Marcos Teixeira. Eleven people petitioned
for the position, and two of these mentioned services rendered in North
Africa. A widow named Elena Antunes asked for the position as a dowry for
her new husband. However, in the end it was awarded to Antónia Ramalha,
the widow of Marcos Teixeira. Marcos had only been awarded this post because it was Antónia's dowry, granted in recognition of her father's and
brother's services in Mina. This position was renewed as Antónia's dowry, at
least partially because Marcos had only occupied it for three months.[31] In another example, in 1593 a second position of secretary of the probate court
was created in Alenquer and awarded to João de Fonseca for his services as a
factor in Mina and in India.[32] Five years later, the same post in Sines was
awarded to Manuel de Abreu in recognition of his seven years in Mazagão.[33]

The Orphans' Chest

One of the more problematic duties of this judge was to administer the estates of minors. Because of the obvious opportunity for abuse, money belonging to minors was to be kept in a special chest and locked with three
keys. In addition, a strict account was to be kept whenever money was de-
posited or withdrawn. A separate custodian of the chest was appointed by

judges and the *câmara*, such as António Barbeiro in Viana do Castelo in 1650, awarded the post "because he is a trustworthy person."[34]

Concerns regarding the unauthorized use of orphans' estates can be found throughout the Portuguese world, including Salvador and Goa. In the case of Brazil, the high court of Salvador noted in 1613 that wherever there was a *juiz dos órfãos* there must also be a special chest for their estates. The *relação* directed in detail who was to guard it and how.[35] In Portuguese Asia, the Crown noted that money belonging to orphans should be retained by Christians, either Portuguese or Goan, and could not be loaned for speculation to Brahmans "or other heathens."[36] Further safeguards stipulated that such inheritances should be protected in Asia as they were in Portugal, since captains and other officials were prone to raiding orphans' chests during times of crisis.[37]

The Crown was also concerned in 1607 that, when widows in Goa remarried, stepfathers plundered children's estates. The Crown ordered that these goods be registered and guarded until the child reached the age of majority. If necessary, the Crown directed, "mothers should be placed in charge of these estates."[38] In addition, orphans in Goa were not to be emancipated before the age of twenty-five. "Some in India have been, and the result was that they spent all their inheritances. This will have to cease."[39] Just a few years later in 1632, the Goan high court ordered the probate judge to keep an orphans' chest in accordance with these laws; either Goa had not had such a chest before that time or it was empty and the regulations ignored.[40] This situation had not improved by the end of the seventeenth century. Domingos de Siqueira Sarmiento, the *juiz dos órfãos* and *provedor-mor dos defuntos* of Goa wrote the Crown that the orphans' chest was empty and that no accounts had been kept.[41] Similar problems were reported in 1655 with money left to the *misericórdia* of Évora for dowries.[42]

What becomes obvious from such documentation is that orphans' estates (especially liquid assets in these chests) were too tempting to overlook, particularly in hard times, and were spent on the pressing needs of the moment. This would explain why such directives were apparently never carried out.

The Guardian or Tutor

A guardian was normally appointed to care for the orphan and to administer his or her estate (under the direction of the probate judge) until the child reached the age of emancipation. How time consuming and expensive was this position? Manuel Pires da Roca of the town of Ouguela (eastern Portugal, near Elvas) acted as guardian for the town's orphans, including his two nephews Pedro and Manuel, the orphaned sons of his brother-in-law Pedro Fernandes Fatagas. For two years during the period from August 1685 to September 1693, an audit of their estates was ordered by Afonso Soares Mexea, the *juiz ordinário* of that town, acting also as *juiz dos órfãos*.[43] As indicated in the regulations for probate justices, this was clearly in line with his duties; another audit was taken six years later. In this second summary, Manuel Pires detailed his expenses in raising these two children. Little Miguel had an illness that lasted three months. In that period, his guardian purchased seven hens, which cost him 250 *réis* each, totaling 1$750 *réis*. He also bought six roosters at a total of 300 *réis*, 400 *réis* of sugar, 200 *réis* of eggs; another 400 *réis* were paid to the pharmacist and the barber. His brother, Pedro, also had an illness that required 1$000 *réis* in chickens, eggs, sugar, and barber's fees. Miguel, Pedro, and three other orphan boys apparently lived with this guardian. Included in the audit of their accounts is a charge of 500 *réis* for rent for three years, deducted from their inheritances and paid to this same Manuel Pires in 1698.[44]

To then answer the questions posed, raising a child was not cheap. This was especially true when he or she became ill and required expensive foods (such as chickens) and medicine. Those who took their responsibilities seriously, such as Manuel Pires, undoubtedly found that these duties occupied much of their time.

A tutor was not just responsible for the physical well-being of his ward but also had to look out for the child's ultimate best interests. Diogo Lobo de Abreu did just that for his two orphaned nieces, D. Angela Estefania and D. Maria Teresa de Albuquerque. In the early seventeenth century, he petitioned the Crown from Goa to award dowries to each of them, which it did.[45]

Orphanages

This system of a guardian working under the authority of a probate judge was one pattern used when the tutor was a relative and could either directly provide for the orphan or later be reimbursed from the estate, as in the case of Manuel Pires. Poor children without such family and money, as well as abandoned children of unknown parentage, formed a separate (and much larger) group of orphans that was outside this guardian system.

Abandoned children (*enjeitados* or *expostos*) were supported by the local *misericórdia* or *câmara* (or a combination of funds from both). In the Goan case, the 1655 revised statutes of the *misericórdia* recognized that it had the responsibility to care for orphaned or abandoned children with the money given to it by the *câmara*.[46] Occasionally the state intervened directly with financial help, as in 1592 when the Casa da India assisted the orphans of Vila Viçosa (east-central Portugal) by selling property it owned there and giving the proceeds to the *provedor dos órfãos* of that city.[47]

In yet another link established among orphans, nuns, and other single women and the empire, the state subsidized charitable and religious institutions with periodic payments made from the Casa da India. In 1636, the boys' orphanage in Lisbon was specifically put on the list of institutions receiving royal subsidies. Payment came from the sale of pepper, cloves, cinnamon, ginger, and malaguetta pepper.[48] Most charitable institutions in Goa were funded from a special 1 percent trade tax, specifically created for this purpose.[49] Later, when these funds proved insufficient, a percentage from the royal monopoly on tobacco was added. A similar tax on trade was in place in Macau. State expenses in Diu in 1635 show large sums going to its *misericórdia*.[50] Similar taxes and royal subsidies for charity were in place in a number of other cities in the Portuguese world during early modern times.

Male Orphans

Male orphans in the larger cities were frequently placed in orphanages when spaces became available. Évora, Lisbon, and Porto all had shelters for male orphans. In the case of Porto, the Colegio dos Meninos Orfãos da Nossa Senhora da Graça was founded in 1586.[51] Their revised statutes of 1739 noted that, as in the case of other shelters, they were modeled after identical homes in Évora and Lisbon.[52] A second orphanage for boys was founded in Porto by Prince Regent D. Pedro II in 1679.[53] In the same manner as the *misericórdia*, these institutions were deliberately modeled after each other and often copied the statutes of the parent institution verbatim.

The number of boys in Graça was limited to twenty; furthermore, the statutes noted that they must, as a minimum, be fatherless. In the eyes of the law, children were orphans if they had lost their fathers only, even if their mothers were still living. Boys entering Graça had to be of "pure blood" (that is, not of New Christian, Moorish, or Gypsy parentage). In addition, they had to be poor, from the city, and "ideally, should know how to read and write a little." In order to enter, they had to be between four and twelve years of age, since "if they are older, they are not as easy to subjugate." The boys wore a uniform; when they went around the city, they were required to go in pairs and could not sleep outside the college. *Porcionistas* (paying boarders) were accepted from the community at the rate of 20 *milréis*, doubled in 1735 to 40 *milréis*. The boys were allowed to remain in the orphanage until they reached the age of fifteen, when they were to be placed in a job or apprenticed as sailors (*grumetes*). Those "who study or demonstrate talent in singing" were retained by the orphanage until they could be ordained as priests at the age of twenty-one or twenty-two. Those who were "naturally bad, who played cards or other illicit games, carried knives or other arms, lied, eyed or approached women after being punished by the rector" were sent to Brazil or India to serve the Crown and were not allowed to return to Porto or the orphanage. These were not just theoretical regulations. Four boys went to Brazil in 1653, and another sixteen were sent there from 1693 to 1715. In the same period, fifteen others became priests.[54]

The state was eager to enlist "soldiers" as young as eight. Sailors still in their early teens were not uncommon. This practice of using orphan boys as sailors was common throughout western Europe; the French navy had a similar experience. "Boys from eight to ten years old—often brought from orphanages—formed most of the trainees. Many deserted by early adulthood."[55]

The safety of these little boys who arrived in Goa on the ships was the subject of a curious letter from the Crown to the viceroy in 1601. In it, the Crown complained that it had been informed that "some people meet the arriving ships and take away the little boys who go to India on them. These people later take them away or sell them to nobles or soldiers and these boys end up as captives." The Crown further directed that boys too young for royal service be taken to the hospital and taken care of from funds from the royal account.[56] A few years later in 1624, the Crown wrote Goa that it had been informed that Christian children were being kidnapped in Goa and sold to the Moors. Although from this statement alone it is impossible to tell if the second group of little boys were Goan or Portuguese, the Crown directed that "anyone caught doing this will be executed and if not captured, will lose all his goods."[57]

Training orphan boys to become sailors was an idea put forth by no less a figure than Manuel Severim de Faria in his well-known social and economic commentary, *Noticias de Portugal*, first published in 1655. In his first chapter, Faria discussed Portugal's lack of manpower and possible remedies. He also suggested collecting orphan boys in port cities, such as Lisbon, Setúbal,

Porto, and Viana in order to train them to become apprentice sailors. "In this way, they would become useful and the Kingdom [of Portugal] would avoid the masses of poor and *vadios* which roam the country."[58] Faria also stressed the importance of awarding dowries to all female orphans, "so that they will marry and produce children."[59]

The practice of using orphan boys as apprentice sailors was popular during early modern times and continued well into the nineteenth century. In 1794, Cunha de Azeredo Coutinho addressed this problem when he suggested that the navy's manpower shortages could be overcome by training the Brazilian Indians to fish in large boats, which they would also instruct the Indians to build. "Although we have prisoners to man the army, we have none to augment the navy. . . . From this background will spring sailors trained in all the arts to sail in those waters."[60] In 1832, the Royal Orphanage in Lisbon petitioned the Crown to allow seven boys between the ages of thirteen and seventeen to be placed on ships as apprentices bound for the Estado da India.[61]

Other orphan boys were used for missionary activities in the colonies, especially Brazil. The Jesuits noted that the participation of orphan boys in the conversion process yielded mixed results. Their main fear was that the boys were too young and therefore easily corrupted by the local women.[62] However, to the contrary, several orphans sent to Brazil became Jesuits and grew up with the Indians, learning their languages and teaching them the Christian faith. These young boys thus acted as cultural and religious intermediaries. António de Pina and João Pereira were specifically mentioned in Jesuit correspondence as performing exemplary jobs in Salvador.[63] Other orphans who followed this path by 1568 were: Simon Gonçalves, also working in Salvador; Luís Valente in Rio de Janeiro; and Manuel Viegas working in São Paulo de Piratininga.[64]

Female Orphans

Perhaps a clearer distinction in the treatment and expectations of male and female orphans can be drawn by contrasting the rules of male and female orphanages in Porto at the same time. The 1685 statutes of the Recolhimento das Donzelas Orfãs da Rainha Santa Isabel stated that it was founded by D. Elena Pereira after the death of her husband, Gonçalo Borges Pinto. The *câmara* of Porto donated the land. The statutes were the same as those of the *recolhimento* for young ladies (*donzelas*) of Évora. Orphan girls were allowed to enter at the age of twelve and could stay until they reached forty. The maximum in residence at any one time was set at twenty-one. No woman of Jewish, mulatto, or Moorish background could enter. The girls had to be from the city or born to noble parents and grandparents. The shelter was also open to married women, whose husbands were absent, and to widows, who were allowed to stay until they reached the age of forty. Paying boarders were charged 20 *milréis* annually and some needy women were allowed in at a lesser rate, "as a refuge from their poverty." [65]

The daily routine in such an institution demanded that all rise at five o'clock from Easter until the fourteenth of September. During the winter months until Easter, they awakened at six. A total of three maids were allowed for the entire orphanage, but an individual orphan could have her own servant if she paid her salary. In either case, servants who worked in the shelter had to be women of "good virtue." [66]

Institutional Problems

This particular orphanage in Porto had two difficulties in the late seventeenth century that are instructive, since both were typical of such shelters. In the 1680s, it was short of funds and had to begin a process of arm-twisting to collect money it was due, specifically a long-standing debt from Francisco de Brito Freire. In April 1674, he had promised to pay 40 *milréis* annually.[67] In the decade that followed, he had not paid a *tostão*, so he owed 400 *milréis*. At that point, the orphanage requested the assistance of Father João de Faria (in Setúbal, where Francisco was presumably residing) to help the orphanage collect this debt. Although Francisco made partial payments during the next few years, by 1689 he owed the orphanage more than 450 *milréis*. They were still trying to collect whatever they could a decade later; their accounts show that his failure to pay prevented them from awarding all the dowries they had promised.[68]

A second common difficulty was maintaining order and discipline within the institution. In 1691 the bishop of Porto, D. João de Sousa, sent D. Francisco Monteiro, his inspector, to investigate the Recolhimento da Santa Isabel because of the various complaints he had received regarding their failure to follow their statutes. His report stated that the orphan girls and others must follow the orders given to them by the assistant regent. All persons who were not orphans, paying boarders, or who did not have the bishop's written authority to be there were to leave within a month because "they are breaking the rules of the *recolhimento* and causing it harm." Those who remained were specifically forbidden from receiving or sending notes, speaking with men—even brothers or fathers—or conversing with people from the windows of the orphanage.[69]

The same bishop had similar discipline problems with the sisters of the convent of Bom Jesus of Valença (extreme northwestern Portugal). Sister Mariana de Purificação informed the bishop that two sisters were involved in a feud and requested that he intervene because their actions were beginning to detract from the harmony of the convent. In her letter of complaint sent to the bishop in December 1697, she mentioned the behavior of Sister Maria Ursula do Espirito Santo and asked for a secret inquiry. This was reinforced by a letter (dated the next day) from the mother superior of the convent, Francisca de Chagas, in which she also complained of the behavior of Sister Ursula and requested guidance from the bishop. In return, D. João de Sousa sent an investigator, João Gomes Pereira. In his report, Pereira mentioned that Sister Maria Ursula do Espirito Santo and Sister Mariana de Purificação had been fighting, and Sister Ursula was the guilty party. Specifically, Sister Ursula disobeyed the mother superior, refused to follow the rules of the convent, drank (too much?) wine, and on two occasions insulted Sister Mariana by calling her "a whore and a pig in front of all the other sisters in the choir." All agreed that Sister Mariana was a humble and quiet soul and that Sister Ursula should be punished. Six weeks after this report was made, Sister Ursula was disciplined, probably by being locked in her room.[70] Two other nuns, this time in the convent of São Francisco in Monção (extreme northwestern Portugal), were upsetting the other sisters with their "illicit conversations." The bishop's investigator suggested that Sisters D. Maria de Abreu and D. Angela de Magalhães, the two "educated" ones in the convent, had a suspicious relationship ("uma amizade de mã suspeita") with an unnamed sister and refused to follow the convent's rules or obey the mother superior.[71]

Obviously, in spite of the rules and regulations that outlined a life of reflection and virtue, the day-to-day life in such orphanages and convents could be one of intrigue and infighting, which was all the more embittered by the (sometimes forced) isolation of these women. One social commentary from the mid-eighteenth century dealt with this issue when it stated what many women, such as Sister Maria Ursula, may have felt: "My parents put me in this convent when I was very small, and now I see myself condemned to a perpetual jail, without being guilty, if it is not a great crime to be a woman born to a noble but poor father."[72]

Female Orphanages

A second orphanage for girls was founded in Porto in 1731: the Recolhimento de Orfãs de Nossa Senhora de Esperança. Its statutes were similar to those already discussed, but they added that orphan girls would only be admitted if they were not blind, did not have any sores on their faces, or were not otherwise deformed. Daughters of nobles would be given preference over commoners, and daughters of brothers of the *misericórdia* would be given preference, all other factors being equal. Little girls could enter from the age of seven until they were fourteen and had to leave the shelter when they reached twenty-five.[73]

In the case of Évora, in 1620 the king permitted a shelter for young ladies, the Casa das Donzelas, to be founded and asked to be kept informed of its progress. Five days later, he was petitioned by the *câmara* and contributed to it.[74] Its 1625 statutes stated that it could hold up to twelve young ladies who were fatherless and at least sixteen years old. They were allowed to remain in the shelter until the age of twenty-five when "they should assume another state" (that is, marry or become nuns). If at the age of twenty-five they did not, they were required to leave the shelter within six years to provide spaces for younger women "who are in greater danger because of their ages." Paying boarders, married women, and widows could stay as long as they could pay, to the age of forty-five, "because at that age, the danger to them begins to diminish." Their annual rate was set at 20 *milréis*, increased to twenty-five by 1659.[75] The statutes required everyone to eat together: "beef, lamb, or pork depending on the season." On fish days, they also were to have vegetables. Something was to be served before and after the main dish, and they were to be provided with fruit daily, bread, figs, olives, and cheese. All residents were to rise at half-past five through the summer months until the end of September. During the winter, they got up at seven.[76]

The ultimate objective of these institutions was marriage for these girls. Orphans such as these would be given dowries by the *misericórdia*, and the process could be further expedited by showing them to prospective husbands, if need be. Guidelines were issued on the delicate process of how to accomplish this.[77]

Girls could be expelled from the orphanage for a variety of reasons: possessing letters (to or from anybody) without the initials of the mother superior; having friendships (either inside or outside of the orphanage) that caused scandals; attempting to talk to forbidden persons; having an incurable

disease; injuring anyone seriously (or the regent in any way); failing to ad-
here to the wishes of the *misericórdia* or the headmistress; possessing any
key to the orphanage; having papers written in code; and speaking with men,
hiding them inside the building, or promising marriage.[78]

A similar array of orphanages was founded in the colonies. In the early
1600s, the Crown decreed that it was against the establishment of any convents in Salvador or Pernambuco since, like Goa, "we annually send orphans
there in an effort to populate these cities. A shelter for young ladies is fine,
but no convent." [79] Such an orphanage was founded in Rio de Janeiro in 1695,
with a maximum of thirty young ladies allowed to join.[80] Two additional
shelters were established by the *misericórdia* in Rio in the 1730s, one for
abandoned infants and another for orphan girls.[81] In 1694, the Crown agreed
to a shelter for orphans in Damão modeled on Nossa Senhora da Serra in
Goa, but stipulated that it was not to be a convent, "since the two already ex-
istent in the Estado da India were already a great expense." [82] A temporary
shelter for widows and orphans was begun in Macau in 1726. The *câmara*
endowed it with one half of one percent of the city's overall trade. The shelter was reorganized in 1782 and given the name Recolhimento de Santa Rosa
de Lima.[83]

The noteworthy differences between the treatment of male and female
orphans as shown in these statutes are the duration the *misericórdia* was
willing to support them (boys to age fifteen, girls to twenty-five or forty under some circumstances); the greater emphasis placed on the physical appearance and parentage of the girls; and restrictions placed on the ability of
the girls to communicate freely. Meanwhile, boys were only directed to remain in pairs when they wandered around the city.

In both cases, orphans who caused trouble or refused to obey orders
would be expelled, but girls remained in town while orphan boys were made
into child *degredados*. It also becomes obvious that the mission of orphanages for boys was straightforward: tend to their needs while they were
young and then make them useful (as sailors, in other trades, to aid in missionary activities, or as priests). Orphanages for girls had distinct goals:
marriage for younger women and shelter for widows and those whose husbands were absent. Furthermore, the number of female orphanages and their
small sizes, as well as the distinct goals, were reflected by differences in their
social standings in their communities. That is, some orphanages were richer,
more desirable, and more closely associated with the nobility. This same pattern reappeared with convents.

Dowries and the Misericórdia

Awarding dowries left to it in legacies was of one of the *misericórdia's* most important social and financial activities.[84] How this body selected women to receive these is of more than passing interest. The detailed instructions on this delicate matter were listed in the revised statutes of 1646 of the *misericórdia* of Porto. This passage is of particular importance because, as it notes, it was the system used by all *misericórdias* that award dowries, and almost all of them did or could. Even in small towns, local *misericórdias* would have been able to occasionally award a dowry or two. In the larger cities such as Porto, Évora, Salvador, and Goa this would have been an annual event, with a number of dowries.[85]

The detailed procedure on how to select the young ladies and award dowries included a schedule and safeguards for both the *misericórdia* and the orphan. The process began each year during Lent and concluded with the awarding of dowries to those selected around Pentecost.[86]

In the case of Évora, in the one fiscal year of 1622–1623 (the fiscal year started and ended on St. John's Day), the *misericórdia* paid 56 *milréis* for five dowries: three for 12 and two for 10 *milréis*.[87] The same *misericórdia* awarded sixteen dowries in the period from 1657 to 1658: three were valued at 20, nine at 12, and four at 10 *milréis*.[88] The value of dowries in Évora did not appear to increase much. Thirty years later, they ranged from 10 to 20 *milréis*, but the vast majority were set at 12 *milréis*, a situation that remained unchanged ten years later and continued until the mid-eighteenth century.[89]

This contrasted sharply with the maximum allowed for dowries for the wealthy in the mid-seventeenth century, set by the state at 12,000 *cruzados* (4$800 *milréis*).[90] These were also the crisis years of the Luso-Dutch struggle and the Wars of the Restoration of Portuguese Independence, the latter largely being fought in the Alentejo countryside not far from Évora. Under these circumstances it is truly remarkable that the city's *misericórdia* was able to offer these dowries in the midst of such political instability and long-term high inflation.

In the capital, three men, Dr. Ignácio Pereira de Sousa, Dr. João Carneiro de Morães and Dr. Luís Gomes de Castro, left money in their wills for ransoming captives, having masses said, helping prisoners, and awarding dowries to needy young ladies. Some thirty-four dowries (valued at 30 *milréis* each) were awarded from this fund during the decade from 1668 to 1678. Five of these were given to orphan girls in one of the shelters in Lisbon.[91]

Wet Nurses and Abandoned Infants

Many babies were abandoned shortly after birth, and caring for them became a major responsibility for local authorities. The same blending of *misericórdia, câmara,* and imperial funds can be found in many cases relating to abandoned infants and payments made to wet nurses (*amas*). Although these orphans did not duplicate the local and imperial roles occupied by older children, orphans they were. Of course, the major distinction between older orphans and abandoned infants was that, in the latter case, the parents were unknown. Because of this, as Pullan states, their future "career as soldier or colonist or mere husband can be molded entirely by the state."[92] A few words about these infants are in order to demonstrate the closely related activities of the institutional trio of *misericórdia, câmara,* and agencies of the state.

An example of this blending can be seen in a *consulta* of the Desembargo do Paço, which in 1587 reminded the *câmara* of Évora that it was their responsibility, and not that of the *misericórdia,* to take care of abandoned children in that city. The Crown had given some funds to the hospital of São Lázaro, and it was through it that these babies could be supervised. The *câmara* could no longer claim that it was, "very poor . . . and has many needs" but was now obligated to take on this responsibility as it had been ordered to do in the past.[93]

In spite of the limited economic opportunities available to many urban women, authorities frequently had difficulty finding a sufficient number of wet nurses to match with these foundlings. The salaries paid to these women were 400 to 500 *réis* monthly. For example, the *misericórdia* of Évora in 1616–1617 paid 500 *réis* monthly to forty-nine wet nurses, such as Maria da Cruz, a widow living on Rua do Duque. Maria took care of Ana, who had been abandoned at the door of the head wet nurse (*ama das amas*) on May 25, 1616. Maria was paid 1$500 *réis* to watch over little Ana during the months of June, July, and August 1616.[94] The next year (1617–1618), the *misericórdia* of Évora listed fifty-four wet nurses, each being paid 500 *réis* monthly. One such woman was Brazia Dias, a married women who lived on Rua do Borralho and who took care of Isabel for the months of March through July 1617. For that service, she received 2$500 *réis* and another 2$500 as an advance payment for the next five months.[95] Another woman named Margarida, the wife of Francisco, lived in the Mouraria (a neighborhood in Évora) and received 2$000 for taking care of João for the four months of May through August 1617. Little João at that time was five years old, having been abandoned on June 15, 1612. Margarida continued to care for him at least until January of 1618 and was paid six months later for these last months of service.[96] In 1620–1621, the *misericórdia* was paying thirty-nine wet nurses. For reasons that are not clear, their monthly fee had suddenly decreased from 500 to 400 *réis*.[97] The next year, the number of wet nurses decreased to thirty-five, but payments at 400 *réis* remained the same.[98] In March 1622, the *misericórdia* of Évora spent 3$850 in payments to wet nurses: seven women were paid 400 *réis*, one was paid 350, two were paid 200, and three were only given 100 *réis*.[99] These payments of less than 400 *réis* resulted from the infant's death that month; the wet nurse only received payment for the portion of the month she actually fed the child.

The city of Elvas provides a number of examples of the burden these infants placed on municipal resources. The monthly rate for wet nurses in Elvas during most of the seventeenth century was also 500 *réis*.[100] In 1686–1687, the *câmara* of Elvas paid another 500 *réis* to João de Deus and 1$500 to the doorman (*porteiro*) to find these women. In this second case, the *porteiro* performed this duty for three months.[101] In the month of May 1687, the *câmara* had expenses of 13$600 *réis*: 760 for baptisms and funerals; 500 to the *porteiro* for finding wet nurses, and 200 for the hospital. The remaining 12$140 went to the wet nurses themselves.[102] The next month (June 1687), the *câmara* of Elvas had twenty-three abandoned infants (twelve girls and eleven boys) under its wing.[103]

Given these modest payments made to individual wet nurses, in 1654 the Crown found an ingenious method of ensuring a steady supply. Husbands of wet nurses working for the *misericórdia* were excused from military service. In this way, "the *misericórdia* will not lack *amas* and the children will not lack the means to be raised and will not die from lack of help, as can happen in these cases."[104] This exemption was later renewed and, in 1696, extended to the sons as well as the husbands of *amas*.[105] The recruitment process for soldiers was something dreaded by the *povo* (peasantry) in every *comarca* in the land. Once the Crown made this exemption for both husbands and sons of wet nurses, pressure must have been placed on wives and mothers who were able to tend to these infants. Such exemptions from military service were few and deliberately limited to a handful of critically needed professionals and individuals: students at the University of Coimbra, woodcutters in the Leiria area, sailors and their sons in Setúbal, the only child of a worker or widow, familiars of the Holy Office, and members of the household of the Desembargo do Paço.[106]

Another method of ensuring a steady supply of *amas* was to increase

TABLE 4

Abandoned Children in the Real Hospital de Todos os Santos
of Lisbon, 1770–1777

Year	Number Present	Added	Grown Up or Given Away	Died	Remaining
1770–71	24	1,244	825	288	155
1772–73	14[a]	1,319	1,209	95	29
1774–75	29	1,513	1,216	301	25
1776–77	22[b]	1,493	1,296	181	38

SOURCE: AHU, reino, maço 31.

[a] Discrepancy of 141 not explained in data

[b] Discrepancy of 3 not explained in data

their salaries, which was apparently done by the early eighteenth century. The *câmara* of Viana do Castelo paid 600 *réis* a month to *amas* to take care of *enjeitados* in the three years from 1705 to 1708. The city kept careful records of the names of its wet nurses as well as their civil status and the names of their husbands, if married; where they lived; the names of their parishes and places of residence; dates of any payments made; and the names of the infants they tended.[107]

In Lisbon, feeding abandoned babies was also a major expense of its *misericórdia*, through the Real Hospital dos Todos os Santos. In 1706, the *misericórdia* of Lisbon spent around 7 percent of its annual income on abandoned children.[108] By 1736 its expenses had soared to 21,164$130 *milréis*, paid to eighteen wet nurses, one servant, as well as on meat, bread, and other related expenses for the abandoned children of Lisbon. Two years later, that figure was 27,307$100 *milréis* paid to twenty-six wet nurses.[109] The shelter for *expostos* (*casa da roda*, ultimately also the *misericórdia*) in Porto faced similar expenses for wet nurses in the early eighteenth century.[110]

A brief glimpse of the magnitude of this problem can be seen in data from the 1770s, detailed in table 4.

Reformed Prostitutes

Two quite distinct groups of single women in early modern Portuguese society remain to be incorporated into this discussion: nuns and prostitutes. In conjunction with these hospitals, orphanages, and other shelters, the *miseri-córdia* in many of the larger cities in the Portuguese world began homes for prostitutes who wished to change their profession. These homes were not unique to Portugal and were found in a number of Catholic countries, in particular after the Council of Trent in 1563. The appearance of these shelters is a complex social phenomenon that can be partially explained by the increased attention being placed on marriage and family by the Catholic Church and Catholic states. Around this same time, marriage manuals appeared in Portugal and outlined the qualities of a perfect marriage, the duties of the husband and wife, and related issues.[111] This emphasis resulted in the repression of sexual activities outside this one legally recognized union and was one of several reasons the legislation on sodomy, for example, was so severe.

In regard to prostitution, an early example of this new intolerance can be seen in legislation from 1559 directed at the inhabitants of the island of São Tomé, where prostitutes were ordered to separate themselves from the rest of society. If they failed to do so, they would face a series of fines and ultimately be removed from the island and exiled to Portugal.[112] Just a few years later, the Crown noted that in Goa, "women of ill-repute, both Christian and Hindu cannot live together as they presently do."[113] Whether it was the Hindu and Christian women living in the same neighborhood or their activities (or both) that the church found objectionable, one cannot be certain. Nevertheless, when the Counter Reformation reached Goa, the resulting legislation forbade this mixing of peoples and placed Christian goals at the forefront. Nowhere is this more clear than in the treatment of prostitutes and Hindu orphans in Goa. By the late 1500s, this message was also made quite clear to those in the European homeland. By 1570, King D. Sebastião attempted to regulate all women in Portugal who taught young girls how to read, sew, or embroider. Women engaged in these activities were to obtain a license that would verify their good moral standing. Single women in Lisbon who rented out rooms to men were to relocate to one of the streets or alleys on a short list, drawn up in 1570. Young girls older than seven years of age were forbidden to live in such homes. Those who failed to obtain the required licenses, refused to move, or who rented homes to such single women (outside the approved area) faced heavy fines and *degredo* to São Tomé for two years.[114]

Institutional homes with the objective of "reforming" such women were invariably named after Mary Magdalene; these shelters are known as "Magdalene Houses" in the literature. An excellent example of this reforming effort and the general theory behind it can be found in the handbook by Father Pedro Malon de Chaide, published in 1600. It contains a mixture of biblical quotations, psalms, and essays on the life of Mary Magdalene and how she redeemed herself in God's grace. This same process is represented visually in paintings from the period; the great Spanish artist Murillo has completed what are perhaps the best-known examples of the "Penitent Madalene."[115] Shelters such as these appeared in a number of cities, including Évora, Lisbon, Castelo Branco, Braga, Goa, and Macau.[116] In this last and much later case from Southeast Asia, the "shelter" acted as a combined jail and reformatory for women who had been denounced as prostitutes.[117] The proper upbringing of the children of these women was also a concern of the local *misericórdia* and *câmara*.[118]

In the case of Lisbon, the Pious House of Converted Women, or Casa Pia das Convertidas, was founded in 1587 by King D. Filipe II. This institution was also known as the Recolhimento da Natividade or the Recolhimento da Santa Maria Madalena and had as its goal "regenerating women and channeling them into the honest life for possible marriage." Originally located on the Rua do Loreto, it was transferred in the mid-eighteenth century to the Rua do Passadiço in São José de Entre-as-Hortas.[119] It too had an important colonizing role to play in the Portuguese Empire.

Glimpses of the day-to-day lives of the *convertidas* can be seen in the rules and regulations of such a shelter. The headmistress (*regente*) had complete authority over these women, and their days were long, filled with prayer and reflection, and solemn, with little in the way of frivolity, joy, or outside contact.[120]

On a number of occasions, women from this shelter were sent to one of the colonies. Twelve ladies from this shelter arrived in Angola in 1595 with the new governor, D. João Furtado de Mendoça, to begin their new lives in Luanda. "These were the first white women to be sent to that colony, and all were to marry during his governorship (1595–1602)."[121] In 1620, the *provedor* of this institution wrote the Crown and noted that, "at the moment, there are over thirty women in the shelter and it has been some time since the Crown sent any women abroad." The *provedor* now requested, and the Crown agreed, that several women be sent to Maranhão and given 12 *mil-réis* to assist them in beginning anew there, as had been done in the case of other women sent to Angola from this home in 1609.[122] A widow and nine *convertidas* from this shelter left for the same destination (Angola) five years later in 1614, and another six women went to Angola in 1649.[123] In 1677, the same shelter petitioned the Overseas Council and received 20 *mil-*

réis and permission to allow eight women to leave for the "Rios de Sofala" (Mozambique).[124] The women in this last group formed part of a major colonizing effort, which included fifty married couples possessing a wide variety of skills that would be needed in the colony.[125] In fact, by the late 1600s, the Crown directed that Sofala be the primary destination for "women who are prejudicial to the Kingdom, who are in jail or [recently] out of it."[126] The highlands of Mozambique had been a neglected area of the empire until the late seventeenth century. Its especially difficult terrain and associated tropical diseases made it a remote region for the Crown to effectively incorporate. Women such as these reformed prostitutes were one attempt to colonize this region. Sending Goans to the region was another; in fact, Goans relocated in the highlands of Mozambique during early modern times formed much of the economic and social backbone of Portuguese East Africa.[127]

The institutions of the *misericórdia* and *câmara* implemented throughout the empire were used to supervise aspects of colonization. In a continuation of this process, charitable subunits, each autonomous but under the *misericórdia*, were established in the European homeland and then duplicated overseas. Many of these were local institutions with no imperial schemes behind them. Others, notably the Magdalene houses and the Shelter of the Castle of Lisbon, were clearly designed with both local and imperial needs in mind. While the underlying motives were quite distinct, both institutions were ultimately under the same supervision and sent much-needed single Portuguese women to the empire with the desired goal of marriage and long-term colonization. As such, the links established between these institutions and the empire—both financial and social—provide another view of the state's systematic use of individuals as reluctant colonizers.

A parallel effort, which connected these institutions and the individuals in them with state-sponsored colonization, was the awarding of dowries, a complex process that has thus far only been discussed in relation to the *misericórdia*. I now turn to the next two chapters to view the manner in which not just the *misericórdia* but the state linked orphan girls with its empire through dowries of minor positions in the imperial bureaucracy.

SEVEN

Orphans, Dowries, and Empire

The good and diligent woman is her husband's crown because with
her hands she augments her husband's things. . . . The woman who is
lazy, careless, and slothful in completing her obligations, rather than
being her husband's crown of honor and esteem, is transformed into
a crown of thorns of insults and torments for her afflicted husband
and children.

—BERNARDO BENTO PIMENTEL CASTELLO-BRANCO,
Vida da Mulher Prudente, 1750

In one of the crowning achievements of seventeenth-century Portuguese di-
plomacy, Princess D. Catherine of Bragança, sister of Kings D. Afonso VI
and D. Pedro II, married King Charles II of Great Britain in 1661. This union
supported the Portuguese struggle with Spain during the last years of the
War of the Restoration of Independence and bolstered Portuguese peace efforts in the related simultaneous Luso-Dutch conflict.[1] Catherine's dowry,
large enough to ensure English acceptance, consisted of payment valued at
"£300,000 in sugar, cash, Brazilian mahogany, plus the port of Tangier, the
island of Bombay, and valuable trading privileges in the New World."[2] This
dowry and the related payment to the Dutch for a peace settlement were
largely collected in the empire; each city had a quota, which in the case of
Salvador in 1688 was a hefty 90,000 *cruzados* yearly.[3] Although this was the
most famous example in seventeenth-century Portugal, dowries that linked
women with the empire were common and remain an unexplored area of
inquiry.[4]

Dowries were actually rather complex economic transactions and could
consist of money, goods, real estate, a mixture of any of these, or, when

awarded by the state, title to an office for the prospective husband. Under Portuguese law, if the marriage took place with a contract (*contrato de dote*), the woman's dowry was inalienable. To put it another way, under this system the dowry was the wife's contribution to the marriage and not the husband's property.[5] Dowries awarded by the state reverted to the wife in the event she outlived her husband. In the *Ordenações Filipinas*, married women were able to make contracts in their husbands' names as long as these financial obligations did not extend to their dowries.[6] By contrast, the wife was not obligated by her husband's debts nor could her goods be confiscated to pay them.[7] For example, D. Mariana de Noronha, the widow of D. Estévão de Ataide, and her daughter, D. Ana de Noronha, petitioned the Council of State in 1619 to direct the Casa da India to return the jewelry her late husband sent her, in spite of any of his outstanding debts.[8] The state even went so far as to refund money already spent by a husband when the wife could prove her dowry had been the source of these funds.[9] Interestingly enough, the word *dote* (dowry) could also mean a payment made to a woman for violation of her honor and virginity when the offending party did not marry her.[10]

The *misericórdia* often stepped forward to award dowries when the bride's family clearly could not. However, the state was a key source of dowries for another set of deserving young ladies. At the same time, the theoretical restrictions it placed on these awards limited the pool of prospective husbands to a handful of men born in Portugal. A parallel system awarded dowries to convents when novices entered; these were important and far-reaching economic transactions controlled by women. While the state awarded dowries to women in both these groups, it was confronted with the contradiction of sponsoring marriage and colonization or promoting convents in its empire.

The Recolhimento do Castelo of Lisbon

Some female orphanages, such as those in Porto, the Casa Pia das Moças Desamparadas in Coimbra, and Recolhimento de Nossa Senhora dos Anjos in Chaves, were clearly designed to meet local needs.[11] Although important social institutions at the municipal level, they had a minimal impact outside their communities. Other shelters developed a global reach. The most important girls' orphanage in Portugal that also functioned as part of a larger imperial colonization scheme was the Recolhimento do Castelo (de São Jorge) in Lisbon. Although the city had other orphanages for women, and other institutions in Portugal from time to time sent orphans overseas, this Shelter of the Castle was initiated with the motive of rewarding orphan girls with dowries in the empire.

The statutes for this shelter stated that the girls were to be between twelve and thirty and had to have lost both parents, since legally one could be an orphan with the loss of one's father. Preference for entry was granted to those whose fathers had died in service overseas. These were not just any orphan girls. The title used to describe them made that clear: orphan girls of the king (*órfãs do rei*). These royal orphans were sent overseas on an ad hoc basis to both Brazil and India in batches during the second half of the sixteenth century.[12] No less a figure than Father Nóbrega himself wrote King D. João III in the early 1550s to suggest sending orphan girls to Brazil, especially to captaincies other than Pernambuco, "because all of them will marry."[13] Father Nóbrega continued discussing this subject the following year when he urged the king to send any Portuguese women to Brazil, since "any white women here are so desired that they will do well for the land and will gain [a husband] and the men will become separated from sin."[14]

For much of this period, the authorities in Lisbon alternated between sending orphans to Brazil or India. In correspondence directed to the viceroy of Goa, in 1563 the Crown noted that it was not sending any orphan girls to Asia that year and asked to be kept informed about the personal and marital status of those orphans already in Goa.[15] Ten years later, the Crown noted there were numerous orphans in Goa that the viceroy needed to assist and decided not to send any more that year from Lisbon.[16]

Around 1583, the Crown systematically began to award dowries of posts in the empire and send these young ladies abroad.[17] In the years that the viceroy was to depart for Brazil or India (that is, every third year), two or three orphans were to accompany him. In the intervening years, two orphans were to leave for India with the fleet. Other orphans were to be sent to sites in Portugal and elsewhere overseas.[18] The Shelter of the Castle was designed as the central point of collection for this process—a transient staging area where these women would live for a few years until departure. Being selected was an honor awarded only to the deserving few, daughters of fathers who had died in royal service. The usual exclusions were applied; those girls with New Christian or Gypsy ancestors were denied admission. While it is true that this requirement was not strictly upheld, at times these rules were enforced; in 1615 the daughter of Furtado de Brito was awarded and then denied a place in the shelter because her father had been a New Christian.[19]

Clearly, the general idea was to award these girls with minor bureaucratic positions and to process them through this institution as quickly as possible. At the receiving end in Goa (and elsewhere), from the very beginnings of the system, the Crown urged that the girls marry as quickly as possible after arrival.[20] In order to achieve this, the agencies of the Crown had to coordinate their efforts, share information, and in general cooperate—a requirement that fell by the wayside in the penal exile system. This lack of coordination was the source of a complaint made by the Mesa da Consciência e Ordens in 1616.[21]

Entering this shelter was clearly perceived as an honor, as well as a relatively quick and easy method of obtaining a dowry of a minor government post. In 1636, João de Barros da Silva went to a great deal of effort to petition the Desembargo do Paço for places in this shelter for his two nieces.[22] Most of these young ladies came from the lower ranks of the nobility; several may have been commoners. Many more wanted to enter than could possibly be accommodated. This, coupled with the reality of many young girls neither marrying nor leaving the shelter, caused two of the first bottlenecks in the system.

One of the basic issues was not *what* to do with them, but *where* exactly to send them. This explains the alternating destinations of Brazil and India. It would appear that the voyage to Portuguese Asia was considered too long and difficult, or the number of local orphan girls in Goa was too high to allow additional ladies to depart from Lisbon. In either case, in 1603 the king agreed with the Mesa and ordered that only three girls should be sent annually and then only to Brazil.[23] The authorities then vacillated and sent some to India and others to Brazil during the early 1600s. In 1605 alone, the Crown ordered a total of six orphans from Alcáçova and other places to India and then, later in the same year, commented that it would abandon the imperial aspects of the system and only use the orphans within Portugal.[24] The authorities continued to be leery of sending these girls to India well into the 1620s, claiming that Portuguese Asia was too distant. Instead, the Mesa suggested awarding positions in Portugal under the same system, when suitable posts were available.[25]

The "problems in sending them to Brazil," mentioned in the documentation were not just logistical; they represented a failure on the part of the authorities in that colony to cooperate in this marriage scheme. By all indicators, European orphan girls were simply not needed in the more central regions of Portuguese America, and the Crown was hesitant to send them to the fringe regions where they were. Nevertheless, in 1606 the viceroy of

Portugal, D. Pedro de Castilho wrote the Crown in Madrid that minor positions in the newly formed high court of Salvador would be awarded to men who married these orphan girls. Domingos Santos, António de Costa Fragoso, and two or three others were offered positions as a doorkeeper, secretary, or royal secretary with this specific provision.[26] Among these men was Christóvão Vieira Ravasco, father of the well-known Luso-Brazilian literary figure Father António Vieira. Christóvão married Maria de Azevedo and was later awarded the post of appellate clerk with that court.[27]

A few years later, in a clear indication that some were not following past resolutions, the Mesa da Consciência e Ordens issued a reminder that posts overseas should be given to those who married girls from the Recolhimento do Castelo.[28] The Captain of Paraíba was then only following orders when he petitioned the Mesa to send an orphan girl in 1611.[29] The Crown continued to remind its agents that these orphans should be recognized when positions were available overseas and that suitable people (that is, in terms of social background) should marry them.[30]

By 1616, India was once again one of the destinations for these girls. The Mesa noted that these orphans should be sent to either Portuguese America or Asia but, in either case, be awarded bureaucratic offices for dowries.[31] What then developed was a two-tiered system: those who could do so married in Portugal and were awarded dowries in the European homeland; those who did (or could) not arrange such a marriage were then sent to India. Brazil as a destination was dropped.[32]

Typical of the first group was the orphan Catarina da Silva, daughter of the late Pedro de Lerna, who had served the Crown. In 1614, the Desembargo do Paço noted that she was in the Shelter of Castelo and would receive a dowry in Portugal when "one of the *letrados* approved for royal service marries her."[33] Two years later, she married Luis de Figueiredo. The marriage was later annulled, but her dowry was renewed.[34]

Marriage in India may have been a distant second choice for many of these girls, but to Goa they went nevertheless. Although orphan girls haphazardly departed for India during the second half of the sixteenth century, more systematic annual shipments of three or four girls left from this shelter during the early 1600s. In royal correspondence sent with the three orphans who left in 1608 (see table 5, below), the Crown noted that these young ladies were entrusted to the viceroy's care as were those already in India since it was only with the intention of marriage that they had been sent.[35]

In March 1619, the Crown sent another three orphans from the Orphanage of the Castle to Goa. When they arrived in Goa, they were placed in the

TABLE 5
Examples of Orphan Girls Sent to India

Date	Name	Comments
1588	Catarina Leitoa	Left Lisbon in the company of other orphans from the Lisbon shelter.[a]
1589	D. Bernarda Pereira D. Elena de Ataide Viçença Rebella D. Mercia Pereira D. Maria de Meneses Joana da Osequa Catherina Goudinha and Maria Vallente	All eight were from the shelter in Alcaçova.[b]
1605	D. Maria de Almeida D. Briniz de Azevedo and her sister D. Isabel da Costa D. Juiomar de Carvalhosa D. Briniz da Cunha D. Briniz da Cruz	All six were from Castelo.[c]
1608	Custodia de Costa D. Margarida da Fonseca Jeronyma de Torres[d]	
1618	D. Maria Cabreira	An orphan in Castelo in Lisbon, awarded the position of secretary to the treasurer of Goa.[e]

[a]HAG, MR 2A, f. 41.
[b]HAG, MR 2A, f. 52, 25 March 1589.
[c]HAG, MR 6B, f. 27, 13 March 1605
[d]DR da I, 1:243, Crown to Viceroy, 26 March 1608
[e]HAG, códice 413, f. 96, 6 August 1618.

Shelter of Nossa Senhora da Serra and, "as was the usual custom, three hundred *xerafins* were given to each for clothing and other costs for one year," during which time the viceroy promised to work to arrange their marriages.[36] An additional three orphans from the castle and another awarded a certificate with which to enter the orphanage (*alvará da lembrança*) left for India with the viceroy in 1622.[37] Although the young ladies in the shelter must have felt some pressure to leave and marry, the year before (1621) one girl was allowed to stay in Lisbon and was not forced into marriage in India.[38] In such cases, when a young lady was awarded an office but decided not to marry, she was placed in the custody of her mother.[39] The *misericórdia*, the Mesa, and the Crown's agents clearly combined their efforts to provide for these girls. For example, in 1631 the Crown ordered the royal pharmacy to provide the shelter with any medicine required, to a maximum of 12 *milréis* yearly.[40] Table 5 lists a number of examples of such orphans sent overseas from the European homeland.

In fact, the Crown was guilty of indecision regarding the exact destination of these girls and several times changed its mind about sending them to India. This indecision was compounded by the number of girls already in the shelter. Not only had young ladies been entering in the usual way, but also the provision that women must be under thirty in order to enter was removed, at least temporarily in 1625.[41] A few years earlier, the Crown further bent the rules to allow a widowed daughter of an official, whose deeds merited a reward, to enter "even if she is old and poor."[42] Women such as D. Maria de Freitas, widow of Gonçalo Lourenço do Carvalho, received a pension of 300 *xerafins* and were allowed to reside in this shelter.[43] The result was that by 1629, the entire system apparently reached a crisis point that required swift action. In 1626 and again in 1629, King D. Filipe IV decreed that no more orphan girls should be sent to India. In addition, the king wished to be informed when suitable offices become vacant in Portugal as well as overseas.[44] That same year, the Mesa da Consciência e Ordens, in a lengthy commentary on this problem, noted that the lack of spaces meant that no new girls could enter. This was caused by not enough being sent to India, "where they marry well."[45] The royal commentary in the margin noted that "it is good that the order already given be followed." In an obvious effort to clear out as many girls as possible, a decree passed at the same time by the Mesa ordered that orphan girls could not remain in this shelter after they reached the age of thirty, and they would be given preference when posts overseas, as well as in Portugal, become vacant.[46]

On the one hand, the Crown worked toward rewarding these women as quickly as possible and therefore opening new places in the orphanage. On the other hand, by the mid-1600s, the Mesa and other bodies had lowered the admission criteria, which only exacerbated the overall problem. This process began in 1622 when the shelter bent its own rules to accept a bastard daughter, since her father had served the Crown.[47] Two years later in 1624 the Mesa allowed the daughter of a poor *fidalgo* serving in the military into the shelter, even though her father was still alive.[48] Three years later (1627), the Mesa stretched the rules a bit more to allow the governor or viceroy of Portugal to use the Shelter of the Castle as a holding place for "any woman acting badly."[49] A married woman was allowed to enter in

1633, and any woman thinking of leaving her husband could be detained there.[50] In 1645, the king ordered the shelter to accept the widow of a *desembargador*.[51] The next year, the king ordered another wife of a *desembargador* into this shelter, against her will. When her husband refused to pay for her meals, the king ordered that he either do so or she would be moved to another shelter.[52] In another incident in 1648, a certain woman was "acting badly" and was placed into the Recolhimento do Castelo. The Mesa later ordered her moved to the Recolhimento de São Cristóvão.[53] Given this leniency on the part of the Mesa, it is not surprising that the shelter began to run out of room; another institution, the Recolhimento da Nossa Senhora das Mercês was asked to take the overflow from Castelo.[54]

In the middle of the seventeenth century, the Mesa was still clearly watching over these young girls and attempted to provide what it could for them. The Mesa asked to be informed when one of the girls from this shelter married so that it could reward her with royal favor.[55] As late as 1682, the Mesa awarded 50 *cruzados* to assist someone going to India who had married one of these orphans.[56] The same year, the Mesa also decided that it would not object if a gentleman, for his own reasons, wished to place his wife in the Recolhimento do Castelo.[57]

This last decree began the transition from an imperial to a local orphanage concerned with little beyond Lisbon. In 1705, the Mesa declared that any woman in this shelter who ran away would be captured, expelled, and placed in the custody of her mother or another relative. The person to whom she fled would be put in jail.[58] Two years later, the number of places was reduced to thirty.[59] By the middle of the 1700s, the Crown stopped the practice of sending these girls overseas or using them within the country, and the *misericórdia* of Lisbon began awarding them dowries directly. In one case, twenty-six women were listed as marrying a variety of workmen, including cobblers, coopers, and barbers. Of these brides, twenty-four had names listed for both parents.[60] In another list from the same approximate time, forty-seven others married tailors, fishermen, sailors, and stonecutters. One black woman was also included in this list; she married a black tailor.[61] In the brief six-year period from 1770 to 1776, the *misericórdia* of Lisbon awarded 373 dowries, 80 of which went to orphans in the Shelter of the Castle.[62] At the same time, Lisbon orphanages were making self-supporting steps, such as selling embroidery.[63] Clearly, by this time the connections that linked the minor nobility, this orphanage, and imperial dowries had been severed. The Shelter of the Castle had evolved into a municipal orphanage, similar to those elsewhere in Lisbon and around the country.

Orphan Girls Sent to Goa

When the *órfãs* first began arriving in Goa with some regularity in the 1570s and 1580s, they were placed in private homes of "good, honest, people" and supported by the Goan *misericórdia*.[64] In his study of that institution, Ferreira Martins also noted the tripartite nature of the assistance they received; "the support for each orphan that came from the Kingdom [that is, Portugal] . . . was distributed among three entities: the *Misericórdia*, the *câmara*, and the viceroy or governor."[65] The *misericórdia* provided food and shelter until the orphan married, and the *câmara* contracted marriage-makers or *casamenteiros*[66] to facilitate the union. The viceroy completed this process by awarding the dowry. In short, everything possible was done to make the transition from single to married life as smooth and as swift as possible.

It is not clear just when the policy of placing *órfãs* in private homes stopped, but by 1598 their number—both from Lisbon as well as local—had grown to the point where this was no longer possible. In that year they were already under the wing of the church and were staying at the Convento da Nossa Senhora da Graça (Convent of Our Lady of Grace). In 1598 construction of a shelter for female orphans was approved by the governing board of the *misericórdia*. Known locally as the Recolhimento das Orfãs, but officially as the Recolhimento da Nossa Senhora da Serra (the Shelter of Our Lady of the Mountain), it was founded for the purpose of "gathering and protecting [these *órfãs*] where they will be occupied in works of virtue and away from occasions of offense to their dignity and loss of their honor and fame, from where they will leave to marry and be protected."[67]

Taxes from two villages were set aside to support this home, and King D. Filipe III sent the first annual royal subsidy of 1,000 *cruzados*.[68] Construction was completed in 1605, and the *órfãs* transferred to the new building.[69] The *misericórdia* agreed to administer the orphanage in the same manner that it directed several other shelters and hospitals in Goa, but with the clear understanding that Serra would have to support itself.[70] From time to time, the Crown noted that the 1,000 *xerafins* the shelter received was not enough to meet all its needs. For example, in order to take care of the three daughters of João Rodrigues Camelo and other daughters of João Pereira Pinto, whose fathers were both killed by the Dutch in Malacca, the viceroy had to give the shelter extra money.[71] By 1620, Serra's income had been stabilized by earmarking the revenues from a total of seventeen villages around Goa to support it.[72]

Figure 10. The Shelter of Our Lady of the Mountain (Nossa Senhora da Serra), Panaji, Goa. This shelter was founded in the late 1500s to house and protect orphan girls sent from Lisbon. Since its inception, the shelter has moved three times and is currently located in downtown Panaji, where it serves as a training institute for nurses. Photo by author, 1991.

This orphanage was only one of three begun by a remarkable archbishop of Goa, D. Aleixo de Meneses. In his first two years in Goa in the 1590s, there were an alleged fifty-two *fidalgas* (noblewomen) killed by their husbands because of adultery. To remedy this situation, the archbishop created this shelter for orphans, a Magdalene house (modeled on Lisbon's), and the convent of Santa Mónica and dedicated each to an aspect of the Holy Trinity.[73]

Both Serra and Goa's Shelter of Mary Magdalene had similar administrative structures. In fact, most of the shelters under discussion here shared a common internal organization that consisted of a headmistress, doorkeeper, chaplain, surgeon, and lawyer. In the Goan case, one person often held the same position (such as lawyer) for both shelters.[74]

It was the Recolhimento da Nossa Senhora da Serra that was central to the history of this colonization effort made by the Crown through the *órfãs del rei*. It was also in this shelter where that policy faced its third major problem. Well before 1598, when Serra was founded, the authorities in Goa informed Lisbon that no more orphan girls from Portugal need be sent, because the colony did not lack its own daughters of men who had died serving the Crown.[75] By 1564 the archbishop of Goa informed the king, "Every year Your Majesty sends to these parts many orphan girls . . . [while] Goa's own orphans need attention as well."[76] Five years later in 1569 the Crown wrote the city council of Goa that it was aware of the needs of the many orphan girls in that city, daughters of men who had died in service, and that it would write to the viceroy regarding this matter.[77] Finally, the viceroy also wrote Lisbon on this subject and was answered in 1573 when the Crown noted, "We have seen what you [the viceroy] have said regarding not sending any more orphans there and the reasons you have given for this. We will respect your wishes when possible."[78]

By the time the construction of Serra was beginning, it would appear that the local authorities in Goa had grown accustomed to accepting orphans from Lisbon, in spite of the increasing number of its own orphaned young ladies. At this time authorities in Lisbon made the important concession that, since many of the orphans it had sent to Goa with dowries had married, local girls (whose fathers had also died in royal service) were also eligible to enter Serra and receive dowries.[79] That is, the two groups of orphans would be treated the same.[80] It was also at this point that Lisbon began to vacillate as to *where* to send the girls from Castelo in Lisbon. The number sent could also vary; some years Lisbon sent eight girls, in other years they might send none.[81]

In the case of those sent in 1618, on the viceroy's outward trip to Goa, he took with him three orphans: D. Maria Cabreira, who married Joseph Cabreira; D. Chorobina de Santo Payo, who became the wife of Sebastião Veloso; and D. Antónia de Castro, who was not married at the time of the report. D. Chorobina was awarded several offices for her dowry, among them the captaincy of lands around Naroa, which could be renewed in the event that she became a widow.[82] D. Antónia de Castro, according to the report, had not married because she was too old.[83]

Actually, correspondence between Lisbon and the viceroy in 1623 suggested that orphan girls were difficult to marry because the dowry had become increasingly abstract with the decline of the Asian empire.[84]

The *órfãs* would later be joined by "virtuous women." By the middle of the seventeenth century, the Shelter of Our Lady of the Mountain would take on an additional function as a place where "many noblemen left their wives and daughters . . . when they traveled."[85] This practice did not seem to be limited to members of the nobility but was available to any husband who would pay the *misericórdia* for sheltering his wife. Thus, the functions of Recolhimento da Nossa Senhora da Serra paralleled the Shelter of the Castle in Lisbon when it extended its charitable duties, concerned with the welfare of orphan girls, to include much broader monitoring of wives for absent husbands. Serra even accepted poverty-stricken, childless widows such as Samoa Teixeira, who entered in 1619.[86] This pattern is not surprising and is very much in line with that of parent shelters in Portugal. The outcome was much the same as the European model, as well; too many women were allowed to enter and not enough left.

In two examples, both the shelters of Serra and Magdalene accepted married women as temporary boarders. Ines Pereira, wife of Diogo Rebelo of Damão, entered Magdalene in 1612 in fear of her husband and "because of her sins." Her husband's friends and emissaries had been harassing her, one of whom was Luís da Costa Lobato. Her husband was now a *renegado* in the lands of the Moors, so she petitioned the *misericórdia* for help.[87] In 1625, Ana da Silva, the wife of D. António Telo was staying in Serra, away from her husband and unhappy marriage, while the viceroy paid the *misericórdia* her costs. The *misericórdia* directed that she should stay in Serra for the time being, until her marriage was annulled.[88]

One of the first problems to develop with the *órfãs* sent from Lisbon was that they were pampered, protected, and promoted at the expense of local orphan girls. Not until the middle of the seventeenth century did the Crown stop sending contradictory instructions and both groups were truly treated equally.[89] In 1635 local orphans were allowed into Serra upon nomination of the Goan *misericórdia*. The Crown encouraged this body to continue nominating and placing local orphan girls into that orphanage "as they have done until now."[90] The progression that allowed this had three important steps. First, women born in Portugal were given preference over all others. In fact, this entire scheme that connected Lisbon with Goa was designed specifically for these women. Then, in 1595, the Crown stated that local orphaned daughters of men who also died in service to the Crown would be given dowries in the same manner as those from Portugal.[91] This was further extended in 1682 to local daughters whose fathers had served but not died in office.[92]

The Crown quite clearly had a "white," *reinol-castiço* colonization plan in mind as desirable, although there was some debate on this issue at the time of its conception.[93] This becomes obvious when the local alternative was available from the very beginning of the *órfãs del rei* policy, but the Crown went to great lengths and expense to promote its daughters from Portugal.[94]

In spite of its preoccupation that these women marry quickly, several cases demonstrate the concern the Crown showed for these women and their dowries. In two cases in 1625, orphans sent to India were married and then separated. They petitioned the Mesa and received return passages to Portugal in lieu of dowries.[95] In another case from 1657, Diogo Pereira wrote the Overseas Council asking to marry D. Cecilia de Mendoça, daughter of D. Luís de Castelo Branco, one of the orphans in the Shelter of Serra. However, the Overseas Council responded that he was too young and inexperienced to be rewarded with a position of the *capitania* of Goa as a dowry. If that were to happen, they claimed, it would set a bad example. As a result, the Overseas Council refused, stating that it would be better if he were to apply again in a few years.[96] Another issue was raised when Rafael Mendes Thomas married Antónia Correia de Magalhães, an orphan from Serra who died suddenly after marriage. Her dowry had been the two positions of inspector of customs and of the dockyards, both in Goa. Even though his wife had died and the laws (assuming this was a marriage by contract) made these positions the possessions of her estate, her husband asked to occupy them because he had not yet done so. The Crown approved his petition.[97]

In regard to rewarding illegitimate daughters, the Crown seemed to be of two minds on this matter. At the beginning of the seventeenth century, the "natural" daughter of Rui de Sousa de Larcão, former governor of São Tomé (of Mylapor) was in Serra. In spite of her background, she was awarded a dowry of a village in Sri Lanka, with the provision that she and her husband move there.[98] The same question of illegitimacy resurfaced in 1687 when Manuel Martiniz de Matos married D. Mariana de Andrade, the daughter of Gonçalo Andrade and one of the orphans in Serra. Since she was illegitimate, she would not inherit from her father. The *relação* and *misericórdia* of Goa were consulted and agreed that all the "numbered" (that is, official) orphans in Serra should be awarded dowries if their fathers had served the Crown. In this case, her father had been a judge on the high court for more than ten years, a fact that certainly did not hurt her case. The Overseas Council was consulted and agreed to award her a dowry, in spite of her background and to do the same for all the "numbered" orphans in Serra.[99]

In spite of this ruling, in 1691 when D. Fernando de Castelo Branco died with no legitimate heirs, his illegitimate daughter was denied her father's former position (*tanador-mor* of Goa) for her dowry. She was so poor that she only received the 3 *xerafins* monthly allowance that Serra gave all its orphans. Her male cousin was then allowed to inherit her father's position with the condition that, since no nobleman would marry her given her status, he would provide her with 200 *xerafins* annually.[100]

In 1719, the *misericórdia* complained that illegitimate daughters were entering Serra.[101] Some women there, it noted, were staying too long and had passed the age of thirty.[102] By 1733, the *misericórdia* redefined the requirements to enter Serra, making it much more of a local, than an imperial, shelter. In order to enter, a girl had to be known to the Mesa (not only personally, but her parents as well and where she was from); fatherless as a result of his death in office; poor; at least fourteen and not over thirty years of age; a daughter of a brother of the *misericórdia*; and born to *reinois* or *castiços*. In addition, she had to inform the Mesa of her parents' backgrounds, if known.[103] By 1736, King D. João V ordered the *misericórdia* of Goa to follow the statutes of the Shelter of Serra, particularly in regard to the entrance requirements.[104] Thus this shelter and Castelo in Lisbon were both transformed from imperial to local orphanages around the same time, once their link was severed.

Dowries of Offices

Orphan girls were to receive a dowry from the viceroy or governor of a position in the bureaucracy of *factor* or lower for three years, money, land, taxes from villages, or any combination of these.[105] The state awarding dowries in Portuguese Asia was actually a tradition begun by Afonso de Albuquerque. In 1511 the wives of Bras Gonçalves, Salvador Fernandes, Jorge Fernandes, and Dinis Homem were each given a *pano* of silk from the royal treasury for their dowries or as a part of their dowries. Similar gifts for dowries continued for the next three months.[106] From these modest beginnings this system developed into one that awarded dowries of other state properties, such as offices and lands.

Typically, in the early years of the system when the Estado da India was

at its economic peak, dowries consisted of one position in the imperial bureaucracy, land, or income from a couple of villages. In a typical case such as
this, Isabel Francisca da Silva requested a payment of 40 *milréis* to honor the
military services of her recently deceased husband and the post of secretary
on the India fleet as a dowry for their daughter. Her case was considered by
the members of the Overseas Council in January 1644, and King D. João IV
awarded her request. By the end of the seventeenth century, dowries more
typically consisted of two bureaucratic positions and little else.

A typical Portuguese fortress and factory was administered by an array of officials.[107] At the top of these was the captain of the fort, closely followed by the *factor*. In a large outpost, such as Mozambique Island, there
were several other important posts: secretary to the *factor*, judge (*ouvidor*),
bailiff, secretary to the bailiff, and barber-surgeon. In addition, someone
was required to tend the gunpowder and several companies of soldiers were
present, with their officers.[108] In a smaller outpost, these positions might be
limited to a captain, *factor*, his secretary, a clerk in charge of weighing and
registering goods, a doorkeeper, and a handful of soldiers. In Bassein, for example, in addition to these, there was a second secretary for the *factor*, and
a supervisor of the dry dock.[109]

Positions in this bureaucracy awarded as dowries were normally minor
posts, such as a secretary. The two most lucrative positions of captain and
factor were normally occupied by nobles appointed directly from Lisbon, but
even these were occasionally awarded as dowries, particularly in smaller
outposts. From the very beginning of the Estado da India, state positions
were limited to three-year periods and could only be occupied by married
men.[110] At the height of the Asian empire, income from these positions
would have made them attractive. Unfortunately, during the course of the
seventeenth century the Portuguese lost most of their Asian holdings to the
Dutch, the Omanis, and a list of other enemies. At the same time, the number of positions awarded as dowries stayed constant. As a result, the reality
of actually holding one of the remaining posts decreased sharply. This situation was further compounded by the practice of awarding two posts as a
dowry, one as the actual dowry and the other in lieu of the traditional cash
payment made by the governor.

Originally, dowries had excluded the post of captain. However, in 1694
one of the orphans in Serra, D. Antónia Francisca de Melo, was given the
captaincy of Bassein for her marriage to Pedro Rebelo de Almeida. This ex-
clusion was dropped for all but the largest captaincies in Portuguese Asia
(Chaul, Bassein, Diu, Damão, Macau, Mozambique, and Goa).[111]

By 1632, the Crown directed that sons or wives were to inherit these positions in the event that a father or husband died while in office.[112] An example of such a case occurred only two years later in 1634, when the son and daughter of D. Pedro Mascarenhas were each given a three-year appointment of the captaincy of Hormuz, to honor services rendered to the Crown by their father.[113] Hormuz, however, had been out of Portuguese political control for twelve years when the award was made. This system was further modified by a 1704 royal letter to the *câmara* of Goa. The Crown stated that if the officeholder were killed in the line of duty fighting against European or Asian threats to the Crown, the position was to automatically pass to the son. If there were no sons, then the position was passed to a nephew, even if there was a will stating otherwise.[114] As a result of common practice, and perhaps only reenforced in this law, positions frequently become tied to a particular family.[115] One position could stay in a family and act once as the bride's dowry, be occupied a second time by a son, and then serve a third time as a daughter's dowry. This was the case for the wife of António Soares de Madureira. In 1652, she petitioned the Overseas Council for the position of judge of the customs house of Goa, a post both her mother and sister had been awarded for their dowries. In another case in 1664, Margarida da Costa requested the same dowry both her aunt and mother had been awarded: secretary of the India fleet.

In examining the materials in both the Historical Archives at Ultramarino (AHU) and the Historical Archives at Goa (HAG), a total of more than 111 such state-awarded dowries were found; almost all were awarded posts in seventeenth-century Portuguese Asia. Many went to orphans in Serra, while others were given to deserving women outside such shelters. Positions in the bureaucracy were for three-year terms, and a number of men were often appointed for the same post around the same time. This practice, combined with the concurrent loss of many outposts, resulted in long delays for husbands to occupy the promised position(s). Because of these practices, a number of certificates required extensions of the time limits to occupy the offices. As the number of posts in the Asian empire declined, certificates were reworded to allow the holder to sell the position or shift its location to one remaining in the Portuguese political orbit. Such extensions and modifications became more numerous after 1635 and are true reflections of the political reality of the time. The value of the dowries, the prime motivating factor for many men to marry these women, became increasingly abstract as both the reality of obtaining them and their projected incomes declined with the fortunes of the empire.

The Goan *misericórdia*, in correspondence with the Overseas Council, mentioned that the Crown established the policy of awarding dowries to orphans in Serra in 1583. This policy was later amended in 1595 to read that these positions could also be occupied by locally born daughters of nobles whose fathers were deceased and had, at some point, served the Crown. Later, 1,000 *xerafins* was added to these dowries. After Archbishop Meneses returned to Portugal, the administration of this shelter was handed over to the *misericórdia*.[116] By the 1660s the Crown noted that dire financial times in Portuguese Asia necessitated awarding an extra position for the dowry, in lieu of the traditional cash payment. Given the long delays, which were increased by this practice, the young ladies in Serra actually received nothing.[117]

In order to make it more attractive to marry one of the orphans in the Recolhimento da Nossa Senhora da Serra, an *alvará* in 1674 doubled the years of credit for military service of any such husband; thus, four years of service would count as eight.[118] Two additional royal decrees were designed to improve the lot of these orphans: their dowries could be renewed in the event that they became widows, and would be awarded even if they did not marry.[119]

Examples of this shift in the nature of the dowries can be seen in the case of Manuel de Campos, who married Clara Teixeira in the 1690s. Clara was an orphan in Serra and for her dowry received the captaincy of the fort in Mozambique. In lieu of the 1,000 *xerafins*, she was awarded an additional captaincy in Goa.[120] Another orphan in Serra, D. Ana da Silva, in 1693 was awarded two positions for her dowry, the captaincies of Chaul and of Campo de Bela Flor (near Bassein).[121] In the same year, Maria da Costa, another orphan in Serra was awarded two positions for her dowry: tax collector in Salcette and *factor* of Congo (a post near Hormuz).[122]

Dowries of Land

Other than positions in the imperial bureaucracy, dowries were awarded by the state in the form of land or taxes from villages. Specific villages could often be tied not only to individuals but also to institutions, as in the case of the Shelter of Serra. Extended examples of the use of such South Asian villages to support individual Portuguese can be found during the early years of the seventeenth century in Sri Lanka and a bit later in the *praças do norte*, the chain of Portuguese holdings along the northern half of India's western coast. Lands such as these were awarded by the Crown to deserving orphans and soldiers. When awarded to women, ownership of lands in the Bombay regions was exclusively matrilineal for three lives by 1610.[123]

A similar set of laws determined who would be rewarded with lands on the island of Sri Lanka. In 1610, Lisbon informed the local authorities that Portuguese men and women should be awarded villages for two or three lives, with the stipulation of female inheritance.[124] In a list of the annual dispatches from Sri Lanka for the year 1615, twenty-eight Portuguese received income from specific villages, orchards, or plots of land on the island. Four of these were orphans; three others were husbands receiving these lands as dowries. The remaining twenty-one were soldiers, rewarded for their many years of service (ranging from five to twenty years).[125] Luisa de Palhares, daughter of João de Palhares, was one of these orphans awarded the village of Eliviche in Sri Lanka for three lives as her dowry.[126]

A few years later, Lisbon insisted that villages in Sri Lanka were to be awarded to Portuguese already resident there, not to outsiders.[127] In this way, these villages were rewards as well as a method to ensure a long-term Portuguese presence on the island. Actually, the Portuguese modified an earlier system of tribute to fit their own requirements. The traditional system of awarding villages or their incomes in Kotte (Sri Lanka) retained royal ownership while dividing them into three types: royal (Crown), service, and temple. Some royal villages were retained by the Portuguese authorities, as they had been previously. Both royal as well as service villages were awarded to deserving soldiers and orphans. Temple villages were frequently reassigned to support the Franciscan missionary efforts on the island.[128]

In 1626, dowries of land in the Estado da India, specifically around Bombay and Bassein, were awarded to Portuguese women on the condition that they marry men born in Portugal, a requirement renewed by the Goan high court the next year and extended to include all lands in the North.[129] Twenty years later, that condition had been removed for women in Bassein, and they were free to marry whomever they wished.[130] Nevertheless, land or villages given to women for three lives as dowries for marriages to *reinois* were designed for long-term colonization and could not be sold.[131]

These *praças* were some of the richest lands in all of Portuguese Asia. In two examples of lands given to women for three lives, in 1627 D. Catarina de Vasconcelos had her land in Bassein recognized and registered with the notary. Noted in the registration was the fact that this was the second life and that she could pass this land on to her daughter as a dowry, if her daughter married a man born in Portugal.[132] Dona Margarida Teles de Meneses

Ferreira was another woman who registered her lands around the same time for the same reason.[133] D. Francisca de Lacerda, a widow, was awarded the village of Balegão da Pragama (Damão region) for two lives in 1640.[134] The same year, D. Isabel de Silva was awarded the village of Bilvarim, near Tarapor (Damão), for two more lives, "with the usual stipulations and obligations."[135] This process was still active at the end of the seventeenth century. In 1693, D. Maria de Moura was awarded the village of Dantora, near Maimjuelme (Damão), for three lives, hers being the first. These lands were to be passed to her daughter on the condition that she marry a *reinol*, and this was also a condition placed on the holder for the third life.[136]

The land registers were apparently not kept current, because in 1680 the high court of Goa commented that the taxes and titles for lands in the North, including those awarded as dowries, were not in order.[137] Around this time, and perhaps as a method of clearing up any confusion, men who wanted to marry and inherit these lands were required by the *relação* to show certificates to verify at least eight years of military service before they would qualify.[138] By 1690, the *câmara* of Goa had written several times to ask Lisbon that the *reinol* requirement and the clause limiting lands for three lives be lifted, the reason given being "that there are many good men around here," but had not received a definitive answer.[139] Given the value of the land under consideration and the increasing number of *castiço* nobles in Goa, this was an understandable concern. For example, in 1682 the Crown was making annual payments to *fidalgos* in Goa, both born there as well as in Portugal. The payments made that year show forty-five born in Portugal and sixty-four born in India.[140] Nevertheless, it was not until 1737 that this requirement was eventually removed.[141] Many of these lands were lost to the Marathas in the War of 1737–1740. Their loss, diminished profits, and increased competition in trade marked the real decline in Portuguese India.[142]

Husbands and Wives

The Crown was specific as to what sort of man the young lady was required to marry. At a minimum, he was to be born in Portugal (*reinol*). *Reinol* men in the Estado da India were available, but frequently such *soldados* did not make suitable matches for these young ladies. This conflict is the crux of Luso-Indian (particularly Luso-Goan) intermarriage in the early modern period. For quite distinct reasons, Portuguese men and women found marriage to Goans and other South Asians more desirable than to each other. On the one hand, many of these single Portuguese women originated from the minor nobility and would not have considered marrying the common rabble that composed *soldados*, much less *degredados*. Nor would this group of Portuguese men have been attractive to other orphan girls who were commoners. On the other hand, *soldados* were faced with increasing economic difficulties if they failed to marry and establish support outside official Portuguese circles. The promised dowries might have been attractive in the early years of the Estado da India, but, after the 1630s, any attraction would have faded. Goans, however, had something to gain by marriage with their Portuguese rulers. As a result, orphan girls, when they did not marry Portuguese, turned to Goan Christians, usually higher-caste individuals with financial resources and status. Portuguese *soldados* married Goan and other South Asian women, sometimes Christian, sometimes not. For example, in 1650 the king informed the viceroy in Goa, in response to a letter addressed to him by the Goan city council, that he had been informed that Portuguese men had been marrying rich Hindu women with estates and these women must be baptized.[143] In both cases involving Portuguese men or women, the best-laid colonization plans of Lisbon had derailed; however, the result was an ongoing process that began Luso-Indian communities in Goa and elsewhere in South Asia.[144]

Some incidental evidence from 1621 indicates that *soldados* may have not been marrying Portuguese *donzelas* but rather local Christian women. The viceroy writing to the Crown stated that he had been around those parts for a while and had noted a change in the marriage habits of Portuguese soldiers. While in previous years these soldiers had not married, more recently they married quickly after arrival and adopted Asian manners, spending their wives' money in the process.[145]

Seventeenth-century travelers' accounts of women and marriage in Goa, such as those of Tavernier, Mandelslo, and Pyrard, are of particular interest. Tavernier mentioned the economic and social decline he noted between his first and second visits, while commenting on the Goan women.[146]

Many travelers mention the loose morals of the women in Goa. Comments on married women reveal that they led a cloistered life but one with some interesting twists. The previously mentioned *solteiras* were a notoriously jealous bunch. If one thought a *soldado* was about to leave her for another woman, "infallibly they will poison him with a certain drug, which can keep him alive for six months, but at length will kill him."[147] Married men did not hesitate to do the same. These same travelers believed that the Portuguese were "vindictive and jealous" and would use poison with no hesitation.[148]

Both Mandelslo and Pyrard commented on the secluded life of Portuguese women and on the jealousy of their husbands, noting that few Portuguese women could be easily seen around Goa.[149] Mandelslo also recounted a dinner given by a high Portuguese official that he found unusual because "the Portuguese ladies are as seldom seen as the Muscovites and Persians, yet . . . we were served by four handsome young maids of Malacca."[150] Pyrard described an idle life for the married women: "[Their] most ordinary pastime is to remain all day long at windows . . . so that they can see without being seen."[151]

Some Portuguese women may have been idle, but they too shared in the wealth of the Estado da India. In 1546, to assist in the defense of Diu, the women of Goa and Chaul offered their jewels to the Crown. "There are jewels [owned by women] in Chaul which are sufficient to carry on the war for ten years."[152]

One of the more bizarre aspects of daily life in Goa was the use of the drug called "madman's herb," used by both husbands and wives to render the other party senseless and to thus be free for extramarital affairs.[153] Pyrard and others make reference to its frequent use for this purpose.[154] In addition, "opium was supplied as part of the food ration to those employed in the galleys and in gunpowder manufactory."[155] One could assume that it was also sold to the residents.

Not only in the use of drugs had the Portuguese acculturated to life in India. In his article on dancers in Goa, Boxer describes the uproar caused by the presence of "lewd, base, and vile" dancers in Goa during the seventeenth and eighteenth centuries.[156] Indian dancers were prohibited in Goa as early as 1598, but continuing royal edicts against them, lasting at least until 1734, would indicate their continued presence.[157]

These dancers were of greater importance to the nobility than to *soldados*. Slavery, however, did affect all classes of Portuguese society. Slaves in Goa were numerous and, judging by the treatment some received, not expensive.[158] A general discussion on the role and nature of slavery in Goan society is beyond the scope of this work.[159] What is important here is that slaves provided *soldados* with yet an additional option to marriage with *órfãs* or local Christian women. It was an option that was explored since "we read in a Jesuit report that there were innumerable Portuguese in India who bought droves of slaves and slept with all of them."[160]

Given that this was a slave society, that social stratification was based on religious and ethnic background, and that Goa was a frontier society thousands of miles from the European homeland, one could make the argument that the institution of marriage itself was being encouraged by both the church and the Crown through the use of *órfãs* and *soldados* to bolster the Portuguese presence. The Crown promoted the status of married men at the expense of *soldados* in several ways. *Casados* were exempted from military duty and from several municipal taxes.[161] Only married men were allowed to hold offices. Single Portuguese women in this society had few options; the state went to some lengths to ensure the marriage of at least these female orphans by attempting to provide dowries. The fact that the dowries proved to be worthless or, at best, abstract realities, does not detract from this overall effort put forth by the *misericórdia* and the Crown. In fact, the longevity of this imperial dowry scheme is remarkable in view of the realities of Portuguese Asia. How and why the entire system was derailed demonstrate the system's original motives in light of the declining fortunes and size of Portuguese Asia, the problems faced by these colonizers, and the development of Luso-Indian society in general.

I now turn to two other types of single women in the Portuguese world to see the important imperial links they established.

EIGHT

Reformed Prostitutes, Nuns, and Empire

I only have the name of wife because the rest is slavery. I acknowledge that the man should be the head, but I am not sure the woman should be the feet.

—JOSÉ DA SILVA DA NATIVIDADE, *Confortaçam*
para os Queixozos, 1752

The Shelter of Mary Magdalene of Goa

Two other institutions of importance to women were concurrently established with Serra. The Convent of Santa Mónica was the second while in 1610 a third institution, modeled on Lisbon's and called the Recolhimento de Santa Maria Madalena, was founded in Goa. The "disgraced women" living in the shelter had originally been placed with the *órfãs* in their shelter of Serra, but pointed letters from the archbishop of Goa and from royal authorities in Lisbon made it clear that the practice of mixing the "vile and suspect" women of Goa with the *donzelas* of Serra was to stop at once.[1] The *misericórdia* was ordered to stop allowing women of ill-repute into Serra in 1615.[2] Later decrees attempted to put as much distance as possible between the two shelters, although both remained under the jurisdiction of the *misericórdia*, and the funding for the two became somewhat interconnected. For example, payments made to Magdalene, also known as the Casa das Convertidas, in 1612 included 20 *candis* (400 *alqueires*) of rice, 10 of wheat, and 5 *corjas* (bundles of 20 pieces) of cotton cloth. The Recolhimento da Nossa

Figure 11.   Penitent Magdalene by Bartolomé Estebán Murillo. One of Murillo's favored subjects, the Penitent Magdalene represents the mystical transformation anticipated by residence in the shelters of Mary Magdalene. Reproduced with the kind permission of The Minneapolis Institute of Arts.

Senhora da Serra received (among other goods) 200 *xerafins* and 10 *corjas* of cotton cloth.[3] Annual cash payments made by the Crown to both shelters were 300 *milréis* to Serra and 90 to Magdalene.[4] Later in the mid-seventeenth century, when income from lands was insufficient, the Crown earmarked a percentage of profits from the royal tobacco monopoly to help both Serra and Magdalene meet their expenses.[5]

One of the major problems with these two shelters was a familiar one: too many women entered and not enough left. In 1611, the *misericórdia* noted that the way to preserve Serra was to charge paying boarders 100 *xerafins* annually, paid in advance.[6] The number of women in each shelter was limited to twenty in 1680.[7] At the same time, *porcionistas* were required to pay (in advance) 60 *xerafins* to stay in Serra and 50 to remain in Magdalene.[8] These figures should be interpreted as goals rather than reflections of reality; a census conducted in 1697 showed forty-three women in Serra and twenty-eight in Magdalene.[9]

The financial relations between the Estado da India and local chapters of the *misericórdia* were complex. At the same time the state was setting aside part of profits from the tobacco monopoly (above), the Goan *misericórdia* received a separate subsidy of almost 240 *milréis*.[10] Chapters of the *misericórdia* in Damão, Diu, and Chaul were receiving large sums of money from local *factors*. The *misericórdias* in Chaul and Goa were also both owed a large sum of money by the state; some of these loans were more than sixty years old by the early eighteenth century.[11] From time to time, a local chapter might benefit from a sudden windfall, such as what happened to the Goan chapter in 1610. Around 280 pieces of ivory were salvaged from a sunken ship coming from Mombassa and were given to the *misericórdia* to help support orphans, widows, and the sick.[12] Another tactic was to spread responsibilities to a larger number of people, which is just what that Goan chapter attempted in 1609. The Mesa noted that it was expanding the number of brothers from 300 to 400 "because the men leave and go seek their fortunes elsewhere, others are ill and the needs and responsibilities of the *misericórdia* are growing."[13]

In the same manner as their counterparts in the parent house in Lisbon, the women of Magdalene in Goa had their own roles to play in Portuguese colonization. "Many of them . . . renounced their vice which had led them down the wrong road . . . and conducted themselves in ways which compensated for their past."[14] In the statutes of this shelter, it was noted that it was designed for "women who have erred and want to change their ways. No adulterous women nor women who have been publicly chastised or accused of witchcraft may enter."[15] Certainly part of this "reforming" effort required the women to abandon their former lives. In order to ensure this, in 1648 the *misericórdia* noted that men who talked with the women in Magdalene would be excommunicated.[16] For similar reasons, male visitors were forbidden in Serra.[17]

In addition to funds from the *misericórdia* and state, individual orphans could be supported by officeholders. Ursula de Miranda was one such woman in Magdalene. The city council suggested awarding the position of bailiff to Francisco Rodrigues de Pina, with the provision that he then provide 7 *xerafins* monthly for her upkeep.[18] In a number of cases, the brothers of the *misericórdia* arranged passage for these women to other areas within the Portuguese Empire. Colombo, Luanda, Brazil, and Malacca all received Goan *convertidas*.[19]

Goan Orphans

Much of the state's involvement with single women as colonizers originated from the ideology of the Counter Reformation. This is especially true in the "reforming" efforts represented by the Magdalene houses. One other activity must be mentioned in this context: the interest of secular authorities in the upbringing of non-Christian Goan orphans.

In 1559, King D. Sebastião passed a law regarding these children, stating that those without mothers, fathers, or grandparents and who "were not old enough to have an understanding of reason" should be turned over to the *juiz dos órfãos* and placed in the College of São Paulo, where they were to be baptized. Little Goan orphan boys were suddenly at the forefront of missionary efforts and became the responsibility of the Father of the Christians, the Pai dos Cristãos: the individual charged with guiding recent converts to Christianity.[20]

In 1567, this law was reinterpreted by Bishop D. Jorge Semedo to read that being fatherless alone was sufficient grounds to declare a child an orphan and separate him or her from remaining family, even if the child's mother and other relatives opposed it. Baptism could be enforced with a justice official present, if necessary. Some orphans attempted to evade this new understanding by marrying, but boys under fourteen and girls under twelve years of age were not allowed to marry and were forcibly converted as well. This law was enforced by having all such children turned over to the captain of the area (that is, Goa, Bardez, Salcette). The captain entrusted the child to the authorities of the College of St. Paul. Anyone hiding such children was threatened with loss of his or her property and indefinite exile.[21] Many Hindu residents of Goa left for the lands of the Moors (such as Bijapur) because they tired of dealing with the Portuguese on such issues. The practice was stopped when it threatened the economic interests and social harmony in Goa and later applied only to orphans with no families.

In a later investigation of these charges, the response from the Pai dos Cristãos was that the father of the Christians "had never done this . . . but people often hid such orphan children, whose parents were dead, from them when they visited." The Pai dos Cristãos enforced a series of laws, known as the Laws in Favor of Christianity, aimed at the forced or coerced conversion of a number of South Asian communities under Portuguese political control. For example, the Father of the Christians noted Hindus marrying outside their districts or on days forbidden by the church. Many had been marrying during Lent, with "pagan processions." All this was to stop. In some communities, Hindus were forced to attend public sermons.[22]

In a related incident in 1680–1681, the Crown wrote to Goa that it was concerned about the Portuguese and Goan Christians who were responsible for the "great parties people there have to honor the births of sons." The Crown complained, "These parties went on for too long, cost too much, and resulted in offensive acts to God. They must therefore be stopped." The Overseas Council, in a *parecer* on this subject, stated that these parties went on for days, "imitating in this the ways of the heathens, who have a party for eight days to honor the birth of a son." In order to curb this practice, the Overseas Council decreed that if any Portuguese man had such a party, he would lose his office and years of service. If a Goan did this, he would be fined 100 *xerafins*.[23]

By 1736, the Holy Office of the Inquisition had assumed many of these duties and decreed exactly what the local Christians could and could not do in regard to their local customs, weddings, songs, and other aspects of daily life. Practices that appeared to imitate Hindu ways, such as hosting extended parties, were especially discouraged.[24]

The Convent of Santa Mónica of Goa

The third institution of importance to women in Goa was the Royal Monastery of Santa Mónica. This was a cloistered Augustinian convent founded between 1606 and 1610 only after overcoming protracted royal opposition.[25] It formed the final link in the trinity of shelters and homes for single women in Portuguese Asia. While both the shelters of Serra and Magdalene offered dowries and promoted marriage as the basis of Portuguese colonization, the sisters of the convent of Santa Mónica linked far-flung outposts of the Asian empire with the convent's economic base (mostly) in Goa. As a result, its impact was powerful in Goa and felt throughout the Estado da India.[26]

Figure 12.   The Convent of Santa Mónica of Goa. Founded in 1610, it was the earliest European convent in Asia. It survived until the nineteenth century and currently serves as a training center for nuns. Photo by author, 1991.

At first, the Goan city council argued for its creation, but the Crown refused to allow a convent in Portuguese Asia. In 1605 the *câmara* discussed at some length the benefits of having a convent filled with nuns in that city, completing the good deeds of the other shelters.[27] The reasons why the Crown was initially against the creation of this convent were not stated but became clearer after it prospered. At that point, interestingly enough, the *câmara* and Lisbon reversed their standing on Santa Mónica; the Crown became its principal protector, and the city council attacked it.

In the early 1600s, the great costs of building and maintaining the convent might have been one legitimate concern of the Crown. However, in the context of colonization, Santa Mónica provided young ladies with a respectable alternative to marriage. Relatively quickly, Santa Mónica was accused by the city council of two serious and interconnected charges: being too wealthy and sabotaging the possibility of marrying Portuguese women by drawing an excessive number into their convent.

In the context of attracting *soldados* away from royal service, the Crown was concerned that the number of monasteries in Goa was excessive. For example, in 1635 the Carmelites started a convent without royal authority and were ordered to stop.[28] A few years earlier, the city council had complained to Lisbon that Santa Mónica was "draining Goa of its wealth and young ladies."[29]

Lisbon feared this second possibility, which was probably the source for initial royal opposition. That is, Lisbon felt that a convent in the Estado da India would thwart Portuguese marriages and thus frustrate colonization plans, such as the rationale behind sending orphan girls.[30] However, once the convent was founded, the Crown went to great lengths to protect it, while attempting to balance these two conflicting requirements by limiting the number of nuns who could enter. The city council, by contrast, was concerned that Santa Mónica was not only decreasing the number of eligible Portuguese wives but simultaneously becoming too wealthy.

In a series of exchanges in the 1620s, the Crown and the viceroy discussed Santa Mónica and its newly acquired riches. The viceroy wrote that the convent "had eighty nuns and numerous novices and was getting too wealthy and too big for Goa and had even allowed in some women forbidden by its own statutes."[31]

Around the same time (1620s), the Crown ordered the number of nuns in Santa Mónica limited to a total of forty, in accordance with the wishes of the *câmara*. This total was increased to fifty in 1624.[32] Nuns were also not to inherit goods without royal authority. Furthermore, the Crown ordered that the convent be discontinued after the death of the present occupants, after which time it was to serve as a shelter supported by the convent's current sources of income. Lisbon noted its best efforts toward colonizing Goa were being thwarted by the economic growth of Santa Mónica, as well as the continuing increases in the number of nuns.[33]

In the *pareceres* from Goa that the king requested and that followed this order, the Inquisitor Francisco Borges de Sousa defended Santa Mónica, noting that it played an important role in Goa, allowing some women with modest dowries to enter. The real threat, he felt, was from the Dutch.[34] In the second *parecer*, the chancellor of the Goan high court, Gonçalo Pinto da Fonseca, attacked the convent, claiming that the number of marriages had decreased since it was founded, that Santa Mónica had drained large sums of money from the economy, and that it drew its novices from the richest strata of Goan Christian society.

One of the rich widows the judge may have had in mind was D. Catarina de Lima, the widow of Sancho de Vasconcelos and a native of Malacca. She entered the convent in 1609 and was known by the name of Catarina de

Santa Mónica. In honor of services to the Crown rendered by her husband, two dead brothers, and dead son (all of whom died in royal service), the convent was awarded one of the lucrative official voyages to China. Catarina and her three daughters in Santa Mónica were awarded 400 *pardaus* for life, and the crown made a good faith effort to remedy her financial difficulties caused by its chronically slow payments.[35]

An inventory of the properties owned by Santa Mónica in 1618 tends to support the charges of excessive wealth. In just ten years, Santa Mónica owned an impressive list of real estate in Goa, which yielded an annual income around 4,000 *pardãos*. These properties included the taxes from villages in Salcette, Ilhas, and Bardez, pharmacies and lands scattered throughout Goa, and a long list of houses and commercial properties in the city of Goa itself.[36] With some justification, in 1635 the city council called Santa Mónica's holdings "the lion's share of the patrimonies of the city."[37] Only five years later, the mother superior of the convent, Sister Ursula de Encarnação, was adding to the convent's holdings when she purchased some additional lands with palm trees.[38] Complaints fingering Santa Mónica as the principal reason for the decline in married *soldados* were made again in 1644 and 1650.[39]

How is it possible to reconcile these two different views of the situation regarding Santa Mónica and the nature of the nuns? The third *parecer* in this most revealing series, from the *câmara* of Goa, explains that while the motivations for starting the convent were noble, the greed of parents and relatives made it attractive to place daughters with a modest dowry in Santa Mónica. In this way, the parents and relatives were left with the difference in what would have been a more generous dowry; siblings would be left with portions of their sister's inheritance. As a result, the city council explained, the number of nuns has grown remarkably because "no one tries to marry their daughters, but just to place them in the convent.[40]

In 1629 the mother superior of the convent responded to the charges of excessive wealth. She claimed the convent was not as well-off as many believed it to be; since they were now limited to one hundred nuns, they barely were able to meet their expenses. In addition, they had taken in several women with no dowries at all or with small children to raise, as well as the one hundred nuns.[41]

There appears to be some truth in the charges that families attempted to swindle nuns out of their lawful inheritances, in the manner described above. In 1646, the mother superior wrote to the Overseas Council to complain that one of the nuns in Santa Mónica (then deceased), the daughter of Luís de Brito and D. Catarina de Vilhena, was robbed of her inheritance. Specifically, her father inherited and then sold some lands, without giving anything to his daughter or to the convent. At the same time, he owed it money, since he only made a 200-*xerafim* deposit when his daughter entered.[42]

Santa Mónica appears to have become a victim of its own early success, both economic and social. In 1625, just a few years after its beginning, Santa Mónica had ninety-six nuns in residence and had acquired 129 dowries. The number of nuns in residence and dowries accumulated by Santa Mónica from its beginnings in 1610 until in 1874, when the last nun was in residence, is condensed in table 6, below.

Data presented here indicates that the number of nuns in Santa Mónica very quickly peaked in the 1650s at 104. The cumulative number of dowries exceeded 300 before the close of the seventeenth century. Given the reality of these figures in the context of the sharp economic downturn faced by Portuguese Asia during the same period, the complaints made by the city council and others take on a new validity. Only after 1730 the convent began a gradual decline, which extended into the late nineteenth century.

Complaints of Santa Mónica's excessive wealth continued at least until 1702. At that time, the *câmara* complained to the Crown that Santa Mónica made a loan to the Crown attorney of the Estado da India and that in doing so had not listed all its properties nor had it revealed all its dowries. In addition, Santa Mónica had exceeded the number of sisters allowed as well as its limit of 8,000 *cruzados* in income. Specifically, the *câmara* accused the convent of not listing its land holdings in the North and failing to mention that the required dowry for entry was 2,000–3,000 *xerafins*, which "had to be paid or they would simply refuse admission with no scruples whatsoever."[43]

This economic growth of Santa Mónica occurred at a time of general decline in the rest of Portuguese Asia and was undoubtedly a factor causing the envy expressed by the *câmara*, courts, and governors. Santa Mónica prospered, but by 1687 the *câmara* commented: "We see every day in the city houses falling into decay, not on account of the antiquity of the building, but for a lack of money . . . which proceeds from the great poverty and general misery of the inhabitants."[44] The next year, the same body noted that there were a lot of houses in disrepair; the formerly "sumptuous homes were, for the greater part, destroyed."[45]

Nor was the *misericórdia* of Goa immune from these same economic pressures. In 1651, the *misericórdia* informed the Crown that it was no longer able to fund orphanages and hospitals and requested help.[46] A few

TABLE 6

Nuns in Residence and Cumulative Dowries
Obtained by the Convent of Santa Mónica
of Goa, 1610–1874

Year	Nuns in Residence	Cumulative Dowries
1610	32	33
1630	100	152
1650	104	214
1670	67	262
1690	55	298
1710	53	339
1730	57	376
1750	43	396
1770	51	435
1790	42	458
1810	40	479
1830	24	489
1850	10	493
1874	0	493

SOURCE: Moniz, (first series) XV:177–98; XVI: 284–94, 354–63; XVII:92–102, 188–97; (second series) II–III:111–19.

years later in 1664, the *misericórdia* was granted the right to keep money belonging to absentees who died there, provided there were no heirs. This privilege was granted as a special favor to the Casa because of its great poverty and to provide it with enough income to care for the many widows and orphans from the southern forts and the city of Cochin who were being sheltered there.[47] By 1666, the Crown had already been informed by the *misericórdia* that both Serra and Magdalene were on hard times.[48] In 1676, the *misericórdia*, still claiming poverty, was awarded income from some lands in the North specifically to support the shelters in Goa.[49] In that year (1676), the *câmara* reported that Serra had "more than 100 daughters of nobles and Magdalene had seventy orphans and *convertidas*."[50]

The real problem underlying Santa Mónica's wealth was that it was accumulated in spite of (and in sharp contrast to) the economic decline surrounding it. To put it another way, its wealth was comparative rather than absolute. The prestige enjoyed by such a convent in Portuguese society meant that it drew its novices from the wealthy and upper classes. In the case of the former, Goans and *mestiços* could buy respectability; in the latter case, impoverished Portuguese could place their daughters in Santa Mónica to avoid large dowries and possibly to increase the inheritances of other siblings. The combination of these two distinct elements only made the union stronger, until its economic base truly eroded. This occurred by the late eighteenth century, when the Crown noted that Santa Mónica had fallen onto hard times and deserved all the assistance available.[51]

Where did these young ladies come from? When one examines their origins, a telling outline emerges. One of the original complaints against the convent was that it attracted too many women from Portugal, including some orphans sent from Lisbon. There does not appear to be much truth to that charge, since the total number of *reinol* women who entered Santa Mónica was between nine and twenty-four, or between 2 and 3.6 percent of all those who entered. Almost all of these were novices in the first years of the convent's history. Between 65 and 70 percent of the ladies who entered were *castiço, mestiço,* and Goan women from lands around the city; the remainder came from virtually every corner of the Estado da India.[52] Only a handful were from areas outside Portuguese political control. As a result, Santa Mónica was firmly attached to Goan society and enjoyed a reputation throughout the Asian empire as a convent of distinction. It proved to be one more link that united the scattered outposts of Portuguese Asia. In this case, the link was a powerful social and religious institution for women and the first Christian convent in Asia established by the Portuguese.

As a real indicator of its success, several other cities petitioned to be allowed their own convents, but the high court of Goa and the authorities in Lisbon ensured that no additional convents were started in the Estado da India. For example, in 1608 the high court noted that the shelter for young ladies in Bassein was allowed because it was not a convent.[53] By 1627, the *relação* forbid any more shelters or convents without specific royal authorization.[54]

In spite of these problems, Lisbon did allow one additional convent in the Estado da India: Santa Clara in Macau. It, too, faced the same charges as Santa Mónica—thwarting the marriage possibilities of Portuguese *soldados.* In 1686, this convent was forbidden to allow any more women to enter. This law was renewed in 1687, with the penalty of 500 *pardaus* if broken. "The intention was to end this convent."[55] The viceroy renewed this law in 1718, directly blaming Santa Clara for the lack of marriages in Macau.[56] The maximum number of nuns was set at thirty-three and increased to forty in

1731.[57] At the same time, the first orphanage in Macau was started in 1726, and the girls were also given dowries by the *misericórdia*.[58]

Around this same time, the Crown perceived that convents in Portugal were subverting colonization in Portuguese America. In 1732, the king required that young ladies leaving Brazil with the intention of joining a convent in Portugal would only be able to do so with special licenses.[59]

These convents were perceived as alternatives to marriage both by the women concerned as well as by the authorities, which explains the Crown's rationale behind limiting the maximum number of nuns, or, in the Brazilian case, their ability to leave the colony. By contrast, the authorities did not wish to suppress the convents altogether; two years after the viceroy wrote the letter concerning Macau quoted above, he wrote the mother superior of the convent of Santa Clara, concerned that the convent was not receiving all of the money due it: "I specifically ordered that city to continue to pay and not attempt to evade [paying the convent] the [proceeds from a special] one percent [tax]."[60] In the same letter, Dom Luís de Meneses asked to be remembered in the nuns' prayers.

In other words, the Crown was caught on the horns of a dilemma. On the one hand, it wanted convents to flourish. On the other hand, if they did prosper, *soldados* would be hampered in making the best possible matches with Portuguese ladies. By the late 1600s, the authorities in Lisbon had decided that the most effective method of colonization was to use families.

Colonizing Families

Reinol families living in the colonies do appear from time to time in the literature and probably were not as rare as this material might lead one to believe. Several examples show their presence, even in places considered extremely undesirable, such as Angola and São Tomé. For example, Domingos Guedes was awarded the captaincy of the fort at Massanango in Angola and in 1651 went there with his wife and children.[61] Unfortunately, the children became orphans when both he and his wife later died. The Overseas Council agreed to have them brought back to Portugal in 1653.[62] Lopo da Fonseca Henriques, who also lived in Angola with his wife, children, and mother-in-law, petitioned the Crown to be allowed to return to Portugal because of his ill health.[63] Rodrigo da Costa de Almeida was another Portuguese living in Angola with his wife and children.[64] Matias de Almeida lived with his wife, Antónia Pinta, on the island of São Tomé. When she died, the *juiz dos órfãos* sold his property there at a considerable loss, and he obtained permission to leave Angola to reclaim his property.[65] António Lobo, of Évora, requested and was awarded the post of *juiz dos órfãos* on the island of São Tomé for the principal reason that "he says that he will be taking his wife and family with him."[66]

By the middle of the seventeenth century, the authorities in Lisbon realized that the best way to ensure the long-term growth of a colony was not to use *degredados*, orphans, prostitutes, or other unattached individuals, but rather to send ready-made families. Two efforts along these lines were notable; both took place at roughly the same time but in very different regions of the former Império Português.

The authorities in Lisbon in 1635 detailed a plan to colonize Monomotapa (modern-day Zimbabwe) with two hundred soldiers and two hundred married folk.[67] Just a few years later in 1651, Lisbon organized an equally complex colonization scheme for the interior of Mozambique, known as the Rios de Cuama. The Overseas Council noted in 1651 that married couples from the Entre Douro e Minho (the most densely populated region in Portugal) should be enlisted.[68]

In yet another effort to populate this region in the 1670s, the Crown drew up a list of the type and number of each tradesman that would be needed.[69] The Overseas Council reviewed it and made a few minor revisions.[70] One woman named Antónia Pereira requested permission to join this last expedition to the Rios de Cuama. The Overseas Council and Crown agreed and gave her 20 *milréis*, sending her with the married couples.[71] Given the destination and the cash payment, in all likelihood Antónia was from the Magdalene House in Lisbon.

Unfortunately, families such as these sent to colonize Mozambique in the seventeenth century suffered the same high rates of mortality on ships as other families sent elsewhere; many died a few months after their arrival in the Zambesi River valley.[72]

In 1678–1679, the Crown sent twenty-six married couples and sixteen children to Sena (Mozambique).[73] In response, the viceroy wrote to inform Lisbon the next year that the Crown could save a lot of money by sending people from Goa to Mozambique and the Rios. Instead of sending colonizers from Lisbon, the viceroy suggested using women in Serra and Magdalene, who could be given dowries there, "since they usually marry soldiers or other white men born in India." In addition, the viceroy suggested using Goan couples as colonizers.[74] Around this same time, an informal census of Portuguese in the region revealed some eighty-nine Portuguese men and children living in nine outposts, plus "around 160 people living on Mozambique [island]." [75]

At roughly the same time, the authorities in Lisbon were concerned about populating Maranhão and Pará. In spite of this royal eagerness, the Crown was reluctant to allow foreigners to settle there, even other Catholics such as the Irish.[76] D. Mariana Josefa, wife of Nicolau da Costa e Melo, secretary of state for Maranhão, had the Crown pay the transport costs for her sons to come to Maranhão. The Crown noted that this would "help to populate that place." [77] The Crown did not appear to be quite as concerned with Irish settlers elsewhere in the empire, such as in Mozambique. In 1677, the Overseas Council approved the petition of the Irishman Monator Sid, his wife, and three daughters to move there.[78]

At this time the first waves of families emigrated from the Azores to Maranhão and Pará. By the middle of the seventeenth century, overpopulation and volcanic activity made emigration necessary. In 1649, Martis Filter, a German merchant and owner of the ship *Mercurio,* was given permission to take one hundred married couples from Santa Maria in the Azores to São Luís do Maranhão. He was then to proceed to Brazil and load sugar.[79] However, an English ship was also authorized to make a similar transport of fifty such couples from Santa Maria to Maranhão in 1647.[80]

Judging from this experience, the Overseas Council noted in 1693 that married couples would be better colonizers than soldiers for the cities of São Luís and Belém do Pará.[81] Free emigration to Brazil from the Azores and Madeira was encouraged and organized by the Crown in the eighteenth century. In 1722, 294 people, mostly couples, were ready to leave the islands of Pico and São Jorge for the Nova Colonia (do Sacramento).[82] João Rodrigues Lisboa was given permission to transport an additional 500 people from Madeira to Santa Catarina (Brazil) in 1754.[83]

In this context one can note a 1755 broadside on the resettlement of persons from the Azores to Brazil.[84] In it, the Crown offers to pay transportation costs, a lump-sum payment on arrival, and to equip each couple with the tools they would require to begin their new lives. Noteworthy is the requirement that the men must be under forty and the women under thirty years of age. Single women between twelve and twenty-five were especially encouraged to emigrate.

In a rather extended commentary on the causes of the decline of the Portuguese state of India and cures for these, the viceroy Francisco de Távora mentioned in 1696 that some local Christian widows, in imitation of Hindu ways, were not remarrying. He felt that as a result, the Estado was placed in great peril. He decreed that from that point, all local women regardless of their caste could remarry and that no one was to attempt to stop them in word or deed, specifically not their parents, brothers, or other relatives. Those who attempted to do so would lose everything he or she owned. Another recommended cure for the decline of Portuguese India was to promote the use of Portuguese and to suppress the use of Konkani (the language of Goa). The viceroy decreed that everyone, particularly local women, was to speak and use Portuguese within three years.[85]

In making this list of problems and their possible solutions, the viceroy recognized the inevitable with regard to Portuguese women and the variety of *reinol-castiço* colonization plans hatched in Lisbon for Portuguese Asia. The first element was that Portuguese and *castiço* women were too few to allow such schemes to ever work. In response to this, the logical alternative was to encourage Luso-Indian intermarriages, something that had been taking place informally since the arrival of Albuquerque and that had periodically been officially encouraged.[86] The third revealing aspect of the viceroy's complaint, above, is his definition of empire through the mandated use of the conqueror's language and customs. That is, if the homeland's population is insufficient to control a global empire, mold the people in the colonies to the closest resemblance possible: Portuguese-speaking Christians who can share additional cultural traits with Europeans. By extension, to be Portuguese is then defined by language, religion, and culture—not by ancestry.

Orphan girls and prostitutes sent abroad probably totaled only a handful. If three to five *órfãs* were sent annually from Lisbon during the period of this study (1550–1755), they would have totaled between 615 and 1,025. If an average of two women per year left the Magdalene houses in Lisbon or Goa for other destinations in the Portuguese Empire, they would have added 410 more women to this picture. That would mean a grand total of 1,025 to 1,435 state-sponsored single female colonizers were relocated in the Portuguese Empire from 1550 to 1755. In the great sea of population that was early modern South Asia, these numbers have little meaning. What is of great interest is this organized effort to get marriageable Portuguese women to India (and elsewhere), how and why that effort was derailed, and the solutions to contradictory demands faced by the Crown.

Conclusion

ALVIANO: We know that Brazil was settled first of all by persons
of evil ways and men who had been banished from Portugal for
their crimes.

BRANDÔNIO: The first settlers who came to Brazil had many
opportunities to get rich in a hurry on account of the liberality
of the land. As they prospered, they promptly shed their evil
nature, which the necessity and poverty they had suffered in the
Kingdom [of Portugal] had brought out. And the children of those
men, having those riches and enthroned as rulers of the land,
sloughed off their old skins just as a snake does, and adopted in
everything the most polished manners.

—AMBRÓSIO FERNANDES BRANDÃO, Dialogues
of Great Things of Brazil, 1987

This study has attempted to present a picture of criminals and single women,
principally orphan girls, as forced or state-sponsored colonizers in the early
modern Portuguese Empire. The state and church-related systems that
guided these efforts were complex and based on Portuguese (and ultimately
Roman and occasionally Visigothic) law as well as long-standing Iberian social customs. In spite of the numerous cases cited here, the fact of the matter is that these individuals and their sentences (and the remaining masses
of legal data) do not make any sense in isolation. I have no doubt that I have
left out many examples and numerous individuals from this study of forced
colonization. However, after an extensive archival search, I believe that I
have assembled more than sufficient data to demonstrate these imperial
structures and their underlying rationale.

The general subject of emigration is one of the great themes in Portuguese history. Unfortunately, the vast majority of the literature on the
subject concentrates on the nineteenth and twentieth centuries, when the
data becomes more frequent and reliable. Demographic figures for many locales during the early modern period are scanty; Portugal itself, as well as

the empire, are no exceptions. Early modern figures can best be understood as impressions rather than statistics; nevertheless, they do provide some idea as to the overall population of the empire.

Magalhães Godinho has calculated the following number of people leaving Portugal during the periods indicated: from 1500 to 1580, 280,000; from 1580 to 1640, 300,000; from 1640 to 1700, 120,000; and from 1700 to 1760, 600,000.[1] After 1580, the majority of these departures were probably for Brazil; they certainly were after 1640. The number of Portuguese in the entire Estado da India in 1540 was estimated to be 6–7,000.[2] Thirty years later, at the height of Portuguese power in Asia, Diogo do Couto estimated a maximum of 16,000 Portuguese present in the Estado da India.[3] Winius, by contrast, estimates that no more than 10,000 Portuguese were ever present in Portuguese Asia at one time.[4] Figures complied by Subrahmanyam indicate that in 1635 there were around 4,900 "white" *casados* and 7,400 "black" *casados* in all of Portuguese Asia.[5]

In contrast, one estimate of the total Portuguese emigration to the New World during the sixteenth and seventeenth centuries places it at 100,000.[6] This is clearly low, since it would indicate that 600,000 of Magalhães Godinho's totals (above) would have been destined for Portuguese Africa and Asia. Other estimates from 1498 to 1700 suggest an annual average of 815 Portuguese departing Portugal and average annual arrivals in Portuguese Asia of 482.[7] Table 7, below, lists several (admittedly contradictory) population estimates for locales in the Estado da India. Table 8 outlines the population of Macau, the second city of Portuguese Asia, from 1583 to 1822.

In 1718, the Royal Academy of History requested a detailed census from all regions under Portuguese control.[8] The responses to this inquiry from both Goa and Macau were encountered in the Goan archives and are presented in table 9, below.

In spite of the contradictory and fragmented nature of this data, it is clear that by the eighteenth century, the *reinol* and *castiço* percentages of populations of Goa and Macau, the two largest and most important cities in Portuguese Asia, were small. In the case of Macau, Europeans and their direct descendants may have totaled 7 percent of the population. In Goa, their percentage was even lower.

On the other side of the globe in Portuguese America, Cabral de Mello presents demographic figures for the Brazilian Northeast around 1630 as 95,000 for the *capitania* of Pernambuco, a central region in the colony. Of these 95,000, only 8,000 were free people who could be mobilized for service. He suggests a population of 20,000 to 25,000 for the remaining *capitanias* of

TABLE 7

Population Estimates of Various Locales in the Estado da India

City/Region	Date	Comments
Goa (city)	1500s	225,000, of which there were 800 Portuguese families
	1540	10,000 Indian Christians and 3,000–4,000 Portuguese[a]
	1580s	60,000
	1600	75,000, of which 1,500 were Portuguese and *mestiços*
Old Conquests of Goa	1630s	around 250,000
	1635	800 "white" *casados* and 2,200 "black" *casados*[b]
	1848	European descendants, 451 males and 470 females.[c]
Cochin	1663	4,000 "whites"
Praças do Norte	1600s	400 "white" families; 200 in Chaul,
		2,000 "whites" in Bassein; 60 families in Diu
São Tomé (Meliapore)	1600s	more than 400 families of Portuguese descent
Columbo	1600s	more than 2,500 families of Portuguese descent

SOURCES (unless otherwise indicated): Rodrigues, "Portuguese-Blood Communities."

[a] M. N. Pearson, "Goa During the First Century," and the sources cited therein, principally, T. R. de Souza, *Medieval Goa*.

[b] Bocarro and Magalhães Godinho, cited in Subrahmanyam, *Portuguese Empire*, 222.

[c] Kol, 328.

Itamaracá, Paraíba, Rio Grande, and Ceará. This would total 110,000 to 120,000 inhabitants around 1630. Cabral de Mello also discusses the number of the soldiers brought over from Portugal, which was not very great when compared to the native militia—580 men in 1631 (compared to more than 4,000 locals). Less than one-third of the militia in 1646 and 1648 were from outside Brazil. Even this figure may be inflated, since many of these soldiers were probably residents of the area.[9] Magalhães Godinho has estimated the population of Brazil in 1612 as around 50,000 white colonists and 120,000 black and Indian slaves.[10]

Other estimates of regional populations of the empire in the mid-seventeenth century include observations such as that made regarding the factory at São Jorge da Mina. In 1621, the population was composed of 300 residents and 200 soldiers. The island of São Tomé had 800 "white" residents and another 2,000 *mestiços* and Africans (*creolos da terra*).[11] Military lists for Cape Verde in 1664 show 1,248 *soldados*—of these 55 were "whites."[12] In 1696 the total population of the city of Santiago (Cape Verde) was listed by the governor as 327 hearths or 1,885 souls.[13]

TABLE 8
Demography of Macau, 1583–1834

1583	900 Portuguese men [a]
1601	600 Portuguese *casados* and visiting merchants [b]
1622	700–800 Portuguese *casados* and *mestiços*, 10,000 Chinese
1634–37	600 *casados*
	About 600 young males (capable of bearing arms)
	600 *gente da terra* (*mestiços* or Chinese), and 5,000 slaves
1635	850 *casados* [c]
	150 single men and married men with wives in Portugal
	5,100 slaves (6 slaves average / *casado*)
1640	600 Portuguese *casados*
	600 sons capable of bearing arms
	500 native-born *casados* and soldiers
	5,000 slaves
	20,000 Chinese
1643	2,000 *moradores* (Portuguese inhabitants)
1644	40,000 total inhabitants
1662	200–300 Portuguese and other Christian males, around 2,000 widows and orphans
1669	300–320 *casados*
1690s	19,500 inhabitants [a]
1800	8,000 Chinese [d]
1822	Christian population listed as males fourteen or older: 604; boys fourteen or younger: 473; women: 2,701; slaves: 537; total Christian population: 4,315. [e]
1830	4,636, including 1,202 "white" men, 2,149 "white" women, 350 male slaves, 779 female slaves, 38 men and 118 women of mixed races. [f]
1834	Total Portuguese residents in the city: 90. [f]

SOURCES: [a] Ljungstedt, 27.

[b] Data from 1601–1669 are from George B. Souza, 32.

[c] Figure also mentioned in Pedro Barreto de Resende, Descripções das Cidades e Fortalezas de India Oriental (1635), BACL, azul 267, ff. 221v.–22.

[d] Data from 1800 and 1822 are from Guimarães e Freitas, 4:1, 14–15.

[e] Ljungstedt (27) places the figure for 1821 at 2,693, not including 186 soldiers, 19 friars, and 45 nuns.

[f] Ljungstedt, 28.

Although these figures are impressionistic, they do reinforce the idea that the *reinol* and *castiço* elements of the overall population in a given colony could be quite small. When the *degredado* element is considered in this light, some of the complaints that reached Lisbon suddenly take on new meaning. While the overall numbers of convicts in the Portuguese world during early

TABLE 9
Population of Goa and Macau, 1718–1719

	brancos (whites)	clerics	naturais (Goans)	cafres (slaves)
GOA				
Ilhas	303	207	19,131	1,674
Salcete	76	348	24,874	212
Bardez	172	107	19,983	267
MACAU	274 males	68	864 males	
	730 European or mestiça women			
	1,178 females			
	263 widows			
	306 unmarried women			

SOURCE: HAG, MR 84B, ff. 333–35, and MR 88, ff. 106–39v. Lista das pessoas que ha nesta cidade de Macao, 29 December 1722.

modern times may have been modest, in many colonies so too was the percentage of Portuguese and *castiço* populations. As a result, *degredados*, as well as single Portuguese women, could have formed 10 to 20 percent of the *reinol* population. That is, it is not a question of a colony having too many resident *degredados*, as the complaint would have one believe. Rather, there were so few Portuguese in some regions that all *reinois* become noteworthy in the overall population, and *degredados* composed an important percentage of that total. Their presence in numbers would have varied greatly from colony to colony. In places such as the North African presidios, São Tomé, coastal Angola, Mozambique Island, and Maranhão, *degredados* would have formed a high percentage of the European population, perhaps as high as 80 or even 90 percent. In central regions of the empire, such as the cities of Salvador and Goa, their percentage would have been low. Elsewhere in places such as Diu, Sri Lanka, and São Paulo the figure would have varied greatly over time, as suggested in this study.

Degredados, the single male criminal-soldiers, were supervised by agents of the Crown from jails in their hometowns to their assigned sites of exile. *Degredados* were collected in local jails throughout Portugal. In groups of six or more, they were brought to Lisbon's main jail of Limoeiro where they faced a number of possible sentences, depending on the nature of their crimes and the pressing needs of the state. In the first stage of this process to 1415, and for those convicted later of minor crimes, internal exile was the usual punishment. Throughout the early modern period until the middle of the nineteenth century, internal exile in Portugal became identified with the town of Castro Marim, although other towns were used from time to time. Exile overseas quickly became the common punishment after 1415 for serious offenders, and those guilty of the many serious crimes were sent to work in the galleys. However, manpower in the galleys was frequently reassigned overseas in emergencies. In most sites, such as Brazil, Maranhão, or Angola, the *degredado* had some relative freedom serving in the military for a given number of years. In Goa, the *degredado* faced a number of options, including staying with a single Goan woman or with a group of other soldiers under the care of a captain. In either case, soldiers could join monasteries, marry, or become *renegados* before ever obtaining their certificates of completion of *degredo*. Given its vast size and its wide range of economic opportunities, Brazil offered even more options to convicts.

The high courts in Goa and Salvador adopted this framework from the European courts and incorporated both internal exile and galleys into the colonial legal system. Lower courts elsewhere in the empire also used an established order of exile sites for their criminals, imitating the ways of Lisbon and Porto. Convicted sinners from tribunals of the Holy Office of the Inquisition entered this process at Lisbon's Limoeiro jail (or in Goa), and only added more manpower to the entire system, which was carefully coordinated by the state.

Orphans and prostitutes, the single, female figures under discussion in this study, had fewer options in this colonizing framework. Single women were gathered in a variety of shelters in Portugal, including Magdalene houses, the Orphanage of the Castle of São Jorge, and other institutions. Orphans from Lisbon sent to Goa were placed in the Shelter of Our Lady of the Mountain, while some other single women entered the Magdalene House, or made their way through other means. Local women from Goa and elsewhere in Asia also entered these institutions. Some of the most eligible women entered the convents of Santa Mónica in Goa or Santa Clara in Macau. Others from the Magdalene houses were relocated in the empire to Brazil or Africa. Orphans from Serra who married were rewarded with dowries, in various forms.

The total number of *degredados* produced by the state and church courts in Portugal and overseas in the empire during the two centuries under study here was around 50,000. The most recent estimates of "convicts, vagabonds, and political prisoners" from the British Isles transported from 1607 to 1775 to the New World are equal to this figure of 50,000.[14] This means that Portugal, with a population base between one and two million (excluding the colonial population) exiled an equal number criminals as the British Isles, with a population between five and ten million souls.[15] Total free and forced French colonization to the New World had the same approximate total of 51,000, based on a population between sixteen and twenty-four million people.[16] The Spanish example is similar.

Although it is true that Portugal was and remains a small country, its penal exile system produced a number of convicts that rivaled other, much larger, European powers. This relatively large Portuguese number of *degredados* gives ample evidence to the pervasive nature of *degredo* in Portuguese law and society. Exile was much more of a real and dreaded fact of life for a much larger segment of the Portuguese population than it was for the French, British, or other European commoner.

All of this would lead the reader to believe that the criminal justice segment of this colonization scheme worked well, and it did. The Crown and church went to great lengths to supervise aspects of this system and to transport, feed, and generally guide these people overseas—with the ultimate intention of punishing the criminal, populating distant regions of the empire, and promoting marriage with state-awarded dowries. If 50,000 *degredados* passed through this system, and *degredados* were only one segment of the male colonizing element, single women, by comparison, were only a handful.

It is tempting to see this colonizing effort as a failure. Perhaps the most fundamental reason for this view is the insufficient number of Portuguese or *castiço* women in the empire. Secondly, these women did not always marry, nor did they wed the men the Crown envisioned. Portuguese and *castiço* men, for their part, also found that it was not necessarily in their best economic interests to marry women from Portugal. The result was a Portuguese presence established in a much firmer and more culturally interactive manner than this original system devised in Lisbon. Because of its fluid nature, the presence extended well beyond the political limits of the Portuguese world.

The lack of Portuguese women and the economic rewards (if not outright necessity) of marriage into local families sparked the creation of Luso-Indian, Luso-Chinese, Luso-African, and Luso-Brazilian communities. *Degredados* were quite active in this process, especially in areas of the Portuguese Empire that were unable to attract free immigration and beyond the political boundaries of the Portuguese world, where *degredados* had become *renegados* or *lançados*.

Was this effort a success or a failure? If one views this system as one created to populate the empire with Europeans and their direct descendants, the modest numbers of convicts and even smaller numbers of female emigrants would lead to the conclusion that the system failed. However, colonization is a complex process that requires much more than the simple transfer of people from one place to another. The exchange of cultural traits is another part of this process; in the Portuguese case, the spread of Catholicism and the Portuguese language are especially important and relevant. Although the numbers of Portuguese were slight, especially in Asia, the global spread of these two cultural aspects and the related creation of Lusophone communities beyond Portuguese America to West and South Africa, the coastal regions of South and Southeast Asia was remarkable.[17]

This was not an easy process. Reference has already been made to the high mortality rates on the *carreira da India*. Given their poverty and exposure to diseases in jail, convicts formed a large percentage of those who died on that journey. However, all Portuguese living in tropical climates faced a range of deadly diseases.[18] Along the coastal regions of West and South Africa, malaria, sleeping sickness, yellow fever, yaws, bilharzia, and smallpox were common during early times and are still problems for public health officials today.[19] Malaria was the primary reason the islands of São Tomé and Príncipe could not be successfully colonized by the Portuguese and, as a result, why the islands came to be so closely associated with penal exiles during early modern times. Malaria has also been a recurring problem in Cape Verde, coastal Mozambique, and much of the west coast of India. Cholera was another problem that periodically swept over Lisbon, Goa, Mozambique, and Salvador. Under these circumstances, the low percentages of *reinois* and *castiços* in Portuguese Africa and coastal western India are understandable. Indeed, it is remarkable that the Portuguese were able to so firmly establish themselves and fundamental elements of their culture in many of these tropical locales.

One aspect that emerges from this discussion of colonization is the issue of a model colony. Perhaps it would be more accurate to speak of a range of models. Table 10, below, presents the timing and duration of Portuguese free and forced colonization in a number of regions throughout the empire.

From the sketch presented in table 10, it is possible to view Portuguese colonization as following one of two models. Madeira is perhaps the best

TABLE 10
A Model of Portuguese Colonization

City /Colony	A	B	C	D	E	F
Castro Marim	1277	1550s	—	1850s	?	—
Ceuta	1415	1415	?	1640	1450s	1640
Azores	1427–1452	1427	1439	1440s	1650s	—
Madeira	1418	1420	1425	1425?	1690s	—
Cape Verde	1441–1456	1450s	1462	1950s	1952	1975
Guiné	1444	1450s	?	1930s?	1952	1974
São Tomé	1471	1480s	?	?	1650s?	1975
Angola	1520	1600s	1880s	1930s	1650	1975
Maranhão	1500	1600s	1650s	1820s	1820s	1822
Mozambique	1498	1490s	1630s	1930s	1850	1975
Goa	1510	1510	1510	1800	1510	1961
Diu	1535	1580s	?	1800	?	1961
Sri Lanka	1518	1550s	1590s	1640?	?	1656
Molucca Islands	1511	1550	?	1600?	?	1623

   A = Initial incorporation by the Portuguese; B = Beginning of forced colonization; C = Beginning of free colonization; D = End of forced colonization/use of penal exile; E = Local exiles sent to other colonies; F = End of Portuguese political control, if applicable.
   SOURCE: For columns A and F, Serrão, *Cronologia.* For B–E, data presented in this study.

example of the first model: a speedy transition from discovery to forced and then free colonization. The African colonies, especially São Tomé, followed a different path and remained virtual penal colonies throughout early modern times, never able to attract free immigration until early in the last century.

   Why did the Portuguese not use a system of indentured servitude? Although there does not appear to be a clear answer, some of the notable differences emerge between Portugal and the countries that did adopt that practice. The indentured system, according to Slicher van Bath, has three defining characteristics: "the existence of a market for white labor, the price of that labor, and the transferability of white labor contracts."[20] It also assumes an excess population in the homeland and a mechanism that can freely transport these individuals. All of these factors were absent in Portugal. The demand for colonial labor, indeed for labor in Portugal itself, was met through slavery. In the Alentejo, Madeira, and São Tomé labor needs were met by black Africans, imported into the country beginning in the middle of the fifteenth century. In Brazil, Indian slavery gave way to black

Africans, as well. In Portuguese Asia, Africans, Chinese, and other peoples were enslaved to meet labor demands. The Portuguese system of forced and state-sponsored colonization placed the government, not private contractors, at the center; the low population base and global manpower requirements for defense excluded the possibility of a system of indentures, a system that was also absent from Portuguese legal tradition.

In fact, the noted commentator Manuel Severim de Faria in 1655 discussed this very issue of manpower requirements: "It is because of the lack of Portuguese that slaves from Guiné and mulattos are required."[21] Faria came to the conclusion that the causes (and remedies) for this situation were three:

1. Portugal maintained an excessive number of overseas outposts and *conquistas*, draining manpower from the country. This could be solved by reducing and consolidating these overseas territories, thus sending fewer men. In addition, he noted that the ships that departed did so with far too many on board. Reducing this number would ensure a safer and healthier voyage.

2. There was a general lack of work in Portugal, which meant that there was no way for men to support themselves, marry, and raise families. Because of this, many men became vagrants and wandered around the countryside, "so many that they seem like an army."[22] Many went to other countries, principally to Spain, especially to Seville. The solution to this problem was to provide training in the trades for these men.

3. There was a lack of suitable land to cultivate in Portugal. The solution to this problem was to create internal, state-planned colonies, especially in the Alentejo.

Severim de Faria was an astute observer of the Portuguese reality. However, as I have discussed throughout this work, many factors are contrary to his points. The transport ships left late and were frequently overloaded. The idea of training schools for vagrants, while in use in northern Europe during early modern times, was contrary to Portuguese culture. Such schools would never have been instituted. Southern Portugal had large estates, and while state-planned agricultural colonies in the Alentejo would have solved a number of problems, this idea would have to wait until the late nineteenth century in Angola, not the Alentejo.

I opened this work with the claim that this was a study of the growing power of the early modern state. What I have explored here is the Portuguese state's application of two very distinct methods to populate its empire. In the first case, the state modified an old tool of penal exile to fashion a method of forced colonization. In the second case, agencies of the state linked charity and dowries to colonization for single women. The result in both cases was more Portuguese overseas, especially in a number of marginal regions unable to attract free immigrants.

The small demographic base and global requirements translated into a reality that each and every citizen was simply too valuable to waste. Holding the criminal for prolonged periods in jail, applying the death sentence, or banishing the convict from the Portuguese world were unrealistic and counterproductive punishments when the state was faced with never-ending imperial requirements. This philosophy was extended to the most marginal figures in early modern Portuguese society: prostitutes, orphans, major and petty criminals, Gypsies, sinners, and New Christians were sent overseas throughout early modern times and formed a sizable element of the European population in many regions. The central issues addressed in this work have been *how* and *why* the Portuguese state identified, collected, and supervised these figures as imperial instruments to support its global empire.

King D. Filipe IV, in a letter of 1622 to the viceroy of India stated, "It has always been necessary for the continuation of the Estado [da India] to establish a Portuguese Nation within it; all possible means of achieving this are worth it."[23] This study has attempted to demonstrate that these were not mere words, but rather a reflection of Portuguese imperial intentions in place on a global basis throughout the early modern period.

Africa.   As used here, one of the presidios under Portuguese control, along the Atlantic coast of (present-day) Morocco.

albergaria.   Inn or hospice.

aldeia.   Village.

alvará.   Royal decree in force for one year, but frequently extended indefinitely.

ama.   Wet nurse.

arrepentidas.   Also known as *convertidas*—women who repented their former lives as prostitutes and who came to reform their lives under the protection of the Santa Casa de Misericórdia (see below).

assento.   Resolution made by one of the courts or councils.

bailadeira.   Female dancer.

caixa.   Box (of documents).

câmara or *senado da câmara.*   Municipal council.

Canarim.   Term used by the Portuguese for Goans.

capitania.   Captaincy.

carreira da India.   The maritime voyage between Lisbon and Goa.

carta régia.   Royal letter, a long-term decree.

Casa de Suplicação.   Appeals court in Lisbon.

casados.   Married Portuguese men.

casamenteiros.   Marriage makers.

castiço.   Person born in the colonies to parents (both) born in Portugal.

códice.   Bound volume of documents.

colégio.   School or institutional shelter.

comarca.   Judicial district.

conselho.   Council; *ultramarino,* overseas council; *do estado,* council of state; *da fazenda,* treasury council.

consulta.   Minutes of a meeting, usually including decision or opinion.

convertidas.   See *arrepentidas* (above).

corregedor.   A superior court judge.

cota.   Another term for *códice:* a book of documents or its reference number.

couto.   Asylum area or asylum city.

cruzado.   Principal money of account during the sixteenth and seventeenth centuries (each *cruzado* was composed of 400 *réis* and was equal to 10 Spanish *reals*).

defuntos.   The deceased.

degredada.   Female criminal exile; plural, *degredadas.*

degredado.   Male criminal exile; plural, *degredados.*

degredo.   Punishment of exile (literally having one's legal status degraded).

desembargador.   A high court justice.

Desembargo do Paço.   Royal council of justice.

donzelas.   Young ladies of marriageable age (damsels).

dote.   Dowry.

enjeitado.   Abandoned child, also known as an *exposto.*

Estado da India.   Portuguese Asian empire centered on Goa.

feitoria.   Factory, trading fort, or commercial-military outpost headed by a *feitor* or *factor.*

fidalgos.   *Filhos de algo* (lit. "sons of somebody"), noblemen.

forçados.   Men sentenced to penal labor in the galleys.

grumete.   Young boy apprenticed as a sailor.

The Islands.   Azores and Madeira, sometimes extended to include the Cape Verdes.

juiz.   Judge; *da fora,* lowest judge in the professional judiciary; *ordinário,* justice of the peace; *dos órfãos,* probate judge.

lançado.   Another term for *renegado* (see below).

letrado.   University graduate.

leva.   (Levy) chain gang.

maço.   Bundle (of documents).

mestiço.   Person born in the colonies of mixed racial origins, one parent being Portuguese.

milréis.   1,000 *reis* (written 1$000).

mitical.   Measure of gold.

órfãs.   Female orphans; *órfã,* female singular; *órfão* and *orfões* are the male singular and plural.

palankeen or *pallankeen.*   Mobile sedan chair used in Portuguese Asia.

pardao (pardau).   Gold or silver coin of Portuguese Asia, valued at 360 and 300 *reis.*

parecer.   Opinion given by a council.

porcionista.   Paying boarder.

povo.   Peasantry.

praças do norte.   The string of Portuguese port cities extending from Diu to Chaul in northern India.

recolhimento.   Institutional shelter, usually financed by a combination of funds from the *misericórdia,* the city, and the state.

reinol.   Person born in Portugal; plural, *reinóis.*

regimento.   Outline of instructions or a collection of guidelines.

relação.   One of the high courts in Porto, Goa, or Salvador.

renegado.   Deserter, Portuguese renegade, man (*renegada*, female) who left Portuguese political control to live with others. Called a *renegado* in reference to his leaving the (Catholic) faith, but also known as *lançado* and in West Africa as *tango-mao.*

Santa Casa de Misericórdia.   Charitable lay brotherhood composed of members of the clergy and local citizens meeting moral requirements. Directed social services such as hospitals and orphanages.

soldados.   Soldiers, unmarried *reinol* men in service to the Crown.

solteira.   An unmarried woman.

tanga.   A silver or copper coin of Portuguese Asia valued at 60 *réis.*

tostão.   A small coin valued at 100 *réis.*

ultramar.   Portuguese overseas territories.

vadio.   A lazy or idle person, a vagrant.

xerafin.   Portuguese money in Asia that equaled 300 *réis* or three-quarters of a *cruzado.*

Sources (other than dictionaries): Boxer, *Seaborne Empire*, 386–91; Boyajian, 319–26; Schwartz, 397–99.

ACL	Academia das Ciências de Lisboa
AD-	Arquivo Distrital (followed by city)
AGC	Agência Geral das Colonias (now known as the IICT)
AGU	Agência Geral do Ultramar (earlier title of AGC, IICT)
AHM	Arquivo Histórico Militar (Lisbon)
AHU	Arquivo Histórico Ultramarino (Lisbon)
AM	Arquivo municipal
ANTT	Arquivo Nacional da Torre do Tombo (Lisbon)
APO-1	*Arquivo Portuguez Oriental*, first series J. H. da Cunha Rivara, ed.
ARGoa	*Arquivo da Relação de Goa*, José Ignácio Abrantes Garcia, ed.
BA	Biblioteca da Ajuda (Lisbon)
BACL	Biblioteca da Academia das Ciências de Lisboa
BGUC	Biblioteca Geral da Universidade de Coimbra (manuscript collection)
BNL	Biblioteca Nacional de Lisboa
BP-Évora	Biblioteca Pública de Évora
BSGL	Biblioteca da Sociedade de Geografia de Lisboa
Cartas	*Cartas de Affonso de Albuquerque*, Raimundo António de Bulhão Pato, ed.
CECT	Centro de Estudos Científicos Tropicais (Lisbon)
CEHU	Centro de Estudos Históricos Ultramarinos
CCLP	*Colleção Chronologica da Legislação Portuguesa*, José Justino de Andrade e Silva, eds.
DH	*Documentos Históricos*
DI	*Monumenta Historica Societatis Jesu: Missiones Orientales. Documenta Indica*, Josephus Wicki, S. J., and John Gomes, S. J., eds.
Documentação-India	
	Documentação para a história das Missões do Padroado Português do Oriente: India, António da Silva Rego, ed.
DP	Desembargo do Paço (a collection in the ANTT)

DR da I	*Documentos Remitidos da India*, Raimundo António de Bulhão Pato, ed.
Elementos	*Elementos para a História do Município de Lisboa*, Eduardo Freire de Oliveira, ed.
f. / ff.	folio/folios or in the pages following (for example, ff. 65)
Gavetas	*As Gavetas da Torre do Tombo*
HAG	Historical Archives of Goa (Panaji, Goa, India)
HMML	Hill Monastic Manuscript Library (St. John's University, Collegeville, Minnesota)
IICT	Instituto da Investigação Científica Tropical (Lisbon)
JFB	James Ford Bell Library of the University of Minnesota
JIU	Junta das Investigações Ultramarinas
Brásio, *Leis Extravagantes*	
	Collecção Chronologica de Leis Extravagantes posteriores a Nova Compilação das Ordenações do Reino publicadas em 1603, desde este anno até o de 1761 . . .
MMA	*Monumenta Missionaria Africana*, António Brásio, ed.
MR	Livros dos Monções do Reino (collection in HAG)
n.s.	not stated
n.p.	place of publication not stated
RJDM	Repartição da Justiça e Despacho da Mesa, correspondence of the DP (ANTT)
n.d.	not dated

PREFACE

1. Decree Law number 39 688 (1954) removed the last penalty of exile in the Portuguese criminal code and substituted it with sentences of long-term imprisonment; see Bender, "Myth," 92–93; and Marinho Homem de Melo, 133–34.

2. Cockburn, 44; Marinho Homem de Melo, 143.

3. Bender, "Myth," 191 and the sources cited therein. Also see Beattie, 87–89, 471–73.

4. Boucher, "France 'Discovers' America," 246.

5. Ibid., 282–83.

6. Cooke, 88.

7. Brasseaux, 48. See also Boucher, "French Images of America," 220–28.

8. See Sturdivant.

9. Huetz de Lemps, 187–89.

10. Boucher, "France 'Discovers' America," 283.

11. Brasseaux, 51.

12. Choquette, "Recruitment," 153, 160. See also Boyer.

13. Bender, "Myth," 191–92.

14. Pike, 135–36.

15. Waley-Cohen.

16. Jennings, 212–39. For the premodern Chinese use of amnesty, see McKnight.

17. *Orders Taken and Enacted.*

18. *A Plea for the City Orphans*, 13.

19. Franck, 22.

20. Choquette, "French Emigration," 573–79.

21. Dumas, 42–44. See also Landry.

22. Proceedings of a colloquium in Coimbra, 20–22 March 1985.

23. For a longer critique of this work, see Boxer, *Women*, 63–64.

ACKNOWLEDGMENTS

1. Published as Coates, *Degredados e Órfãs: colonização dirigida pela coroa no império português. 1550–1755.*

INTRODUCTION

1. Caetano, 23–30.
2. Ibid., 11.
3. Akola, "Demografia"; Alves Morgado, 333.
4. Akola, "Demografia."
5. Ibid., 284.
6. Ibid.
7. Olivença and the lands around it were retained by the Spanish after the War of the Oranges in 1801.
8. Stanislawski, 190, 200.
9. Orlando Ribeiro, *Portugal.*
10. On construction, see Amorim Girão; on family structure, see Jorge Dias.
11. Stanislawski, 207 and 209, figures 14 and 15.
12. Report of two Venetians dated 1580, in Magalhães Godinho, *A Estrutura,* 193–94.
13. Peres, "Actividade Agrícola," 466.
14. Ibid., 465. For the Lisbon case, see *Elementos,* 1:100.
15. For the Portuguese diet, see Oliveira Marques, *Sociedade Medieval,* 1–22.
16. Rau, 67, n. 4.
17. Oliveira Marques, *História da Agricultura,* 50 and n. 90. Cf. modern Portuguese seed yields: 11.4 wheat; 10.99 barley; 8.57 oats.
18. Rau, 67.
19. Peres, "Actividade Agrícola," 472; and Rau, 68.
20. Rau, 69.
21. Saunders, 51, map 2.
22. Ibid., 59.
23. For the debate on this issue, see ibid., 47–48 and the sources cited therein.
24. BA, 44-XIII-32, f. 3v, 9 September 1646; and BA, 44-XIII-50, Leis Varias, ff. 40–41, "Ley sobre a gente da nação . . . ," 13 March 1610.
25. *Elementos,* consulta da câmara, 14 October 1624, 3:119–23.
26. Oliveira Marques, *Sociedade Medieval,* 187.
27. *CCLP,* 7:374, 23 July 1655.
28. ANTT, DP-RJDM, livro 10, f. 103, 30 April 1625.
29. Ferreira, 5:11.
30. BA, 44-XIII-57, ff. 19v–22, printed text of the statutes of the Santa Casa de Misericórdia of Porto, with the new revisions of 1643.
31. Russell-Wood, *Fidalgos and Philanthropists,* 19–21.
32. Ibid., 22–23.
33. Ferreira Martins; Sousa Campos; Brásio, "Misericórdias"; and Russell-Wood, *Fidalgos and Philanthropists,* 21–41.

34. Russell-Wood, *Fidalgos and Philanthropists*, 33–34.

35. Brásio, "Misericórdias"; and Russell-Wood, *Fidalgos and Philanthropists*, 40–41.

36. AD-Braga, fundo misericórida, livros 88, 89, and 674 outline names of prisoners, crimes committed, length of time in jail, and sums spent by the *misericórdia* to feed them in the mid to late 1700s. In the Goan case, HAG, códice 10408, Misericórdia, f. 91v, 28 February 1680.

37. Silveira Cardozo, 226–29.

38. Russell-Wood, *Fidalgos and Philanthropists*, 173–200.

39. Mesgravis, 71; AD-Braga, fundo misericórdia, livro 415 (Pedro de Aguiar and Maria Vieira). See also livros 409 and 410 for the additional example of the donor António Faleiro de Abreu.

40. Boxer, *Portuguese Society*.

41. Ibid., 5; Schwartz, 5.

42. BGUC, manuscript collection, códice 695, ff. 74–76, "Alvará sobre pessoas ociozas e vadias que continualmente nella [Lisboa] ha.," 2 July 1570.

43. BGUC, códice 695, fl. 86., "Sobre a expulsão de ciganos," 15 March 1573.

44. BA, 44-XIV-4, fl. 299, "Sobre os pobres e vadios," 11 May 1592.

45. *CCLP*, 2:264, 18 December 1617, and 6:227–28, 11 December 1643.

46. Arquivo Municipal de Viana do Castelo, livro 763, Actas da Câmara, ff. 20v–21, 29 April 1631.

47. Legislation to this effect was passed in 1641, 1701, and 1750. See Castilho Barreto, 112.

48. *CCLP*, 11:35–36, 10 May 1702.

49. AD-Évora, câmara, 145, ff. 29 and 64–64v, 5 February and 19 July 1497; Arquivo Municipal de Braga, protocolo da senado da câmara; Biblioteca Municipal de Elvas, Arquivo da Câmara, livro das despezas, 1673–1674, códice 939/982, ff. 138v–139. *APO-1*, fasículo 2, alvará of the Viceroy, 19 December 1603; *Documentos Históricos do Arquivo Municipal*, Actas da Câmara, 1669–1684, 5:179–80. Dated 12 February 1776, but placed between documents dated 1676.

50. Arquivo Municipal de Viana do Castelo, livro 51, receita e despezas da câmara 1605, ff. 131–34, expenses of 23 April 1605.

51. AD-Évora, câmara, 145, ff. 1–20, 19 July 1497.

52. HAG, códice 7751, Senado de Goa, cartas patentes, ff. 251–51v.

53. HAG, códice 3025, regimento das fortelazas, f. 28v.

54. Biblioteca Municipal de Elvas, Arquivo da Câmara, livro dos gastos da câmara, 1662, códice 957/983.

CHAPTER 1

1. AHU, Maranhão caixa 9, doc. 57, 28 July 1696.

2. AHU, Maranhão caixa 10, doc. 18, ff. 1–2, 12 November 1698.

3. Caetano Perreira e Sousa, *Esboço,* [unnumbered pages]. See also, Marinho Homem de Melo, 135, 139–41.

4. For an introduction to these two codes and to early modern Portuguese law in general, see Gomes da Camara. The two collections of ordinances were named for the respective kings who saw them codified: D. Manuel I (1495–1521) and D. Filipe II (1580–1598). For the purposes of this study, *leis extravagantes* were those issued after 1602. These have been assembled in two fundamental collections that, in addition to these two *ordenações,* were the legal basis for this study: *CCLP;* and *Leis Extravagantes.*

5. Caetano Perreira e Sousa, *Primeiras Linhas,* 219.

6. Lopes Ferreira, 222–24. This passage actually states there were five levels of exile while clearly listing seven and omitting the most severe form.

7. *Ordenações de D. Manuel I,* livro 3, título 3 and livro 5, título 40.

8. See both Elkiss, 51 n. 14; and Marchant, 59–60, n. 36.

9. Caetano Perreira e Sousa, *Primeiras Linhas,* carta régia, 31 January 1626, 217.

10. Caetano Perreira e Sousa, *Primeiras Linhas,* 219.

11. BACL, azul 269, Leis Várias, f. 299, 28 August 1645. While leaving Portugal without official permission was forbidden throughout the early modern period, this particular law was probably passed in response to the Wars of the Restoration of Independence (1640–1668).

12. *Leis Extravagantes,* 2:508–9, alvará, 26 March 1746.

13. BGUC, códice 488, ff. 279–80. As noted in the sentence, this punishment was in accordance with the *leis extravagantes* of 6 December 1660, ordenaça 5, paragraph 144. An earlier example is in Pissurlencar, 4:448–50, 14 September 1693.

14. The first reference encountered to this substitution dates from the reign of King D. Fernando (1367–1383) and was renewed in 1423. It stated that all sentences other than the death penalty could be satisfied through fines. See *Elementos,* 1:259; and Caetano Perreira e Sousa, *Primeiras Linhas,* 219.

15. *Elementos,* 1:259; and Caetano Perreira e Sousa, *Primeiras Linhas,* 219.

16. The Goan example, undoubtedly working from a metropolitan model, established a schedule of fines from 20 to 40 *xerafins* for these civil infractions (HAG, códices 2655, 2808, 2656, and 1193). A schedule for fines is shown in HAG códice 1844.

17. See, for example, the two general pardons granted on 9 August 1687 and on 30 August 1688, repeated on 26 October 1689, in *CCLP,* 10:125–26, 167–68, 201–2.

18. In 1672, counterfeiting was specifically included in this category, *CCLP,* 8:206–7, 16 and 29 July 1672.

19. These four crimes were considered especially dangerous by other early modern powers, as well. Powers, 43, 117, 210, 217; and Spindel, 125.

20. BACL, azul 103, Leis Diversos dos Anos 1261 à 1734, ff. 25v and 26, 17 April 1506. Portuguese legislation on sodomy is also outlined in Bellini, 93.

21. *APO-1*, fasículo 5, 2:734–37 n. Decree passed by King D. Sebastião, 9 March 1571.

22. *APO-1*, fasículo 5, 2:734–35 n.

23. *MMA*, 3:125–26, 18 February 1575.

24. BA, 44-XIII-50, f. 64v, "[Ley] Extravagante do Pecado de Sodomia . . . ," 12 October 1606. See Mott, 736–38.

25. HAG, MR 12 (1613–1617), f. 27v, Viceroy to the Crown, n.d.

26. BA, 44-XIII-57, ff. 106–106v.

27. Lopes Ferreira, 47–48.

28. Figueiredo, *Synopsis*, 1:396.

29. *Gavetas*, 1:519–20, alvará of D. Pedro II, 21 January 1696.

30. For an example of such a case, see ANTT, DP-RJDM, livro 4, f. 339. In November 1617, João Menezes petitioned for a pardon from two years in the galleys for this crime.

31. ANTT, DP-RJDM, livro 8, f. 127, 4 August 1623.

32. *ARGoa*, 1:15–16, doc. 17, 12 November 1602.

33. BP-Évora, CXV/1–39, 218. Law of 17 February 1623.

34. BP-Évora, CXVI/2–11, number 3, ff. 1–1v, 1563.

35. See Borges Coelho, 1:106–7; and Pieroni, *Os Excluídos*, for an overview of sentencing in Brazil.

36. Soares, 20–21.

37. Alvará of 16 January 1554 in *Documentos para a História do Açúcar*, 1:109.

38. Traces of a similar (but not as comprehensive) collection system can be seen in documents such as BA, 44-XIII-32, number 110–11 of March 1571, which assumes a system to transport prisoners to the galleys. The 1575 version states it is the first comprehensive regiment on the subject. See BGUC códice 695, ff. 94–105, 3 December 1575.

39. The Spanish system is outlined in *Recopilación de las leyes*, 2:203–5.

40. Regimento dos degredados, BA 44-XIII-52, ff. 143–51, 27 July 1582. This *regimento* has been published Figueiredo, *Synopsis*, 2:198 ff. and in outline form in Lopes Ferreira, 225–29. This provides a great deal more information. Cf. Candido Mendes de Almeida, 5:1320–23.

41. Nunez do Leão, 3–11. Leão lists six provinces. Cf. Schwartz, 6, n. 7. The evolution of the *comarca* is outlined in Gama Barros, 3:278–84 and defined in 11:55–6; 11:169–71; and 11:207–17.

42. Schwartz, 398. For the development of the office of *juiz da fora*, see Figueiredo, "Memoria."

43. Caetano Perreira e Sousa, *Primeiras Linhas*, 217.

44. Arquivo Municipal de Coimbra, B-7, Provições Antigas, f. 88, letter from Crown to Câmara, 11 May 1628.

45. Figueiredo, *Synopsis*, 1:196, alvará, 30 October 1514. Another decree dated 11 August 1531 required that criminals from Entre Douro e Minho convicted of murder or theft be sent to exile in chains. Ibid., 1:344.

46. "The *levador dos presos* is to be paid 30 *milréis* and the originating areas are to help," Arquivo Municipal de Coimbra, B-14 livro de correia II, f. 90v, 5 January 1536. The salary for these officials was later incorporated into this regimento.

47. *Gavetas*, 1:870–72, 1568. Ibid., 1:528, 20 August 1703.

48. *Elementos*, 4:389, n. 2. See illustrations.

49. ANTT, DP-RJDM, livro 8, f. 233, 23 October 1623.

50. *Elementos*, decreto of 24 January 1642, 4:452.

51. AHU, India caixa 13A, docs. 139, 142, 146, and 148, dated 2 and 4 March, and 2 and 16 April of 1639. On unhealthy conditions in the jails, see ANTT, DP-RJDM, livro 14, f. 243, 25 August 1632.

52. *Collecção das Leis, Decretos, e Alvarás*, alvará, 21 September 1758.

53. *CCLP*, 4:86, alvará, 18 January 1618, renewed 9 July 1636.

54. *Elementos*, 2:108–18. Prisoners are mentioned on 118.

55. *CCLP*, 7:420, 12 and 30 December 1656.

56. HAG, códice 8779, Indice dos Assuntos da Relação de Goa, f. 86, 1657.

57. *CCLP*, 8:121, 28 August 1666; 8:170, 1 March 1669; 10:126, 9 August 1687; 10:167–68, 30 August 1688; and 10:201–2, 26 October 1689.

58. *Elementos*, carta régia, 4 December 1711, 10:572–73 and n. 2 on 572.

59. Livro dos Livramentos dos Prezos da Cadeia da Corte de que he mordomo O Senhor Conde da Calheta este anno de 1690. BSGL, reservados 146-A-9.

60. Assuming that the book was written in April 1691, the date of the last entry.

61. Lopes Ferreira, 243–44.

62. Hespanha, 18.

63. Cervantes, part 1, chapter 22.

64. *CCLP*, 1:41, 31 January 1604.

65. AD-Évora, Misericórdia 93, Despezas do anno 1622, ff. 120–40.

66. 1,580$335 *reis* of which 40$770 went for prisoners and another 12$000 for their medical expenses—AD-Évora, Misericórdia, livro 1266, ff. 63–64v; livro 1267, ff. 44v, 64–65.

67. AD-Évora, Misericórdia, livros 1269, ff. 63–63v; 1270, f. 93; and 1271, ff. 66–66v. The *misericórdia* of Lisbon was spending from 2 to 4 percent of its total expenses on food and clothing for prisoners, AHU, Reino maço 31. An extensive example can be found in AD-Braga, Misericórdia, books 87–90.

68. *CCLP*, 3:144, alvará, 4 June 1625.

69. *CCLP*, 10:188, 7 March 1689.

70. HAG, códice 10399, Misericórdia, ff. 57–58.

71. *CCLP*, 8:367, 18 April 1674.

72. Biblioteca Municipal de Elvas, Arquivo da Câmara, livro das receitas e despezas da Câmara, 1693, códice 823/82, f. 12.

73. *Leis Extravagantes*, 5:334, Carta do Aviso do Secretário de Estado, 18 May 1734.

74. AD-Évora, câmara, livro 159, alvará, 4 January 1622.

75. AD-Évora, câmara, livro 159, alvará, 30 December 1632. A similar document is BA, 51-X-4, livro do Governo do anno 1632, f. 2.

76. AD-Évora, câmara, livro 159, alvará, 7 February 1635.

77. For a discussion of this recurring problem, see Boxer, *Seaborne Empire*, 206; and Boxer, "Carreira da India," In *From Lisbon to Goa*.

78. For example, boats were not to leave for Brazil without first informing the judiciary. Law dated 7 August 1547, in Figueiredo, *Synopsis*, 1:401.

79. HAG, MR 34, ff. 205 ff. Crown to Council of Government, 4 April 1669; and MR 36, ff. 181–84v, Crown to Council of Government, 31 March 1670. *Lista das Pessoas*. AHU, Madeira caixa 3, doc. 26, ff. 3–6, 17 July 1783.

80. Boxer, *Portuguese Society*, 197–209. These same criminals formed the basis for Martins Vieira, "Registro de cartas de guia."

81. Figueiredo, *Synopsis*, 1:391–92. For examples, see AHU, Angola caixa 3, doc. 58, December 1638 and Angola caixa 14, doc. 63, 28 May 1691.

82. *CCLP*, 2:21, alvará, 17 September 1613; also published in Castilho Barreto, 46.

83. *CCLP*, 8:23, 19 July 1658.

84. Resolução of 2 December 1716, in *Leis Extravagantes*, 5:295.

85. Caetano Braz de Albuquerque, 149–50.

86. AHU, Cabo Verde caixa 6A, doc. 101, f. 5, 10 May 1676.

87. AHU, códice 544, f. 10v–11v, chapter 21, 1676.

88. AHU, São Tomé caixa 2, doc. 110, 19 May 1655.

89. AHU, India caixa 33, doc. 93, 30 October 1685. HAG, MR 34, f. 265, Crown to the Viceroy, 10 April 1668.

90. Gune, vol. 1, part 1:3–4, doc. 3, 21 November 1613.

91. *Cartas*, vol. 6; Estévão Gonçalves, 346, order to the Factor of Hormuz, 22 September 1515; Gonçalo de Évora, 359, 15 October 1515.

92. Payments and maintenance given to *degredado* soldiers are evident in *Documentos Sobre os Portugueses em Moçambique*.

93. HAG, códice 1416, livro de segredo, ff. 30–31, "Cartas para o Capitão-Geral de Ceilão sobre o modo com que ha de passar certidões aos degredados e criminosos," 1639.

94. Boxer, *Portuguese Society*, 119; Martins Vieira, 6.

95. HAG, MR 57, f. 140, Crown to the Viceroy, 22 March 1692.

96. HAG, MR 69–70, f. 47, Viceroy to Crown, 20 September 1706.

97. HAG, MR 72, f. 141, Crown to the Viceroy, 10 December 1707.

98. HAG, MR 72, f. 141, Crown to the Viceroy, 7 February 1708.

99. HAG, MR 158A, f. 310, 15 April 1777.

100. AHU, India caixa 30, doc. 129.

101. AHU, India caixa 39, doc. 67, 13 September 1697. Certificates of completion are rare, but several can be found in ANTT, Casa da Suplicação, livros do Juizio dos Degredados. This series begins around 1750–1755 and ends in 1833 with the creation of the Ministry of Justice.

102. BGUC, códice 695, ff. 255–56, 27 July 1582 and f. 400, 16 April 1586; BA, 44-XIII-32, 110ss is an additional copy of the 1586 law.

103. *CCLP*, 2:246, correspondence dated 6 June 1617.

104. Arquivo Municipal de Coimbra, B-7, Provições Antigas, f. 21, letter from the Crown to the Câmara, 13 December 1600.

105. AHU, Angola caixa 6, doc. 39, 22 February 1656.

106. Lopes Ferreira, 243–44, 30 August 1678. This also appears in *CCLP*, 9:55–56, 13 July 1678.

107. *CCLP*, 9:77–79, 28 April 1681.

108. *Ley para se prenderem os deliquentes.*

109. *Leis Extravagantes*, 3:381–83, alvará, 10 October 1754.

110. ANTT, DP-RJDM, livro 9, f. 264, 31 July 1624.

111. HAG, códice 8791, livro vermelho da relação de Goa, ff. 159–159v, 18 March 1589, published in Basílio de Sá, 5:24.

112. HAG, códice 1416, livro de segredo, ff. 9v–10.

113. *DR da I*, vol. 4, Crown to Viceroy, 13 April 1617.

114. AHU, códice 30, ff. 302v–4, 26 and 28 March 1643.

115. *CCLP*, 10:89, 28 April 1687; and 10:155, 4 March 1688.

116. ANTT, DP-RJDM, livro 18, f. 251, 31 October 1638.

117. HAG, códice 8791, livro vermelho da relação de Goa, f. 217v, 19 August 1597.

118. ANTT, DP-RJDM, livro 10, f. 118, 17 April 1625.

119. See AHU, Baia caixa 17.

120. AHU, Reino maço 31.

121. AHU, Reino maços 2192 and 2193, "Relações dos pressos no presidio de Trafaria."

CHAPTER 2

1. For the Spanish case in Aragón, see Olesa Muñido, 2:749.

2. Barros, 8.

3. *Elementos*, 1:284, carta régia, 26 July 1424 (1386).

4. Russell, 61–73.

5. Lopes Ferreira, 225.

6. *Elementos*, 16:200, aviso to the câmara, 28 January 1756. For a discussion of the Spanish case, see Pike, 88–110.

7. The Spanish case is examined in Pike, 18–20. Penal servitude in France is the subject of Bamford. The Netherlands used a limited form of galley servitude under King D. Filipe II. Galleys patrolled canals acting as both mobile jails and workhouses, see Spierenburg, 259–60.

8. See Mott, 737–38, tables 5 and 6.

9. Figueiredo, *Synopsis*, 1:250, 6 February 1521.

10. Figueiredo, *Synopsis*, 2:4–5, 5 February 1551. Ten years in the galleys was generally understood to equal a death sentence and was frequently stated as such.

11. Figueiredo, *Synopsis*, 2:93, 8 April 1564; BA, 44-XIII-32, number 110cc, 30 December 1567.

12. Chiefly to Brazil; see Donovan, "Changing Perceptions," 34.

13. BGUC, códice 695, f. 86, 15 May 1573.

14. BA, 44-XIV-4, ff. 299–300, "Sobre os Ciganos que andão roubando pelo reino," 16 May 1592.

15. BA, 44-XIII-50, Leis Varias, ff. 54–54v, Lei Sobre os Ciganos, ca. 1610.

16. ANTT, DP, RJDM, livro 5, f. 83, 28 March 1618.

17. *CCLP*, 4:192, alvará, 30 June 1639.

18. *CCLP*, 4:332, alvará, 24 October 1647.

19. Corrêa da Serra, 3:584–85, carta régia, 15 June 1502.

20. *Gavetas*, 1:547–48, 14 October 1708. Also published in *Leis Extravagantes*, 2:364–66.

21. Castilho Barreto, 27.

22. *Leis Extravagantes*, 5:375, decreto, 17 July 1745. See the overview of legislation in Adolpho Coelho.

23. For an overview of the use of Gypsies as forced colonizers in Angola, see Carlos Couto, 107–15.

24. *Leis Extravagantes*, 4:327–29, alvará, 20 September 1760. See also Donovan, "Changing Perceptions."

25. AHU, Reino maço 17, f. 1.

26. BP-Évora, CXV/2–3, livro dourado da relação da Baia, ff. 619–20v, 4 December 1606. The original says, "lingoagem e estilo das galés." BA, 44-XIII-50, Leis Varias, f. 65, 4 September 1606. See also a similar alvará, dated 4 December 1606, which appears in Caetano Perreira e Sousa, *Primeiras Linhas*, 217.

27. *CCLP*, 1:85–86, alvará, 15 July 1604; and 4:171–72, 20 April 1630.

28. AHU, códice 35, ff. 184–184v, 11 October 1623. See Anderson, 68.

29. ANTT, DP, RJDM, livro 8, f. 259, 20 November 1623.

30. ANTT, DP, RJDM, livro 18, f. 158, 18 August 1638. Also published in *CCLP*, 4:171.

31. HAG, códice 8788, livro morato da relação de Goa, ff. 96v–97, 25 October 1597.

32. *Cartas*, 6:322–23, orders to Pedro de Tavora, Captain of the São Vicente, 6 and 13 August 1515.

33. For aspects of shipbuilding in Portuguese Asia, see Boxer, "Almirante João Pereira Corte Real."

34. *ARGoa*, 1:382, doc. 487, 7 September 1627.

35. *DH*, 34 (1936):17–18, 4 July 1692.

36. *DH*, 34 (1936):114–15, 19 July 1693.

37. *DH*, 34 (1936):291, 2 April 1707, 17–18; and Amaral Lapa, 127–28.

38. *DH*, 68:181–82, 19 February 1689.

39. On maritime foodstuffs produced in Lisbon and consumed by sailors, see Vasconcellos e Meneses; and Amaral Lapa, 165.

40. AHU, códice 476, f. 27v–28, 13 February 1630.

41. For an example, see AHU, India caixa 9, doc. 138, 15 October 1626. *CCLP*, 3:29, 22 September 1620.

42. AHU, Guiné caixa 1, doc. 35, 5 September 1644; AHU, códice 275, f. 27v, 19 September 1644, and f. 30, 23 October 1644.

43. BSGL reservados 3-D-18, Letters of D. João IV, 11 April 1652.

44. BP-Évora, CXV/1–39, 210–11, law dated 1626. Published in *ARGoa*, 1:369, doc. 468, 10 April 1626.

45. Selected portions from Dellon's account, in Priolkar, part II, 75–77.

46. Figueiredo, *Synopsis*, 1:2g, 6 February 1521.

47. "Those who flee their places of exile will be sentenced to the galleys," JFB 1603 Portugal-1; BA, 44-XIII-50, Leis Varias, f. 50, 6 September 1609.

48. Anderson, 71–72.

49. Castilho Barreto, 46.

50. Gama Barros, 5:255–64. Asylum cities such as these have their roots in Visigothic and Roman law. See Figueiredo, "Memoria," 1:109–10.

51. *CCLP*, 10:263–64, 13 September 1691.

52. *Leis Extravagantes*, 2:341–42, alvará, 20 August 1703.

53. Gama Barros, 5:260–1; 5:255–64.

54. Ibid., 5:255–64.

55. Figueiredo, *Synopsis*, 1:354, 19 May 1535. BA, códice 44-XIII-52, ff. 127–28, alvará, 25 January 1586.

56. Lopes Ferreira, *Prática Criminal*, 230.

57. *Ordenações de D. Manuel I*, repertório, 33.

58. *Ordenações e leys do reino de Portugal Confirmadas, e establecidas.*

59. *Collecção das Leis, Decretos, e Alvarás . . . D José I*, ff. 587–90.

60. Internal exile and galley service figures complied from BNL, códice 199. Carvalho da Costa, 3:10. I am very much indebted to Dr. Timothy Walker for forcing me to rethink the punishment of exile to Castro Marim and its immediate connection to labor rather than forced colonization, as was the case when applied to overseas.

61. Beccaria, 67.

62. *MMA*, 1:152–53, doc. 36, alvará, 9 February 1493.

63. See Teixeira da Mota, 10.

64. Figueiredo, *Synopsis*, 2:51, dated 1560.

65. Alvará, 10 September 1577, in *Documentos para a História do Açúcar*, 1:29–30, 277.

66. *Registro Geral da Câmara da Cidade de São Paulo*, 1:472, 22 March 1625.

67. HAG, códice 8791, livro vermelho da relação de Goa, ff. 78v–80, traslado sobre as mulheres casadas.

68. HAG, códice 8789, livro verde da relação da Goa, f. 119v, 1624, published in *ARGoa*, 1:336–37, doc. 430, 12 June 1624.

69. HAG, códice 1498, ff. 47–47v, royal orders dated 1634.

70. HAG, MR 84B, ff. 333–35; MR 86A, ff. 82–86v.

71. *ARGoa*, 1:97–98, doc. 120, 12 November 1610; parts of this decree are also in *CCLP*, 1:294.

72. *DR da I*, 8:230, correspondence from Goa to the Crown, 13 December 1622. A more complete history of this fort is the subject of Shirodkar, "Fort of Aguada," 107–22.

73. HAG, códice 8790, livro verde da relação de Goa, f. 62v.

74. HAG, MR 47, ff. 7–9v, 23 March, 30 August and 1 September 1682.

75. Where it is located today (1996). See illustrations.

76. *Ordenações de D. Manuel I*, book 5, title 107, paragraph 4.

77. BNL, códice 427 [F2864], ff. 58–58v and BGUC, códice 466, ff. 35–36.

78. See Armando Cortesão; Luís de Albuquerque; and Damião Peres, *História dos descobrimentos portugueses*.

79. Saunders, 48.

80. For a complete discussion of these aspects, see Magalhães Godinho, *História Económica e Social da Expansão Portuguesa*.

81. Mascarenhas, 94.

82. Oliveira Marques, *História de Portugal*, 1:298–99.

83. Hum dos lugares d'além [lit. "one of the places on the other side"], alvará, 28 March 1519, in Figueiredo, *Synopsis*, 1:234.

84. BA, 44-XIII-57, f. 110v.

85. For this literature, see Pinheiro Marques, 83–86.

86. Dias Farinha, 55–56.

87. Consultas dos Conselheiros de Estado e Portugal sobre as forças que

convirá preparar para expulsar os holandeses do Brasil, Madrid, April 1624 in *Documentação Ultramarina Portuguesa*, 2:524. Also discussed in Dias Farinha, 56.

88. Martins da Silva Marques, 1:265–68.

89. Ibid., 1:375–77.

90. Pardon dated 26 April 1439, in Pedro de Azevedo, vol. I.

91. Pedro de Azevedo, vol. I.

92. Figures compiled from Pedro de Azevedo; António Baião, ed. *Documentos do Corpo Chronológico*; P. M. Laranjo Coelho; and Martins da Silva Marques.

93. Ayres de Azevedo, 117.

94. BA, 44-XIII-57, f. 110.

95. BACL, azul mss. 47, Bernardo Rodrigues, "História da Praça de Arzila, 1508–1561," dated 1561.

96. Redman and Boone, 39–40. Women over forty years of age formed only 5 percent of those whose ages could be determined.

97. ANTT, DP, RJDM, livro 10, f. 185, 24 June 1625.

98. Duncan, 10

99. Ibid., 11.

100. For more discussion on this subject, see Verlinden, 222–23. Verlinden cites as his source Martins da Silva Marques, 2:344; see also 1:517.

101. Oliveira Marques, *História de Portugal*, 1:218.

102. Ibid., 1:222–23.

103. On the initial settlement of the Azores, see also Matos, "Origem e reminiscências."

104. *História Geral de Cabo Verde: Corpo Documental*, vols. I–II.

105. Orlando Ribeiro, *Aspectos e Problemas*, 156–58; Oliveira Marques, *Portugal Quinhentista*, 111–19; António Brásio; Meintel, 32–33; Barata, 921–58; and Teixeira da Mota, 7–11.

106. Conceição Rodrigues, 397–412.

107. Azevedo e Silva, 1:230; Santos Júnior, 71–78; Almeida; and Almada Negreiros.

108. Cf. Carlos Alberto Garcia, 209–21. See also Garfield.

109. Teixeira da Mota, 11.

110. *MMA*, 4:33, doc. 11. Alvará, December 1506.

111. Figueiredo, *Synopsis*, 1:355–56, 19 June 1535.

112. Ibid., 1:408, 5 May 1549.

113. Pedro de Azevedo, 2:18, 7 May 1451.

114. Ibid., 2:108, 22 February 1452. An example of the reverse (sentence reduced by half for service abroad) can be seen in this same work and volume, 49–50, 9 September 1451.

115. Ibid., 2:14–15, 12 February 1451.

116. Ibid., 2:138–39, 27 November 1452.

117. Ibid., 2:66–67, 10 April 1451.

118. ANTT, DP, RJDM, livro 4, f. 116, 1617 and livro 4, f. 116, 11 April 1617.

119. ANTT, DP, RJDM, livro 11, f. 12, 16 January 1627.

CHAPTER 3

1. For an excellent discussion of the relationship between the criminal and the military worlds in early modern Iberian society, see Perry, 95–115. An example of the exchange between these two groups can be seen in *Elementos*, 3:122. Details of the recruitment process from the 1630s can be found in AHM, First Division, First Section, caixa 1, docs. 15–17.

2. *DR da I*, vol. 4, Crown to Viceroy of India, 13 April 1617.

3. AD-Évora, câmara, livro 159, f. 160, 15 June 1640.

4. *Elementos*, 4:344, consulta, 15 July 1638. Along these same lines, it is noteworthy that the Crown was not only eager to round up vagrants but also to compile lists of their names, undoubtedly for future projects. See *CCLP*, 6:236, 19 May 1644; 6:319, 6 June 1646; 7:45, 6 July 1649.

5. *Lista Pessoas que das Cadeas deste Corte vão*; and AHU, Madeira caixa 3, doc. 26, 17 July 1783, "Relação dos redutados para Angola na Ilha da Madeira."

6. AHU, India caixa 34, doc. 117, 1 July 1688. "From this country, only boys go to India and the others are all born in India," AHU, India caixa 35A, doc. 99, 15 November 1691. See also Boxer, "Portuguese and Dutch Colonial Rivalry," 27. For the French case, see Choquette, "Recruitment," 153.

7. *CCLP*, 4:146, 25 February 1638. For the minimum age of slaves, see *APO-1*, fasículo 6, 789, alvará of the Crown, 23 November 1606.

8. *DR da I*, V:294, Crown to Viceroy, 26 February 1619.

9. AHU, India caixa 24, doc. 29, 8 February 1657.

10. HAG, códice 10399, Misericórdia, f. 92, 8 April 1576.

11. HAG, MR 6A, f. 60, alvará, 3 October 1605.

12. HAG, MR 61, f. 9–10, 10 January 1698.

13. *Elementos*, 3:183, consulta, April 1625.

14. *CCLP*, 8:182, 7 June 1670.

15. HAG, MR 68, f. 42, Crown to the Viceroy, 18 July 1703.

16. Duffy, 94.

17. Ibid., 95.

18. AHU, India caixa 4, doc. 85, 3 November 1616.

19. AHU, India caixa 11, doc. 77, 11 March 1635.

20. *DI*, 5:439. Letter from Cochin, 5 January 1562.

21. *DI*, 6:381, 15 December 1564.

22. Boxer, *Seaborne Empire*, 219.

23. Ibid., 218.
24. *Documentação-India*, 2:193, 25 September 1530.
25. Boxer, *Seaborne Empire*, 218.
26. Ibid., 206; Duffy, 94–95.
27. "Letter from Cochin in India" (1580), Matthews, 64–65.
28. AHU, Angola caixa 3, doc. 3, 3 April 1630.
29. HAG, MR 13B, f. 294. Viceroy to the Crown, 16 February 1630.
30. "Because of the lack of people in that place [Estado da India], I order that on the three ships which are leaving that at least one thousand four hundred soldiers should go, 900 in companies and 500 paid for by me ...," AHU, India caixa 10, doc. 97, 14 November 1633.
31. One hundred seventeen were not registered in the original book. Thus, 159 soldiers of the 922 did not arrive. HAG, MR 51A, ff. 131–33v, 22 November 1684. The list is divided by ship and company.
32. This means that 16 soldiers never left Lisbon. Of the 144 who did, 2 died on the voyage and 21 stayed in Mozambique. This means that 121 soldiers should have arrived in Goa, yet only 115 did. They were also short 6 passengers. HAG, MR 54, f. 170, 13 January 1690.
33. *DR da I*, 1:85, 17 January 1607.
34. See Duffy; and Boxer, "Carreira da India," in *From Lisbon to Goa*.
35. *DI*, 15:126, 24 November 1588.
36. BGUC, códice 460, ff. 187v–88v, 10 December 1635.
37. Biker, 5:298 n., Viceroy to Crown, 24 August 1672.
38. HAG, MR 59, f. 195, Viceroy to the Crown, 10 December 1695. See also Boxer, "Portuguese and Dutch Colonial Rivalry," 27–28.
39. *DR da I*, 3:188–89, Crown to Viceroy, 6 February 1615.
40. José Wicki, "Duas relações," 187.
41. *CCLP*, 2:191, 22 February; and 2:226, 17 March 1616.
42. See Chauhan, 29–39.
43. Teotonio de Souza, *Medieval Goa*, 121.
44. Pearson, "People and Politics," 6.
45. Known collectively as the *praças do norte*. See maps.
46. Pyrard de Laval, 2:128–29.
47. Ibid., 2:130–31.
48. Rodrigues da Silveira, 236.
49. Pyrard de Laval, 2:120–21, 124, 131.
50. Ibid., 2:26.
51. *DI*, 1:253, dated 1548 (?).
52. Ibid., 10:628, 3 November 1576.
53. *Documentação-India*, 2:195, dated 1530.
54. Pyrard de Laval, 2:27.
55. *ARGoa*, 1:448, doc. 589, 8 March 1634, n. a.

56. Teotonio de Souza, *Medieval Goa*, 132–51.

57. Pyrard de Laval, 2:125. "They must wear their mantles. . . . "

58. Boyajian, 32–33.

59. Gomes, 131.

60. Braganza, 98.

61. For a further discussion of intermarriage by Goans and the Portuguese and the development of the Luso-Indian community, see McPherson; Winius, "'Secret People'"; and the collection of articles by L. A. Rodrigues.

62. HAG, MR 22B, f. 423, 23 January 1653.

63. HAG, MR 22B, f. 425, 23 January 1653.

64. HAG, MR 23A, f. 151, 15 January 1653; f. 152, 6 January 1654.

65. *DR da I*, 2:423, 26 March 1613.

66. *DR da I*, 9:423, Crown to Viceroy, 19 March 1623.

67. *Documentação-India*, 3:79, n. 2. The *relação* of Goa was founded on 3 April 1544.

68. Priolkar, 22–23. On Jews in Asia and the Portuguese, see *Cartas*, 1:244, 15 December 1513.

69. HAG, códice 8791, f. 217v, 19 August 1597.

70. BSGL reservados maço 4, doc. 52, 3 January 1622.

71. HAG, códice 8789, livro verde da relação de Goa, f. 42, 19 May 1618.

72. HAG, códice 7748, ff. 107–107v, 21 February 1623.

73. HAG, MR 19A, f. 29, Crown to Viceroy, 10 December 1633.

74. HAG, MR 19B, f. 485, Royal Pardon from Lisbon to Viceroy, 6 March 1634.

75. Saint Francis Xavier to King D. João III, 16 May 1546, in Jacobs, 1:20.

76. Letter of Saint Francis to Simão Rodrigues, 20 January 1548, in Jacobs, 1:44.

77. Saint Francis Xavier, to King D. João III, 20 January 1548, in Jacobs, 1:46.

78. Letter to Gomes Vaz, November–December 1566, in Jacobs, 1:496.

79. Jacobs, 1:441, n. 2. See also Faria de Morais, 90.

80. Jacobs, 3:588, n. 1; and Noonan, 37.

81. Pinto da França, 168. On Portuguese interaction on the east coast of Africa, see Freeman-Grenville.

82. Jacobs, 3:588, n. 1. For an overview of Portuguese influence in Indonesia, including linguistic influences on Indonesian languages, see Pinto da França, 161–234.

83. W. H. C. Smith, 92.

84. Boxer, "Portuguese and Dutch Colonial Rivalry," 38. See also Qaisar, 110–12.

85. Israel, 5; Shirodkar, "Dutch-Portuguese Relations," 130.

86. Silva Telles, 12.

87. Boxer, "Raízes de Portugal," 125, 127.

88. AHU, India caixa 20A, doc. 131, 1 November 1649.

89. *ARGoa*, 1:287–88, doc. 352, 22 January 1622.

90. *DR da I*, 9:208–9, Viceroy to Crown, 26 March 1623.

91. *ARGoa*, 1:291, doc. 359, 18 February 1622.

92. Substituting fines for criminal sentences was not new nor was it confined to this example from Goa. See *CCLP*, 8:36, 26 February 1660.

93. Anjadiva Island (Anjediva, Anjediv) off Goa's southern coast. See Gerson da Cunha, "Historical and Archaeological Sketch," 288–310; Shirodkar, "Fortress of Anjediv," 119–33; Teotonio de Souza, *Medieval Goa*, 41–42; and Shastry.

94. HAG, códice 2787, f. 9, 14 January 1777.

95. HAG, códice 650, ff. 69–69v, "Está em observancia até o presente," 14 December 1827.

96. For the West Indies, see Parry et al., 85; for the Portuguese in West Africa, see Rodney; Ogot.

97. AHU, Cabo Verde caixa 4, doc. 45, 6 August 1652.

98. AHU, Cabo Verde caixa 8, doc. 40, 10 November 1696.

99. For the sixteenth century, see Miller.

100. Bender, "Myth," 60–62.

101. *Collecção de noticias para a história*, 3:344–54, part 2.

102. ANTT, DP, RJDM, livro 17, f. 18, 14 February 1636.

103. AHU, Madeira caixa 1, doc. 27, 6 May 1676; AHU, Angola caixa 11, doc. 70, 17 July 1676.

104. AHU, São Tomé caixa 3, doc. 22, 24 September 1674.

105. AHU, Madeira caixa 1, doc. 32, 27 January 1697.

106. AHU, India caixa 28A, doc. 216, 14 October 1671.

107. AHU, India caixa 38, doc. 41, 13 December 1695.

108. AHU, India caixa 39, doc. 10, 25 January 1697.

109. BA, 54-VIII-18, f. 21, "Sentença de expulção de Frei António de Sà contra Frei Diogo Sotomaior," 23 December 1705.

110. See Vieira Ferreira, 127–31; Hemming, 6; Elkiss, 49; and Marchant, 50, n. 3.

111. Figueiredo, *Synopsis*, 1:354, 31 May 1535; 1:355–56, 19 June 1535. See also Viotti da Costa.

112. Viotti da Costa, 8.

113. Marchant, 59–60, n. 36 and the sources cited therein.

114. Vianna, 48; Varnhagen, 1:280.

115. "Soares de Sousa," 102.

116. Léry, 4.

117. Borges Coelho, 1:151, 159.

118. Bivar Guerra.

119. For the overall patterns of cases before the Inquisition, see Viega Torres, 56–59. On *degredados* in colonial Brazil in general, see Diffie, 76.

120. Hemming, 39–40, 119–20.

121. Leite, 2:171, 25 March 1555.

122. Ibid., 1:127, 9 August 1549.

123. *DH*, 37 (1937):14–15.

124. Leite, 1:270, 11 August 1551.

125. Ibid., 2:146, 27 December 1554, and 2:212, 3 April 1555.

126. Ibid., 1:256, 2 August 1551.

127. *DI*, 4:285–86, 12 November 1559.

128. *Livro Primeiro*, 283–84, 20 September 1619. For an example, see AHU, Angola caixa 10, doc. 112, 20/26 May 1673.

129. BA, 44-XIII-57, f. 110v.

130. Malheiro Dias, 3:176.

131. Leite, 3:546, 20 May 1561.

132. BA, 44-XIV-4, f. 194v, Letter of the City Council of Olinda to Crown.

133. BP-Évora, CXV/2–3, livro dourado da relação da Bahia, ff. 44–45, 15 and 20 March 1610.

134. Caetano Perreira e Sousa, *Esboço*, 13 January 1677. Also published in *CCLP*, 9:23, 18 January 1677.

135. BGUC, códice 706, fl. 27, "Assento sobre a Forma dos degredos que se deve praticar na Relação da Baia," 7 June 1655.

136. *Documentos Históricos do Arquivo Municipal, Atas da Câmara*, 3:38, 100, 199, dated 1649 and 1652.

137. *Documentos Históricos do Arquivo Municipal, Atas da Câmara*, 2:104, 1 July 1642.

138. See, for example, Bellini, 35–37.

139. BA, 51-VI-11, f. 125 (number 226), Regimento da Caza da Supplicação, 12 September 1662.

140. *DH*, 67:176–77, 19 June 1675.

141. Pinheiro da Silva, 245.

142. BGUC, códice 707, fl. 29, 26 November 1710; updated on ff. 29–30, 13 September 1715. This same law was later expanded in 1740 to include "anyone causing problems," ff. 31–32. See also Boxer, *Golden Age*, 170, 301, 397, n. 29.

143. AM-Coimbra, B-13, Entrada dos Presos, f. 25v.

144. BP-Évora, CXVI/2–20, Colleção de miscellana, leis relativos ao Brazil, ff. 80–82, 20 March 1720. This *alvará* refers to two passed earlier on 25 November 1709 and 19 February 1711, which were also designed to prevent free immigration from Portugal to Brazil.

Notes to Pages 82–87

145. Figueiredo, *Synopsis*, 1:401, 28 March 1722.

146. Alden, *Royal Government*, 70, n. 31, n. 32. For shipments of supplies made to the garrison there, see 134, n. 80.

147. Lopes Ferreira, 49.

148. HAG, MR 55A, f. 201, Crown asks for the Governor's opinion, 21 March 1690; His reply is on f. 203, 23 January 1691. For recruitment for the Brazilian military, see Peregalli, 100; and Ribeiro Coutinho.

149. See Brito Freyre.

150. For problems with the French in Maranhão, see AHU, Maranhão caixa 2, doc. 117, 6 October 1648.

151. Libâno Guedes and Ribeiro, 3:77–79. For payments made to soldier-prisoners (*soldados e pressos*) in the region in the early 1600s, see *Livro Primeiro*, 348–49.

152. ANTT, DP, RJDM, livro 17, f. 206, 27 August 1636.

153. Severim de Faria, *Relaçam universal*, 25v.

154. AHU, Maranhão caixa 1, doc. 20, 5 March 1619; doc. 39, 24 November 1622; Maranhão, caixa 3, doc. 1, 23 April 1649; Maranhão, caixa 5A, doc. 14, 24 January 1667; doc. 70, 7 October 1673; doc. 81, 9 November 1674; and Açores, caixa 2, doc. 18, 6 August 1677. See also Lisboa, 398; Kieman, 24–25; and Donovan, "Politics of Immigration."

155. Hemming, 373–74.

156. Leite, 1:120, 9 August 1549.

157. Estaço da Silveira, Prologue.

158. ANTT, DP, RJDM, livro 18, f. 247, 13 October 1638.

159. See especially Mello e Souza, 89–101; and Pieroni, "Vadios, Heréticos e Bruxas."

160. Data extracted from BNL, códice 199 (F100) lists of the sentences of the Lisbon, Évora, and Coimbra Tribunals of the Holy Office of the Inquisition, 1662–1699. See also Pieroni, *Os Excluídos*.

CHAPTER 4

1. See Hein; Elkiss; and Blake.

2. João Barreto, 68–69.

3. Elkiss, 46.

4. João Barreto, 68–69, 75.

5. Meintel, 33–35. See also Duncan, 212–15; Carreira; and especially Rodney.

6. In *Documentos sobre os Portugueses*.

7. AHU, códice 545, f. 68, 28 March 1692; Esquemeling, 64–79.

8. For the Portuguese in Spanish America, see Hanke.

9. *Primor e honra*, 5–6.

10. *Cartas*, 1:94, 26 October 1512.

11. Ibid., 1:334, 27 November 1514.

12. Ibid., 6:290–91, orders dated 22 and 25 May 1515.

13. Ibid., 6:292, 26 May 1515.

14. Ibid., 6:292–96, May and June 1515.

15. Subrahmanyam, *Portuguese Empire*, 249–56.

16. *DI*, 16:328, letter from Goa, 15 November 1593. Another example can be seen in HAG, MR 2B, f. 407, 10 March 1598.

17. HAG, MR 2A, ff. 653, dated 1596.

18. See, for example, HAG, MR 3B, f. 477v, where the king states, "Viceroys are pardoning criminals and *degredados* against my Royal orders" (dated 1591).

19. HAG, MR 4, f. 653v, Crown to the Viceroy, 1596.

20. HAG, códice 1185, Provições dos Vicereys. Manuel Veloso Peixote, ff. 348v–50; Bartolomeu Luis, ff. 393–94v.

21. Baião, *Inquisição*, 1:275–76.

22. Winius, "'Secret People.'" In regard to Agra, see Désoulières.

23. On *renegados* in Vijanagara, see Lima Cruz. For the Portuguese in Mylapur, see Subrahmanyam, *Improvising Empire*, 47–67.

24. Winius, "'Shadow Empire,'" 87 and the sources cited therein.

25. *DI*, 7:202 and n. 39.

26. Winius, "'Secret People,'" 3. On reformist tracts, see Moser.

27. Sarkar, 1–6. See also Campos, *History*; and Subrahmanyam, *Improvising Empire*, 96–136 and the sources therein.

28. Subrahmanyam, *Improvising Empire*, 216–40.

29. Boyajian, 75–76.

30. HAG, MR 68, ff. 208–10.

31. HAG, MR 159D, ff. 980–80v, 1780.

32. HAG, MR 6A, f. 60.

33. HAG, códice 8789, livro verde da relação de Goa, ff. 151v–52, dated 1627, is the viceroy's pardon; this is revoked in ff. 169v–70, dated 1628.

34. Biker, 5:298–99, Correspondence of the Viceroy to the King, 17 January 1714.

35. HAG, códice 8791, ff. 78v–80. Royal decree to Viceroy, 15 May 1567.

36. Mendes Pinto, 351, 389–90.

37. *DI*, 16:160–62, letter of 18 July 1593.

38. *ARGoa*, 1:276–77, doc. 337, 29 May 1620.

39. AHU, India caixa 24A, doc. 159, 2 April 1660.

40. AHU, India caixa 25, doc. 43, 4 November 1661.

41. AHU, India caixa 25, doc. 104, 5 May 1662.

42. *ARGoa*, 2:595, doc. 786, 17 April 1677.

43. *DR da I*, vol. 9, correspondence of the Viceroy to the Crown, 20 March 1623.

44. *Cartas*, 5:303, order of Albuquerque's, 11 December 1512. Cf. Subrahmanyam, *Portuguese Empire*, 251–52.

45. *Cartas*, 5:284–85.

46. Ibid., 6:366, order to the factor in Ormuz, 29 October 1515.

47. *APO-1*, fasículo 6, 760, Crown corresponding to the Viceroy, 22 January 1601.

48. Oliveira Marques, *Portugal Quinhentista*, 203.

49. Rodrigues da Silveira, 180–83.

50. Ibid., 183–87.

51. *Collecção das Leis, Decretos, e Alvarás*, 27 February 1758.

52. HAG, MR 83, ff. 17–18, Exchanges between Lisbon and Goa, 12 January 1718.

53. HAG, MR 69–70, f. 19, Crown to the Viceroy, 8 October 1705.

54. HAG, MR 69–70, ff. 20–22v, 15 January 1707. The list indicates names, parents, native towns in Portugal, and dates fled.

55. HAG, MR 93B, f. 615–15v, Viceroy to the Crown, 3 January 1727.

56. HAG, MR 95A, f. 126, Crown to the Viceroy, 13 April 1728.

57. José Wicki, "Duas relações," 169.

58. Ibid., 196.

59. Diogo do Couto, 86–87.

60. BP-Évora, CV/2–7, ff. 70–73v, 17 July 1627.

61. BACL, azul 267, Pedro Barreto de Resende, Descripções das Cidades e Fortalezas de India Oriental (1635), ff. 221v–22.

62. BACL, azul 267, Pedro Barreto de Resende, Descripções das Cidades e Fortalezas de India Oriental (1635), ff. 57v–58. For African slaves as soldiers, see Pescatello.

63. BACL, azul 267, Pedro Barreto de Resende, Descripções das Cidades e Fortalezas de India Oriental (1635), f. 57v.

64. Noonan, 91.

65. BACL, azul 58, Noticias dos Estados da India, 1649–1678, ff. 174–76.

66. HAG, MR 53, ff. 286–286v, 27 August 1688.

67. *Registro Geral da Câmara da Cidade de São Paulo*, 1:469–70, 15 March 1625. ANTT, DP, RJDM, livro 15, f. 161, 1 June 1633.

68. AHU, São Tomé caixa 2, doc. 100, 1 December 1653.

69. AHU, Guiné caixa 2, doc. 39, 20 September 1666.

70. AHU, Angola caixa 10, doc. 43, 27 July 1671. The average annual salary for a soldier in Angola in 1663 was 28$800, AHU, Angola caixa 7, doc. 122, 31 December 1663.

71. *Registro Geral da Câmara da Cidade de São Paulo*, 2:99–101, 130.

72. AHU, Guiné caixa 3, docs.: 67, 11 February 1692; 79, 13 June 1693; and 83, 19 October 1693.

73. AHU, Maranhão caixa 8, doc. 72, 4 November 1692.

74. AHU, Ceará caixa 1, doc. 68, 12 February 1705.

75. *Livro Primeiro*, 252, 12 and 13 October 1617.

76. AHU, Pará caixa 1, doc. 4, 28 February 1617.

77. AHU, Cabo Verde caixa 4, doc. 4, the Governor of Cabo Verde, Roque de Barros Rego, to the Overseas Council, 13 November 1648.

78. AHU, Angola caixa 8, doc. 55, 22 October 1664. For Gypsies, see Donovan, "Changing Perceptions," 39; and Pieroni, "Detestáveis na Metrópole."

79. Boxer, *Golden Age*, 140.

80. *DH*, 34 (1936):293–94. Letter from the King to Luis Cesar de Menezes, 21 January 1708; response, 29 July 1708; repeated on 26 March 1709 and answered 3 August 1709, ibid., 34 (1936):301–2. On this imperial connection, see Amaral Lapa.

81. HAG, MR 14, f. 229, 3 March 1630.

82. Alvará, 9 October 1716 in *Leis Extravagantes*, 2:392–93.

83. BGUC, códice 707, ff. 30–30v, 12 September 1737.

84. Sousa Dias, 46.

85. Cordeiro, first section, 31. An earlier description of these same four forts made in 1618 noted that they "do not provide any income to Your Majesty" (ibid., second section, 11).

86. Brásio, "Misericórdias," 134.

87. HAG, MR 85, ff. 103–19, "Forma em que [ha] de castigar os officiais e soldados," 1717–1719.

88. *Appendix Das Leyes Extravagantes.*

89. Fernandes Pinto Alpoyon.

90. *Compilação de Reflexões de Sanches.*

91. See also Winius, "Portuguese Asian 'Decadência' Revisited."

92. AHU, India caixa 28, doc. 61, 26 March 1669.

93. J. A. Ismael Gracias, 1–2.

94. J. B. Amáncio Gracias.

95. HAG, MR 171B, ff. 299, 321.

96. Silva Rego, *O Ultramar Português*, 329–30.

97. Silva Telles, 13; see also Faria Blanc Junior; and Beleza dos Santos.

CHAPTER 5

1. *Cartas*, 5:249, order of Albuquerque, 27 November 1512.

2. Ibid., 2:117–18, alvará of Albuquerque, 15 November 1513.

3. Caetano Perreira e Sousa, *Primeiras Linhas*, 218, 6 December 1612.

4. ANTT, DP, RJDM, livro 8, f. 170, 31 August 1623.

5. Vallasciin Senatu, 71–72.

6. ANTT, DP, RJDM, livro 3, f. 43 [request for a pardon] and f. 262 [reduces his ten-year sentence in Angola by half], 8 February 1616.

7. Manuel Correa, HAG, códice 1185, ff. 253–253v; António Fragoso de Azevedo, (same códice) f. 92, 1621.

8. BA, 55-VIII-22, f. 140v. ANTT, DP, RJDM, livro 12, f. 97, 25 November 1629.

9. Felicano de Sousa de Meneses, ten years in Angola pardoned, ANTT, DP, RJDM, livro 14, f. 1, 31 March 1631. Sebastião Tavares, five years to Africa and a fine first commuted to Brazil and then shifted to Cacheu, AHU, Guiné caixa 1, doc. 53, 17 May 1647. Clemente Martins sentence of three years to Angola and a fine was commuted to Minas, AHU, São Paulo caixa 1, doc. 25, 28 January 1668.

10. ANTT, DP, RJDM, livro 6, f. 18, 10 January 1619.

11. ANTT, DP, RJDM, livro 8, ff. 287–88, 23 October 1623, and livro 9, ff. 105 and 114, 5 April and 25 April 1624, respectively.

12. ANTT, DP, RJDM, livro 8, f. 40, 23 March 1623.

13. ANTT, DP, RJDM, livro 8, f. 109, 16 June 1623.

14. *DR da I*, vol. 9, 26 March 1623.

15. ANTT, DP, RJDM, livro 7, f. 91, 10 May 1622.

16. AD-Évora, fundo câmara, livro 145, f. 39, 1524.

17. ANTT, DP, RJDM, livro 12, ff. 107–11, 1629.

18. Leite, 2:211.

19. BA, 51-VIII-22, f. 49, 18 April 1628.

20. ANTT, DP, RJDM, livro 17, f. 302, 10 December 1636.

21. *MMA*, 8:540–41, 20 September 1641.

22. ANTT, DP, RJDM, livro 8, f. 184, 1623.

23. ANTT, DP, RJDM, livro 9, f. 39, 3 February 1624; also published in *CCLP*, 3:112–13.

24. ANTT, DP, RJDM, livro 11, f. 97, 29 March 1627 and his pardon, f. 226, 3 June 1627.

25. ANTT, DP, RJDM, livro 11, f. 276, 16 June 1627. He was forgiven "without prejudice."

26. *MMA*, 3:425–26, 22 March 1591.

27. ANTT, DP, RJDM, livro 11, f. 432, 1627. ANTT, DP, RJDM, livro 11, f. 543, 19 October 1628.

28. BA, 51-VIII-22, f. 49, 18 April 1628.

29. ANTT, DP, RJDM, livro 13, ff. 230 and 265, 24 July and 18 October 1630, respectively.

30. HAG, códice 8784, livro azul da relação de Goa, f. 39v, 8 July 1631.

31. AHU, Angola caixa 5, doc. 16, 23 April 1649; and AHU, códice 275, f. 150v, 21 May 1649.

32. AHU, Angola caixa 5, doc. 18, 26 April 1649.

33. HAG, MR 4, f. 653v. HAG, códice 8791, livro vermelho da relação de Goa, f. 226v. Also published in *ARGoa*, 1:6, doc. 5, 28 April 1601.

34. HAG, MR 6A, f. 62, alvará, 11 January 1606. This pardon was not extended to those sentenced to the galleys or to Sri Lanka. In addition to unpardonable crimes, those guilty of murder were excluded.

35. HAG, códice 1185, Provisões, ff. 34v–35, 1614, is a general pardon approved by Lisbon and Madrid in which the viceroy is also given the right to pardon. Also, HAG, códice 8789, livro verde da relação de Goa, ff. 206v–7, 26 March 1630. The viceroy was granted the explicit authority to pardon all criminals, except those guilty of unpardonable crimes, in a memorandum from the Goan high court dated 9 April 1660, HAG, códice 8779, Indice dos Assuntos da Relação de Goa, f. 87.

36. *ARGoa*, 1:179–80, doc. 214, 5 March 1615. This same pardon also appears in *DR da I*, 3:303.

37. *ARGoa*, 1:227, doc. 272, 17 January 1618. An earlier pardon directed at *lançados* in Bengal and Pegu was passed in 1597 and reissued five months later. HAG, códice 8788, livro morato da relação de Goa, ff. 79–82, 20 June 1597 and ff. 101–4, 7 November 1597.

38. *ARGoa*, 1:282, doc. 345, 13 March 1621.

39. Donovan, "Changing Perceptions," 36.

40. Pissurlencar, 3:248–50, doc. 138, 28 April 1653.

41. *ARGoa*, 2:508, doc. 669, 18 February 1654.

42. The pardon of 1657 was from the queen and directed to those in the lands of the Moors and the gentiles, living there "to better their wages or to escape from punishment." HAG, MR 26A, f. 207, 3 March 1657. See also HAG, MR 26A, f. 208, 27 August 1658; *ARGoa*, 2:516–17, doc. 684, 1660; and 2:595, doc. 786, 17 April 1677. The general pardon of 1660 is in HAG, códice 8790, livro verde da relação de Goa, f. 46.

43. AHU, India caixa 28, doc. 60, 26 March 1669. See HAG, MR 34, f. 172, 3 April 1669.

44. *Ordenações de D. Manuel I*, livro 5, tit. 107.

45. BA, 44-XIII-50, f. 66, "Ley Extravagante Numero Seis, Dos que fogem das prisões ou degredo," 30 November 1607. Printed in BA, 44-XIII-55, ff. 122–122v. See also *CCLP*, 1:192, 17 May 1607.

46. *CCLP*, 3:112, 18 February 1624. The *regimento* for the captain of Mazagão of 1692 specifically mentions this problem, *CCLP*, 10:277–90, 6 June 1692.

47. Ibid., 2:91, 30 August 1614.

48. Lopes Ferreira, 233.

49. ANTT, DP, RJDM, livro 11, ff. 475 and 482, 17 November 1627.

50. BA, 54-VIII-16, f. 177, Response by the Mother Superior to a letter of inquiry from Bishop D. João de Sousa, 7 July 1697.

51. Caetano Perreira e Sousa, *Primeiras Linhas*, 220, 26 September 1607.

52. Lopes Ferreira, 231.

53. Ibid., 231–32.

54. *CCLP*, 1:26, 26 September 1603; BA, 44-XIII-50, f. 50, 6 September 1609.

55. BGUC, códice 1734, fl. 53, 1734.

56. Lopes Ferreira, 17–22.

57. BSGL reservados 3-D-18, Letters of D. João IV, 4 October 1652.

58. Lopes Ferreira, 64.

59. AHU, Angola caixa 10, doc. 56, 7 January 1672.

60. AHU, Cabo Verde caixa 4, doc. 15, 17 June 1651.

61. AHU, códice 545, f. 8, 25 October 1674.

62. *ARGoa*, 2:593, doc. 783, 16 June 1676.

63. AHU, São Tomé caixa 3, doc. 66, 8 August 1683.

64. Figueiredo, *Synopsis*, 2:306, 19 June 1535.

65. *DR da I*, 1:270, Crown to the Viceroy, 23 December 1608.

66. *CCLP*, 7:49, 6 September 1649.

67. Pissurlencar, 4:448–50, doc. 168, 14 September 1693.

68. BGUC, códice 488, ff. 279–80, in accordance with the *leis extravagantes* of 6 December 1660, ordinança 5, paragraph 144.

69. BGUC, códice 712, ff. 20–22v, "Ley sobre os que são degredados para sempre para o Brazil e pera as Galés e fugirem dos taes degredos," 1603.

70. *Codigo Penal Português*, 49 article 196, paragraph 2.

71. *DI*, 4:244, Letter from Cochin, 15 January 1559.

72. *ARGoa*, 1:230, doc. 276, 1 February 1618.

73. HAG, MR 6A, alvará, 3 October 1605.

74. *CCLP*, 5:76, 12 April 1641.

75. *DH*, 66 (1944):110–11, carta régia, 11 March 1654. The Crown also stated that if this were to occur, they wanted a certificate sent to Lisbon stating that the death sentence was carried out.

76. Spindel, 125.

77. Hespanha, 16.

78. Ibid., 21.

79. Boxer, "Portuguese and Dutch Colonial Rivalry," 12.

80. Winius, "India or Brazil," 34–42.

81. Magalhães Godinho, "Portugal and Her Empire," 385.

82. Oliveira Marques, *História de Portugal*, 1:490.

83. Ibid., 1:586.

84. Prado Junior, 57.

85. Winius, "India or Brazil," 42.

86. See Ames, "Estado da India."

87. Sousa Ferreira, 31–33.

88. Caetano Perreira e Sousa, *Primeiras Linhas*, 217, decree of 27 April 1795.

89. Caetano Perreira e Sousa, *Esboço*, 27 June 1795 and 2 March 1801.

CHAPTER 6

1. Andrade, 1:224.

2. *Documentação-India*, vol. II, Letter from Goa, 1532.

3. *DI*, 1:155, Letter from Goa, 12 November 1546. "All the ships' captains, officers, and sailors take women on board." See also *Documentação-India*, 2:193, Father Vicente de Laguna writing to the King in 1530 and (same series), 3:21.

4. *Documentação-India*, 3:159, n. 3, Letter from King D. João III to D. João de Castro, 2 March 1545; and 3:500, Letter from the Queen to D. João de Castro, 1547. See also Sanceau, "Uma família." *Documentação-India*, 8:280–81, Letter from Cochin, 13 January 1561. Father Arboleda, who wrote this letter, mentions hearing the confessions of "the orphans who came in our ship."

5. *DI*, 1:384, 388–89, Letter from Goa, 13 December 1548.

6. *DI*, 3:387, Letter from Goa, 18 December 1555.

7. Ibid., 5:489–90, Letter from Goa, 16 January 1562.

8. Ibid., 5:439–41, Letter from Cochin, 5 January 1562.

9. *Documentação-India*, 9:61, Letter of Father Sebastião Gonçalves from Goa, 10 September 1562.

10. *DI*, 6:457, Letter dated 7 and 10 August 1565.

11. AHU, India caixa 8A, 179, 2 May 1625.

12. *APO-1*, fascículo 6, 789, alvará, 23 November 1606. For another example of a Portuguese woman, see AHU, India, caixa 7, doc. 51, 9 and 14 March 1622.

13. AHU, India caixa 7, doc. 79, 1621–1622.

14. ANTT, DP, RJDM, livro 11, f. 77, 22 March 1627.

15. See Campos, *Antiguidades*.

16. *Boletim do Arquivo Histórico Colonial*, doc. 91, 397–99.

17. For an extended example, see the Biblioteca Municipal de Elvas, Arquivo da Câmara, Livro dos Orfãos, 1727–1800, códice 109/82.

18. *Ordenações de D. Manuel I*, livro 1, título 67.

19. Ibid., livro 3, título 87.

20. Paiva e Pona, 23. Nazzari has discussed this process, see 98–100.

21. BA, 44-XIV-4, f. 190, "Sobre o que Pedem os Juizes dos orfãos das villas e cidades deste reyno," directed to the DP and dated 20 July 1591. The *desembargadores* suggested a modest increase in the salary, awarded a few months later in BA, 44-XIII-52, Royal Decrees, f. 178, 7 December 1591.

22. BA, 44-XIV-4, f. 36v, consulta of the DP, 1590.

23. BA, 44-XIV-4, f. 301, consulta of the DP, 1590. BA, 44-XIV-4, ff. 301–2, consulta of the DP, 1590.

24. BA, 44-XIV-4, f. 192, consulta of the DP, 1590.

25. BA, 44-XIV-5, f. 75–76, 24 January 1593.

26. BA, 44-XIV-5, f. 171v, 10 February 1594.

27. BA, 54-IX-8, f. 23, 17 February 1714.

28. BA, 44-XIV-5, f. 205v.

29. BA, 51-VIII-6, "Cartas de D. Filipe II (III of Spain) para o Bispo D. Pedro de Castilho," 1604–1614, f. 132, 24 October 1612.

30. AHU, Macau caixa 1, doc. 2, 24 January 1603. Published in *ARGoa*, 1:16, alvará of the King, 1603.

31. BA, 44-XIV-9, f. 84, consulta of the DP, 1590.

32. BA, 44-XIV-7, f. 39v–40, 30 January and 4 February 1593.

33. BA, 44-XIV-7, ff. 10–10v, 20 August 1597.

34. Arquivo Municipal de Viana do Castelo, pasta 764, book 1003, f. 18, 4 June 1650.

35. BP-Évora, CXV/2–3, livro dourado da relação de Baia, ff. 158v–61, 29 August 1613.

36. HAG, códice 8791, ff. 15v–16, 24 March 1559.

37. *APO-1*, 5.2:913–19; Basílio de Sá, 4:140, V:158. "Proteção dos Orfãos," 1576; BA, 44-XIV-4, ff. 45–46, "Sobre as fazendas dos defuntos da India," 23 February 1590.

38. *DR da I*, 1:118–19, 7 January 1607.

39. *DR da I*, 1:178, Crown to Viceroy, 15 January 1608; also published in *ARGoa*, 1:54, dated one day earlier.

40. HAG, códice 8789, ff. 213–15, 1632.

41. AHU, India caixa 38, doc. 93, 14 December 1696.

42. AD-Évora, Misericórdia, book 2 of Acórdãos, ff. 134v–35, 18 September 1655.

43. AD-Portalegre, Processos Judiciárias de Elvas, maço 153, processo 7665 Auto da Contas for tutors, 26 September 1693.

44. AD-Portalegre, Processos Judiciárias de Elvas, maço 153, processo 7665 Auto da Contas for tutors, 28 January 1699.

45. HAG, códice 1043, f. 28.

46. BP-Évora, CXVI/2–3, Compromiso da Santa Casa de Misericórdia de Goa de 1655, ff. 34–37.

47. BA, 44-XIV-4, f. 292v, 24 March 1592.

48. AHU, Moçambique caixa 2, doc. 10, 9 November 1636.

49. AHU, India caixa 2, doc. 138, 1614.

50. BACL, azul 267, Pedro Barreto de Rezende, Descripção das Cidades e Fortalezas de India Oriental (1635), f. 63.

51. Rededicated on October 19, 1650 by D. João IV and the city council of Porto.

52. AD-Évora, câmara, 160, (unnumbered folios) Royal correspondence to

câmara, 17 August 1649; and AD-Évora, Casa Pia, 1, Minutes of the Hospital Board, 1652–1656.

53. BA, 54-IX-35, ff. 38–38a, alvará of 4 May 1679.

54. See Guedes.

55. McNeill, 67, 230, n. 76.

56. HAG, MR 8, ff. 34v–35, 25 January 1605.

57. *DR da I*, 10:382–83, Crown to Viceroy, 20 March 1624.

58. Severim de Faria, *Noticias*, 27–28.

59. Ibid., 28.

60. Cunha de Azeredo Coutinho, 67.

61. AHU, Reino maço 15, documentos sobre a casa dos expostos no Alentejo, 1780–.

62. Letter of P. Ambrósio Pires in Baía to Diego Mirón in Lisbon, 6 June 1555, in Leite, 2:232. Orphans boys are also mentioned, 2:280–81.

63. Letter from P. António Blázquez in Baía to P. Diego Mirón in Lisboa, 13 September 1564, in Leite, 4:76–77.

64. Catálogo da Provincia do Brasil, from Baía, July 1568, in Leite, 4:473–82. On the role played by Portuguese orphan boys in the conversion process directed by the Jesuits in Brazil, see Alden, "Changing Jesuit Perceptions," 212–13.

65. BA, 44-XIII-8, Cartas do Bispo D. João de Sousa, f. 101v, 20 September 1685.

66. BA, 49-II-27, "Estatuto do Recolhimento das donzellas, orfãs da protecção da Rayinha Santa Isabel, sitto na igreja do Anjo S. Miguel da Cidade do Porto," ff. 1–16, license granted and signed by the Bishop of Porto, D. João de Sousa, 20 September 1685.

67. This appears to have been left to the orphanage by his wife's estate.

68. BA, 54-VIII-6, ff. 194, ca. 1694; and 196, 20 May 1699. For related problems this caused, see BA, 54-VIII-7, f. 266, the Recolhimento do Anjo, 22 August 1693.

69. BA, 44-XIII-8, Cartas do Bispo D. João de Sousa, number 133–f. 113, 20 June 1691.

70. BA, 54-VIII-15, ff. 1–4, letters dated 7, 8, and 28 December 1697; 54-VIII-15, number 86, Letter from the Mother Superior to the Bishop, 17–18 February 1698.

71. BA, 54-VIII-15, number 90, Petition of the Nuns directed to Bishop D. João de Sousa, 1697(?).

72. Silva da Natividade, 8.

73. Pinto Ferreira, 144–45.

74. AD-Évora, câmara, 159, (unnumbered folios) correspondence dated 15 and 20 October 1620. The king gave an *arinhaga* (meaning unknown).

75. AD-Évora, Misericórdia, Acórdãos book 2, ff. 147v 148, 1659.

76. BA, 49-II-28, "Estatutos pera o Collegio das donzellas sitto neste Cidade de Évora," ff. 6v–22, signed and dated by the Archbishop de Évora, Jozeph, 27 September 1625.

77. Pinto Ferreira, 165.

78. Ibid., 168–69.

79. *CCLP*, 1:22, 2 September 1603.

80. *CCLP*, 10:362, 9 January 1695.

81. Almeida Gonçalves, 61–78.

82. AHU, India caixa 37, 68, 16 September 1694.

83. Ljungstedt, 42.

84. On the awarding of dowries and the military orders, see Mendoza.

85. Orphans were given dowries by the Goan *misericórdia* in much the same way as they were in Porto. BP-Évora, CXVI/2–3, Compromiso da Santa Casa de Misericórdia de Goa de 1655, ff. 34–37.

86. BA, 44-XIII-57, the 1646 statutes of the Santa Casa de Misericórdia of Porto, "How Orphan Girls are Selected for Dowries," chapter 27, ff. 42–44.

87. AD-Évora, Misericórdia, livro 93, receita e despeza, 1622–1623.

88. AD-Évora, Misericórdia, 1271, ff. 68–68v.

89. AD-Évora, Misericórdia, livros 1542–1545, livros da receita e despeza, 1680–1684. AD-Évora, Misericórdia, livro 96, livro da receita e despeza, 1692–1693, ff. 95–97. AD-Évora, Misericórdia, 1751, Dotes de Manuel Ramalho.

90. BACL, azul 103, Leis Varias, f. 190v.

91. BNL, códice 427 (F2864), ff. 21–23.

92. Pullan, 6.

93. BA, 44-XIV-3, ff. 69–70, 22 December 1587.

94. AD-Évora, Misericórdia, livro 426, despesas para amas dos enjeitados, 1616–1617, f. 76.

95. AD-Évora, Misericórdia, livro 427, despesas para amas dos enjeitados, 1617–1618, f. 9.

96. AD-Évora, Misericórdia, livro 427, despesas para amas dos enjeitados, 1617–1618, f. 39.

97. AD-Évora, Misericórdia, livro 429, despesas para amas dos enjeitados, 1620–1621.

98. AD-Évora, Misericórdia, livro 430, despesas para amas dos enjeitados, 1621–1622.

99. AD-Évora, Misericórdia, livro 92, despezas-março de 1622.

100. Biblioteca Municipal de Elvas, Arquivo da Câmara, livro das despezas dos enjeitados, 1658–1668; mss. 967/82; livro das despezas dos reis voluntários, 1673–1674, códice 939/82; livro dos gastos dos enjeitados no anno 1677, códice 899/82; livro das despezas pelos enjeitados, 1687, códice 902/82.

101. Biblioteca Municipal de Elvas, Arquivo da Câmara, livro dos gastos dos enjeitados dos annos de 1686–1687, códice 888/82, ff. 3 and 6v.

102. Biblioteca Municipal de Elvas, Arquivo da Câmara, livro das despezas, 1687; códice 890/82, ff. 9–10v.

103. Biblioteca Municipal de Elvas, Arquivo da Câmara, livro dos gastos dos enjeitados do anno de 1687, códice 890/82.

104. *CCLP*, 7:326, 29 August 1654.

105. *CCLP*, 10:382, 20 March 1696.

106. Ribeiro Coutinho, 2:157–84.

107. Arquivo Municipal de Viana do Castelo, livro 978, despezas pelos enjeitados, 1705–1708.

108. BGUC, códice 490, f. 24 v.

109. BGUC, códice 677, ff. 540–51. The basic laws governing this institution can be seen in BNL, códices 8968 (F2363), "Compromisso da Meza dos Engeytados" and 8969 (F 2362), "Roteyro ou Regimento Domestico da Caza da Roda."

110. Guimarães Sá, "Casa da roda," 166.

111. See Angela Mendes de Almeida.

112. *MMA*, 2:443, doc. 155, alvará of King D. Sebastião, 9 November 1559.

113. *Documentação-India*, 10:385, "Concilios Provinciais do Arcebispo de Goa," 1567.

114. *Leys e Provisões*, ff. 177–78, 181–90.

115. See Malon de Chaide and illustrations.

116. Akola Meira do Carmo Neto, "Assistência Pública," 235.

117. Ljungstedt, 42. The shelter in Macau was founded in ca. 1790.

118. BGUC, códice 601, f. 28–29, n.d., but appears to be a seventeenth-century hand.

119. *Grande Enciclopedia*, 6:106.

120. BA, 49-II-29, "Regimento da Caza das convertidas . . . ," ff. 1–9v; neither the location of the shelter nor the date of the regimento is given, but the hand is similar to BA-49-II-28 and this probably dated from the early 1600s.

121. Sousa Dias, 46.

122. AHU, códice 32, ff. 62–62v, 19 May 1620.

123. *CCLP*, 2:91, 14 August 1614.

124. AHU, códice 275, f. 148, 4 May 1649.

125. AHU, códice 48, ff. 67v–68, 23 July 1677. AHU, Mozambique caixa 3, 13, 1677.

126. *CCLP*, 9:71, 16 March 1680.

127. See Hromnik.

CHAPTER 7

1. Boxer, *Seaborne Empire*, 133–41.

2. Shirodkar, "Dutch-Portuguese Relations," 143.

3. Boxer, *Seaborne Empire*, 283. The reaction in Portuguese Asia to the loss

of Bombay was one of shock and bitterness. See Correia-Afonso, *Intrepid Itinerant,* 5–10, as well as his "Postscript to an Odyssey." For the English reaction to this marriage, see Boxer, "Three Sights."

4. In fact, other than Boxer, *Women,* and Sanceau, *Mulheres Portuguesas,* very little has been written on the subject.

5. Nazzari, 15–40, discusses aspects of the dowry system used in colonial Brazil. Marriages such as these, contracted by agents of the state, differed from those with no contract, in which goods (including the dowry) were jointly held in common property.

6. Braz Mimoso, 21.

7. *Recopilación de las leyes destos reynos,* 1:287–88.

8. AHU, India caixa 6, 62, 27 February 1619.

9. AHU, India caixa 19A, 103 and 104, 16 and 19 December 1647.

10. Braz Mimoso, 11.; v. civil code art. 2.391.

11. *Grande Enciclopedia Portuguesa e Brasileira,* 6:106. In a 1703 letter to the archbishop, he was informed that the orphanage in Chaves was falling apart, needed walls and a regent to protect "the little orphan girls inside, who are not very old." BA, 54-VIII-20, f. 430, letter dated 29 July 1703.

12. For a genealogical study of the families in Brazil descended from these first orphan girls and their husbands, see Rodolfo Garcia.

13. Letter of P. Manuel da Nóbrega in Olinda to D. João III, 14 September 1551, in Leite, 1:293.

14. Letter of P. Manuel da Nóbrega in Baia to D. João III, early July 1552, in Leite, 1:344.

15. *APO-1,* fasículo 1, part 1, 59–61, 4 March 1563.

16. *APO-1,* fasículo 1, part 1, 108–11, 27 February 1595.

17. In 1587 the Crown noted that the orphan system was functioning well and would continue, *APO-1,* fasículo 3, 78, Crown to Viceroy, 1587. The Crown, in its correspondence with the Évora city council, mentioned sending orphan girls of noble parents to India and referred to an earlier alvará that started this process in 1583, BP-Évora, CXV/1–39, 147–48, 26 August 1595.

18. *CCLP,* 2:9–16, 8 May 1613.

19. BA, 51-VI-52, f. 280, 12 January 1615.

20. *APO-1,* fasículo 3, 161, Crown to Viceroy, 28 March 1588.

21. ANTT, DP, RJDM, livro 3, f. 34, 8 February 1616.

22. ANTT, DP, RJDM, livro 17, f. 61, 1636.

23. *CCLP,* 1:9, 23 March 1603.

24. Ibid., 1:104–5, 31 January 1605; 2:144, 22 November 1605.

25. Ibid., 3:156, 9 March 1626.

26. BA, 51-V-84, f. 101, D. Pedro de Castilho addressing the Crown, 4 February 1606.

27. Schwartz, 144, 275.

28. BA, 51-VI-52, ff. 272–73, two resolutions dated 26 September 1610 and 11 June 1614.

29. BA, 51-VI-52, ff. 271–72, 3 December 1611.

30. ANTT, DP, RJDM, livro 1, f. 94, 21 May 1614.

31. BA, 51-VI-52, f. 272, 1 March 1616.

32. BA, 51-VI-52, f. 272, 26 December 1618.

33. ANTT, DP, RJDM, livro 1, f. 95, 21 May 1614.

34. ANTT, DP, RJDM, livro 3, f. 434, 29 November 1616. See also *CCLP*, 3:34, 17 November 1620.

35. *DR da I*, 1:243, Crown to Viceroy, 26 March 1608.

36. *DR da I*, 6:202–3, letters dated 30 March 1619 and 7 February 1620.

37. BA, 51-VI-52, f. 281, 3 March 1622. The bishop suggested sending three, and the Crown suggested sending four. AHU, India caixa 7, docs. 38 and 48, 26 February and 10 March 1622.

38. BA, 51-VI-52, f. 272, 8 March 1621.

39. BA, 51-VI-52, f. 276, 25 September 1624.

40. BA, 51-VI-52, f. 276, 27 October 1631.

41. BA, 51-VI-52, f. 281, 10 May 1625.

42. BA, 51-VI-52, f. 281, 4 December 1617.

43. AHU, India caixa 4, 20, 27 January 1616.

44. BA, 51-VI-52, f. 274, 26 January 1626.

45. ANTT, Mesa de Conciência e Ordens, Consultas, livro 31 (1625–1630), ff. 131–32v, 15 November 1629.

46. BA, 51-VI-52, f. 274, 13 November 1629.

47. *CCLP*, 3:72, 24 May 1622.

48. BA, 51-VI-52, f. 282, 20 June 1624.

49. BA, 51-VI-52, f. 282, 19 June 1627.

50. BA, 51-VI-52, f. 282, 14 November 1633. BA, 51-VI-52, f. 283, 18 November 1634.

51. BA, 51-VI-52, f. 283, 1645.

52. BA, 51-VI-52, f. 284, 1646.

53. BA, 51-VI-52, f. 284, 1648.

54. BA, 51-VI-52, f. 284, 1647. See also Belo, and the sources cited therein.

55. BA, 51-VI-52, f. 275, 1648.

56. BA, 51-VI-52, f. 272, 30 March 1607.

57. BA, 51-VI-52, f. 277, 23 November 1682.

58. BA, 51-VI-52, f. 278, 13 November 1705.

59. BA, 51-VI-52, f. 279, 6 September 1707.

60. BGUC, códice 673, ff. 266–67, printed list that appears to be mid-eighteenth century.

61. BGUC, códice 673, f. 287.

62. AHU, Reino maço 31.

63. Ibid.

64. For a brief overview of this subject, see Alfredo Costa, 115–24; Sanceau, *Mulheres Portuguesas*, 109–17; and L. A. Rodrigues, "Portuguese Feminine Emigration."

65. Ferreira Martins, 1:269.

66. I suspect that these were unpaid positions (or they were paid by the *misericórdia*) since they were not listed in several registers of expenses of the Goan *câmara*.

67. Accord of the Brothers of the Misericórdia of Goa, 10 October 1598, as published in Ferreira Martins, 1:269.

68. Santa Maria, 66. See also Ferreira Martins, 2:504 for an example of this figured into the budget.

69. Ferreira Martins, 1:290.

70. See "Recolhimento da Nossa Senhora da Serra," 142–44.

71. HAG, MR 12, f. 279, n.d., the volume is 1615–1617.

72. HAG, códice 10397, ff. 62v–63v, 28 March 1620.

73. Miguel Vicente de Abreu, 6.

74. For examples, see HAG, códice 10408.

75. See Ferreira Martins, 1:257–78 for transcriptions of letters to and from the *câmara* in Goa on this subject. Boxer in *Women* also mentions this problem.

76. *Documentação-India*, 9:315–16, Letter from D. Gaspar de Leão Archbishop of Goa to King D. Sebastião, 20 November 1564.

77. Ibid., 11:27, 16 March 1569.

78. *APO-1*, fasículo 1, part 1, 80–82, 7 March 1573.

79. *APO-1*, fasículo 3, 274–80, Crown to Viceroy, 12 January 1591.

80. *APO-1*, fasículo 3, 501, Crown to Viceroy, 1595.

81. In 1597, for example, the Crown noted that it was not sending any orphans from Castelo, since the few there were too young, HAG, MR 2B, f. 359v, 1 March 1597.

82. *DR da I*, 7:53–54, Crown to the Viceroy, 28 March 1620. This letter is the response to an earlier inquiry from the Viceroy to the Crown in 5:217–19, 20 February 1619, as noted in the footnote.

83. *DR da I*, 5:218–19, Viceroy to the Crown, 20 February 1619.

84. *DR da I*, 9:47, Viceroy to Crown, 15 March 1623.

85. Santa Maria, 66. Ferreira Martins says women were given shelter there against excesses by their husbands. Boxer in *Women*, 69, says they were placed there while their husbands were away.

86. Widow of Agostinho Lobato de Abreu, capitão-mor of Solar. Letter from the Viceroy, Fernão de Albuquerque (1619–1622), to Crown, requesting royal assistance for her. Faria de Morais, 88–89.

87. HAG, códice 10398, f. 32, 1612.

88. HAG, códice 10397, ff. 158–59, 6 and 8 March 1625.

89. This is an important but confused point in the sources. See Ferreira Martins, 1: part 2, chapter 3; and Boxer's comments in *Women*.

90. Pissulancar, 3:538, Letter from the Vicereine to Viceroy, 30 March 1635.

91. HAG, códice 7846, ff. 1–1v, 19 October 1595.

92. HAG, códice 10397, f. 126, 1664. See also *ARGoa*, doc. 816, 639–46, 2 October 1682.

93. "In regard to the orphan girls which we send there, there are various opinions on this matter, since in doing this we fail to reward others who are also needy," HAG, MR 4, f. 754, Crown to Viceroy, 1597.

94. Even at the expense of the Convent of Santa Mónica, if necessary. See *DR da I*, 1:126, 27 January 1607.

95. BA, 51-VI-52, f. 275, 12 February 1622 and 18 January 1625.

96. AHU, India caixa 24, doc. 8, 24 January 1657.

97. AHU, India caixa 34, doc. 45, 20 March 1687.

98. *DR da I*, 2:210–11, Crown to Viceroy, 9 March 1612.

99. AHU, India caixa 32, 154, 11 February 1684; and HAG, códice 10401, f. 95, 1686.

100. HAG, MR 55B, f. 372, 23 January 1691; and AHU, India caixa 36, 2, 10 January 1692.

101. HAG, códice 10419, f. 116, 1719.

102. HAG, códice 10419, f. 153, 1725.

103. HAG, códice 10419, ff. 198v–99, 1733.

104. HAG, MR 105, f. 269, 20 April 1736.

105. See *ARGoa*, 1:255, 19 September 1618; *ARGoa*, 1:390–91, 5 April 1628; and BP-Évora, CXV/1–39, 249–50 for a discussion on this and related issues.

106. *Cartas*, 5:70–71, 17 February 1511, and 143.

107. See Matos, *Estado da India*, 18–22.

108. BACL, azul 267, ff. 22–23.

109. Bragança Pereira, *Arquivo Português Oriental*, vol. 4, part 2, 178.

110. Caetano Braz de Albuquerque, 148–49. Alvará from King D. Manuel to the *câmara* of Goa.

111. HAG, MR 59, f. 125, alvará of the Crown, 22 December 1694.

112. HAG, códice 7846, f. 75, 20 March 1632.

113. BP-Évora, CXVI/2–5, Papers of D. Francisco Mascarenhas, ff. 3–4, 15 May 1634.

114. HAG, códice 7786, ff. 68, 7 February 1704.

115. This was not all that unusual. See, for example, the case of officeholding in sixteenth-century Porto, outlined in Costa Mesquita Brito.

116. AHU, India caixa 25, 49, 17 December 1661.

117. HAG, MR 33, f. 140, 9 February 1665.

118. BP-Évora, CXV/1–39, 326–28, 28 February 1674.

119. BP-Évora, CXV/1–39, 339–41, alvarás, 9 March and 7 November 1675. Parts of these are printed in *APO-1*, fasículo 2, 266–67, 9 March 1675.

120. AHU, India caixa 25A, 217 and 218, 10 May 1663; caixa 26, 123, 15 December 1664.

121. HAG, códice 412, f. 3, 1693.

122. HAG, códice 412, f. 6, 1693.

123. *APO-1*, fasículo 6, 805, Crown to the Vedor da Fazenda of Ceylon, Antão Vaz Freire, 6 February 1610. For modern vestiges of this system, see Saldanha.

124. *APO-1*, fasículo 6, 805, Crown to the Vedor da Fazenda of Ceylon, Antão Vaz Freire, 6 February 1610.

125. AHU, India caixa 3, 127, 18 September 1615.

126. AHU, India caixa 3, 127, 18 September 1615; and 128, 28 September 1615.

127. *DR da I*, 7:40–41, Crown writing to the Viceroy, 28 March 1620.

128. Silva Cosme, 294–98. For additional information on Portuguese settlement plans on Sri Lanka at that time, see Abeyasinghe, 104–6; and Chandra R. de Silva.

129. BP-Évora, CXV/1–39, 415, 14 February 1626. HAG, códice 8789, f. 160, 14 February 1627.

130. BP-Évora, CXV/1–39, 83–85, 12 May 1648.

131. *DR da I*, doc. 863, 692–93, 26 March 1696.

132. HAG, códice 3067, f. 34, 1627.

133. HAG, códice 3067, f. 23. This particular volume is full of such examples.

134. HAG, códice 412, f. 76, 24 May 1640.

135. HAG, códice 412, f. 93, 8 August 1640.

136. HAG, códice 412, f. 9v, 26 February 1693.

137. HAG, MR 44–45, ff. 75–77v, 13 January 1680.

138. HAG, MR 47, ff. 59–60v, 18 January 1680.

139. AHU, India caixa 34, 5, 22 January 1687. HAG, códice 7865, f. 76, 1690.

140. AHU, India caixa 31A, doc. 179, 1682.

141. HAG, MR 107, f. 181, 1737.

142. Pescatello, 35.

143. HAG, códice 7846, ff. 124v–26, 8 February 1650.

144. See L. A. Rodrigues, "Indo-European Miscegenation," and "Portuguese-Blood Communities in India." On women in colonial Goan society, see Correia-Afonso de Figueiredo, 38–132.

145. *DR da I*, 7:150–51, 21 January 1621.

146. Tavernier, 1:151.

147. Pyrard de Leval, 2:129.

148. Tavernier, 1:152.

149. Mandelslo, 78–80.

150. Ibid., 61–62.

151. Pyrard de Leval, 2:115–16.

152. Gerson da Cunha, *Notes*, 43–44.

153. Dewtry or deutroa. Datura Stramonium: "A drug or drink prepared from this employed to produce stupefaction" (*The Compact Edition of the Oxford English Dictionary* [New York: Oxford University Press, 1971], 1:712).

154. Pyrard de Leval, 2:114–15. See note at bottom of his p. 114.

155. Teotonio de Souza, *Medieval Goa*, 160.

156. Boxer, "Fidalgos Portuguêses e Bailadeiras Indianas."

157. Letter of the Viceroy of Goa, D. Francisco da Gama, 27 October 1598 as published in ibid. (Apendice Documental), 94.

158. Mandelslo and Pyrard de Leval mention aspects of slavery.

159. Pescatello. See also Jeanette Pinto.

160. Teotonio de Souza, *Medieval Goa*, 126.

161. Ibid.,132–51.

CHAPTER 8

1. Ferreira Martins, 1:307.

2. HAG, códice 10397, f. 46, 18 March 1615. This also appears in códice 10401, f. 33 and códice 779, ff. 17v–19v.

3. *DR da I*, 2:210–11, Crown to Viceroy, 9 March 1612.

4. *DR da I*, 3:434–35, 6 March 1616.

5. HAG, códice 10399, ff. 165–65v, 1658.

6. HAG, códice 10399, ff. 184–84v, 1611.

7. HAG, códice 10418, ff. 170–170v, 1680.

8. HAG, códice 10418, f. 171, 1680.

9. HAG, MR 86A, f. 10.

10. BACL, azul 267, ff. 143v–44.

11. HAG, códice 2316, f. 20 and 22v, 1667. The *misericórdia* of Goa had made a number of large loans to the state over the course of the 1600s. See the list of these in HAG, MR 68, ff. 39–39v, 5 November 1705.

12. HAG, códice 10396, ff. 185–88, 1610.

13. HAG, códice 10397, f. 137, 12 May 1609.

14. Ferreira Martins, 1:323–24.

15. HAG, códice 10421, ff. 1–54v, 1605.

16. HAG, códice 10399, ff. 156–156v.

17. HAG, códice 10418, f. 178, 1683.

18. HAG, códice 7761, f. 133, 27 November 1688.

19. Ferreira Martins, 1:324.

20. *DI*, vol. 17, ca. 1595. For greater detail, see Trinidade, 1:370–73.

21. HAG, códice 87–88v, Laws in favor of Christianity, 2 March 1575.

22. BA, 46-XIII-31, Collecçõens das ordens Reas antigas e modernas Sobre varios negocios percentes ao governo da India, ff. 1v–39, "Colleção das rezoluções e ordens que hà sobre orfãos gentios e seus casamentos," collected by D. Pedro de Almeida in Goa, 23 January 1678 at the order of Prince Pedro.

23. HAG, MR 46A, ff. 127–28v, 23 March 1681 and 20 November 1681 [?] (last digit of this second date is unreadable).

24. HAG, MR 106, ff. 117–25, 14 April 1736.

25. BGUC, códice 1085, Breve Tratado do Muito Religiossimo Mosteiro de Santa Monica de Goa, ff. 2–2v, n.d. but in a seventeenth-century hand.

26. For a discussion of the importance of such convents in a colonial context, see Russell-Wood, "Women and Society in Colonial Brazil," 11.

27. HAG, códice 7747, ff. 141–43v, 7 September 1605.

28. BGUC, códice 460: parecer, of the Mesa da Consciência e Ordens and the Conselho do Estado, ff. 84–85v, 10 December 1635.

29. *DR da I*, 8:88, 18 February 1620.

30. Boxer, *Portuguese Society*, 37.

31. *DR da I*, 6:121–22, letters 10 February 1620.

32. *DR da I*, 10:363–64, Crown to Viceroy, 23 March 1624.

33. *DR da I*, 8:80–90, doc. 71, carta régia to the Viceroy, 22 February 1622.

34. *DR da I*, 8:83, doc. 71, 20 March 1623.

35. *DR da I*, 2:384–86, Crown to Viceroy, 9 March, 1613.

36. Titulo dos bens do Convento de Santa Mónica, 1618, published in *DR da I*, 8:85–87, doc. 71, Appendix C.

37. HAG, MR 19D, ff. 1303–5v, 25 January 1635.

38. HAG, códice 3045, ff. 18–18v, 1639.

39. HAG, códice 7745, f. 12v, 31 March 1644. AHU, India caixa 21, 14, 1650.

40. *DR da I*, 8:87–90, doc. 71, Appendix D.

41. HAG, MR 13A, ff. 67–68, 7 December 1629.

42. AHU, India caixa 18, 126, 2 March 1646. Vestiges of this appear in the Goan practice of *desistencia*, whereby the bride forfeits any further claims on her parents' property. See Braganza, 96.

43. HAG, MR 67, ff. 63–89, 1702. The letter from the *câmara* is on f. 85 and dated 15 January 1702.

44. Fonseca, 173–74.

45. HAG, códice 7761, ff. 121v–22, 14 August 1688; see also Fonseca, 173.

46. AHU, India caixa 21A, doc. 117, 15 December 1651.

47. AHU, India caixa 28, doc. 24, 30 March 1664.

48. HAG, MR 33, f. 157, 7 January 1666.

49. AHU, India caixa 30, doc. 67, 22 January 1676; HAG, MR 39–40, ff. 95–95v.

50. HAG, MR 39–40, ff. 93–94, correspondence between Goa and Lisbon, 13 August 1674 and 22 January 1676.

51. HAG, MR 164B, f. 440, 1783.

52. Data extracted from Moniz; Telles.

53. HAG, códice 8797, ff. 27v–28, 20 February 1608.

54. HAG, códice 8797, f. 189, 1627.

55. Teixeira, *Macau e a sua Diocese*, 3:500–1.

56. "Ordem para no convento de Maccâo não tomarem mais Religiozas completo o numero (7 de Maio de 1718)," in Boxer, *Asia Portuguesa*, 11.

57. Teixeira, *Macau e a sua Diocese*, 3:500–1.

58. Ibid., 3:511–12.

59. *Leis Extravagantes*, 2:431–33, alvará, 10 March 1732.

60. For specific biographies of early modern women in Macau including the founder of the Convent of Santa Clara, see Teixeira, *Galeria*. Boxer, *Asia Portuguesa*, 98.

61. AHU, Angola caixa 5, doc. 48, 16 January 1651.

62. AHU, Angola caixa 5, doc. 125, 6 September 1653.

63. AHU, Angola caixa 5, doc. 128, 22 September 1653.

64. AHU, Angola caixa 15, doc. 44, 29 November 1695.

65. AHU, Angola caixa 12, doc. 88, 26 November 1682.

66. AHU, São Tomé caixa 2, doc. 127, 28 June 1660.

67. Axelson, "Colonização Portuguesa," 95; and his *Portuguese in South-East Africa 1600–1700*, 97–114.

68. AHU, Moçambique caixa 2, doc. 86, 28 January 1651; Moçambique caixa 2, doc. 87, 11 May 1651 and doc. 107, 19 March 1655.

69. See Axelson, *Portuguese in South-East Africa 1600–1700*, 144–54.

70. AHU, Moçambique caixa 3, doc. 17, 25 June 1677.

71. AHU, Mozambique caixa 3, doc. 18, 8 July 1677.

72. Boxer, "Raízes de Portugal em Africa," 127.

73. HAG, MR 44–45, ff. 133 and 137–38v, 20 June 1680.

74. HAG, MR 44–45, ff. 35–37, 25 October 1679.

75. HAG, MR 44–45, second half, ff. 137–38v, lista dos cazaes mandado para Sena, 20 June 1680. On the prazo system that would develop from these modest starts, see Isaacman; Newitt, *Portuguese Settlement*; and H. H. K. Bhila, "Southern Zambesia," in Ogot; and Ames, "African Eldorado?"

76. AHU, Maranhão caixa 2, doc. 10, 14 May 1644.

77. AHU, Maranhão caixa 9, doc. 36, 12 December 1695.

78. AHU, Moçambique caixa 3, doc. 19, 18 September 1677.

79. AHU, Açores caixa 2, doc. 4, 16 April 1649.

80. AHU, Maranhão caixa 2, doc. 65, 18 June 1647.

81. AHU, códice 274, ff. 88–88v, 12 January 1693.

82. AHU, Açores caixa 2, doc. 35, 22 August 1722. Documentos 36–39 in this same caixa all refer to further emigration in 1722–1723.

83. AHU, Madeira caixa 2, doc. 34, 16 September 1754. For additional data on emigration from Madeira to Brazil around this same time, see "Colonização do Brasil por Madeirenses." Vol. 2 (1932) (of this same journal) outlines two books of "registros para o Brasil" of married couples and others in 1747 and 1751 (2:54–55).

84. *Broadside on Resettlement.*

85. AHU, India caixa 40, doc. 28, 13 March 1696.

86. Correia-Afonso de Figueiredo, 44.

CONCLUSION

1. Serrão, *A Emigração Portuguesa*, 93.

2. Ibid., 103–4.

3. Ibid., 104.

4. Winius, "India or Brazil," 34.

5. Subrahmanyam, *Portuguese Empire*, 222.

6. Altman and Horn, table I.I, 3.

7. Duncan, cited in Subrahmanyam, *Portuguese Empire*, 218.

8. HAG, MR 89B, f. 514., 31 (month unreadable) 1722.

9. Cabral de Mello, 166–73.

10. Magalhães Godinho, "Portuguese Emigration," 24

11. Cordeiro, part 1, 26–27.

12. AHU, Cabo Verde caixa 5A, doc. 182, 24 September 1664.

13. AHU, Cabo Verde caixa 8, doc. 31, 1 August 1694.

14. Ekirch.

15. McEvedy and Jones, 49.

16. Altman and Horn, table 1.1, 3. McEvedy and Jones, 57.

17. On this aspect of the longevity of both the formal and informal empire in Asia, see Scammell.

18. See Curtin.

19. Abshire and Samuels, 190.

20. Slicher van Bath, 29.

21. Severim de Faria, *Noticias*, 7–10, 7

22. Ibid., 9.

23. *DR da I*, 8:81, doc. 71, carta régia to the Viceroy, 22 February 1622.

BIBLIOGRAPHY

ARCHIVAL SOURCES

For commentary on the holdings in various archives and libraries, as well as their locations, hours of operation, services provided, internal organization, and guides to each holding, the reader is referred to the author's article, "Early Modern (1500–1755) Sources" (see below).

I. Arquivo Distrital de Braga, Portugal. Fundo Misericórdia.

II. Arquivo Distrital de Évora, Portugal. Fundos: Câmara, Civeis, Crimes, Casa Pia, and Misericórdia.

III. Arquivo Distrital de Portalegre, Portugal. Livros: 9, 11, 27, 28, 29. Maços: Processos Judiciais de Elvas, Câmara de Alegrete, and Câmara de Portalegre.

IV. Arquivo Distrital de Viana do Castelo, Portugal. Fundo notários.

V. Arquivo Distrital de Vila Real, Portugal. Fundos: Câmara, Convento de Santa Clara, Expostos, Santa Casa da Misericórdia, and Testaments.

VI. Arquivo Histórico de Macau, People's Republic of China. Fundos: Leal Senado and Santa Casa de Misericórdia.

VII. Arquivo Histórico Militar, Lisbon, Portugal. First division, sections 1–5; second division, sections 1 and 5.

XVIII. Arquivo Histórico Ultramarino, Lisbon, Portugal. Fundos: Reino, Açores, Madeira, Lugares da Africa, Guiné, Cabo Verde, São Tomé, Moçambique, Angola, India, Casa da India, Macau, Timor, Ceará, Pernambuco, Paraíba, São Paulo, Espírito Santo, Rio Grande do Norte, Santa Catarina, Sergipe de El Rei, Piauí, Nova Colonia de Sacramento, Alagoas, Pará, Maranhão, and Rio de Janeiro. In addition, selected códices of the Conselho Ultramarino.

IX. Arquivo Municipal de Braga, Portugal. Fundos: Câmara, Livros das cartas dos senhores Arcebispos e Cabbidos, and Cartas dos Senhores Generais, Pessoas e Militares da Guerra.

X. Arquivo Municipal de Coimbra, Portugal. Maços: B–2, B–7, B–13, B–14, and B–16.

XI. Arquivo Municipal de Viana do Castelo, Portugal. Arquivo da Câmara.

233

XII. Arquivo Nacional da Torre do Tombo, Lisbon, Portugal. Fundos: Desembargo do Paço, Repartição de Justiça e Despachos da Mesa; Mesa
de Consciência e Ordens; Chancelaria de D. João III; Chancelaria de
D. Sebastião; Chancelaria de D. Filipe I; Chancelaria de D. Filipe II;
Chanceleria de D. Filipe III; and Cartas dos Governadores dos Lugares
de Africa.

XIII. Biblioteca da Academia das Ciências de Lisboa, Portugal. Various
códices were consulted from the Blue Series.

XIV. Biblioteca da Ajuda, Lisbon Portugal. Manuscript collection, volumes:
44-XIII-7 and 8; 44-XIII-26; 44-XIII-31 and 32; 44-XIII-50; 44-XIII-
52; 44-XIII-55; 44-XIII-57; 44-XIV-3 through 7; 44-XIV-9; 46-XIII-
31; 49-I-77; 49-II-27 through 30; 50-V-39; 51-V-43 and 44; 51-V-84;
51-VI-11; 51-VI-52; 51-VII-15; 51-VIII-6; 51-VIII-15; 51-VIII-22;
51-VIII-48; 51-IX-4; 51-IX-31; 51-IX-43; 51-X-2; 51-X-4; 51-X-12;
54-VIII-2 through 9; 54-VIII-11 through 16; 54-VIII-18; 54-VIII-20;
54-VIII-23 through 27; 54-VIII-37; 54-IX-8; 54-IX-15; 54-IX-17; 54-
IX-24; 54-IX-26; 54-IX-35; 54-IX-42; and 54-X-20.

XV. Biblioteca Geral da Universidade de Coimbra, Portugal, Secção dos
Manuscritos e Reservados.

XVI. Biblioteca Municipal de Elvas, Portugal. Arquivo da Câmara.

XVII. Biblioteca Nacional de Lisboa, Portugal, Secção dos Manuscritos.
Códices: 199 (F100), 219, 274, 427 (F2864), 584, 632, 857, 1534
(F3661), 2298 (F579), 8538, 8968 (F2363), 8969 (F2362), 8974 (F3630),
and 9861. Manuscripts: 207, number 73; 240, number 2; and caixa 25,
document 47.

XVIII. Biblioteca Pública de Évora, Portugal, Secção dos Manuscritos. The
following codices were most useful of those consulted: CIII/2–20,
CIII/2–17, CIII/2–26, CV/2–6, CV/2–7, CIX/1–13, CXV/2–11,
CXV/2–3, CXV/1–39, CXV/2–1, CXV/1–13, CXV/2–8, CXVI/2–20,
CXVI/2–3, CXVI/2–11, and CXVI/2–5.

XIX. Biblioteca da Sociedade de Geografia de Lisboa, Portugal. Manuscripts
consulted from the reservados: 145-Pasta A, A-7; 3-D-18; maço 4,
doc. 52; 146-A-19; and 3-C-13.

XX. The Hill Monastic Manuscript Library, Bush Center, St. John's Uni-
versity, Collegeville, Minnesota. Arquivo da Câmara do Município de
Lisboa, fundos: Chancelaria Régia, Provimento de Pão, Provimento da
Saude, and Obras Públicas.

XXI. Historical Archives of Goa, India. From the city council of Goa
códices: 7695–7704, 7737–40, 7743–48, 7750–52, 7758–61, 7763–
66, 7786, 7809, 7832, 7836–38, 7852, 7856, 7865, and 7870. From the
Goan high court and from lower courts: 1193, 1224–26, 1844, 2494,

2569, 2655–56, 2787, 2808, 8779–80, 8784–85, and 8788–92. Relating to charity and convents: 642, 2044, 2740, 2789–93, 2810–12, 3038–45, 7888, 10396–401, 10408, 10414, and 10417–27. Relating to various western coastal cities: 624, 1247, 2666, 656, 2320, 991, 7962, 1249–52, 1256, 3067, 1376, 2316, 3025, 3030, 4460, and 4463. Produced in Goa relating to job-holding in South Asia: 650, 779–85, 1041–47, 1183–89, 1593, and 2611. Misc. documentation produced in Goa: 860, 1210, 1416, 2439, 2750, 2780, 3031, 7588, 7693 and 9529. Monções do Reino collection: 1–23, 26, 28–47, 49–72, 76, 82–84, 86, 88–89, 91, 93–97, 100–1, 103, 105–9, 118, 120–23, 125, 127–29, 153, 156, 158–59, 163, 171–72, 179–80, and 183. Mercês gerais: códices 412–19, 812–13, 469–75, 1418–25, 1498–1502, 2313, 2358, 2608, 2611, 3033–34, 4461, 4465–69, and 7846–48.

WORKS CITED

Abeyasinghe, Tikiri. *Portuguese Rule in Ceylon, 1594–1612.* Colombo, Sri Lanka: Lake House Investments, 1966.

Abrantes Garcia, José Ignácio, ed. *Arquivo da Relação de Goa.* 2 vols. Panaji, India: Imprensa Nacional, 1872–1874.

Abreu, J. Capistrano de. *Capítulos de História Colonial.* 4th ed. Rio de Janeiro: Sociedade Capistrano de Abreu, 1954.

Abreu, Miguel Vicente de. *Resumo da Vida do arcebispo D. Frei Aleixo de Meneses, Fundador do Mosteiro de S. Mónica de Goa.* s.l.: n.d.

Abshire, David M., and Michael A. Samuels, eds. *Portuguese Africa: A Handbook.* New York: Praeger, 1969.

Akola Meira do Carmo Neto, M. Lourdes. "Assistência Pública," and "Demografia." In *Dicionário de História de Portugal,* ed. Joel Serrão, 1:234–36, II:281–86. Lisbon: Iniciativas Editoriais, 1992.

Albuquerque, Luís de. *Astronomical Navigation.* Lisbon: CNCDP, 1988.

Alden, Dauril. "Changing Jesuit Perceptions of the Brasis During the Sixteenth Century." *Journal of World History* 3, no. 2 (fall 1992): 205–18.

———. *Royal Government in Colonial Brazil, with Special Reference to the Administration of the Marquis of Lavradio, Viceroy, 1769–1779.* Berkeley and Los Angeles: University of California Press, 1968.

Allain, Mathé. *"Not Worth a Straw": French Colonial Policy and the Early Years of Louisiana.* Lafayette: University of Southwestern Louisiana, 1988.

Almada Negreiros. *História Ethnographica da Ilha de S. Thomé.* Lisbon: Imprensa Nacional, 1895.

Almeida, Viana de. *Povoamento e Colonização da ilha de S. Tomé.* Lisbon: Edições Cosmos, n.d.

Almeida Gonçalves, Margareth de. "Dote e Casamento: as expostas da Santa Casa de Misericórdia do Rio de Janeiro." In *Rebeldía e Submissão: estudos sobre a condição feminina,* ed. Albertina de Oliveira Costa and Cristina Bruschini, 61–78. São Paulo: Vértice, 1989.

Altman, Ida, and Horn, James, eds. "Introduction." In *"To Make America": European Emigration in the Early Modern Period,* 1–30. Berkeley and Los Angeles: University of California Press, 1991.

Alves Morgado, Nuno. "Portugal." In *European Demography and Economic Growth,* ed. R. Lee, 319–39. New York: St. Martin's Press, 1979.

Amaral Lapa, José Roberto. *A Bahia e a Carreira da India.* São Paulo: Editora Nacional, 1968.

Ames, Glenn Joseph. "An African Eldorado? The Portuguese Quest for Wealth and Power in Mozambique and the Rios de Cuama, c. 1661–1681." *The International Journal of African Historical Studies* 31, no. 1 (1998): 91–110.

———. "The Estado da India, 1663–1677: Priorities and Strategies in Europe and the East." *Revista Portuguesa de História* 22 (1985): 31–46.

Amorim Girão, A. de. *Geografia de Portugal.* Porto: Portucalense, 1949–1951.

Anderson, R. C. *Oared Fighting Ships from Classical Times to the Coming of Steam.* London: Percival Marshall, 1962.

Andrade, Francisco de. *Chrónica de muyto Alto e muyto Poderoso rey destes reynos de Portugal. D João III.* 4 vols. Coimbra, Portugal: Real Officina da Universidade, 1796.

Andrade e Silva, José Justino de. *Colleção Chronologica da Legislação Portuguesa.* 10 vols. Lisbon: J. J. A. Silva, 1854–1856.

Appendix Das Leyes Extravagantes, Decretos, E Avisos, que se tem publicado do anno de 1747 até o anno do 1761. Lisbon: Mosteiro de São Vicente da Fora, 1760.

Axelson, Eric. "A Colonização Portuguesa no Sudeste Africano, 1505–1900." In *Balanço da Colonização Portuguesa,* 85–107. Lisbon: Iniciativas Editoriais, 1975.

———. *Portuguese in South-East Africa, 1600–1700.* Johannesburg, South Africa: Witwatersrand University Press and the Ernest Oppenheimer Institute of Portuguese Studies, 1960.

Ayres de Azevedo, Diogo Manoel. *Portugal Illustrado Pelo Sexo Feminino.* Lisbon, 1734.

Azevedo, João Lúcio de. *Épocas de Portugal Económico: Esboços de História.* 4th ed. Lisbon: Clássica Editora, 1988.

Azevedo, Pedro de, ed. *Documentos das Chancelarias Reais anteriores à 1531 relativos a Marrocos. Vol. I (1415–1450) Vol. II (1450–1456).* Lisbon: ACL, 1915 and 1934.

Azevedo e Silva, José Manuel. "A mulher no povoamento e colonização de São

Tomé (séculos XV–XVI)." In *A Mulher na Sociedade Portuguesa: Visão Histórica e Perspectivas Actuais*, 2 vols., 2:229–44. Coimbra, Portugal: Faculdade de Letras, 1986.

Baião, António, ed. *Documentos do Corpo Chronológico relativos a Maroccos (1488–1514)*. Coimbra, Portugal: Universidade de Coimbra, 1925.

———. *A Inquisição de Goa*. 2 vols. Lisbon: ACL, 1949.

Bamford, Paul. *Fighting Ships and Prisons: The Mediterranean Galleys of France in the Age of Louis XIV*. Minneapolis: University of Minnesota Press, 1973.

Barata, Oscar. *Cabo Verde, Guiné, São Tomé e Príncipe*. Lisbon: Instituto Superior de Ciências Sociais e Políticas, 1965.

Barreto, João. *História da Guiné, 1418–1918*. Lisbon: Beleza, 1938.

Barros, Eugénio Estanislau de. *As Galés Portuguesas do Século XVI*. Lisbon: Imprensa da Armada, 1930.

Basílio de Sá, Artur, ed. *Documentação para a história das Missões do Padroado Português do Oriente: Insulíndia*. 5 vols. Lisbon: AGC, 1954–1958.

Beattie, J. M. *Crime and the Courts in England, 1660–1800*. Princeton, N.J.: Princeton University Press, 1986.

Beccaria, Cesare. *On Crimes and Punishments*. Trans. and ed. David Young. Indianapolis, Ind.: Hackett Publishing Company, 1986.

Beleza dos Santos, José. "O degrêdo e a sua execução em Angola." *Boletim da Faculdade de Direito* (Universidade de Coimbra) 12 (1930–1931): 161–201.

Bellini, Ligia. *A Coisa Obscura: Mulher, Sodomia, e Inquisição no Brasil Colonial*. São Paulo: Brasiliense, 1987.

Belo, Filomena. "Os Recolhimentos Femininos e a Colonização." *Claro Escuro, Revista de Estudos Barrocos* 6–7 (1991): 123–35.

Bender, Gerald J. *Angola Under the Portuguese: The Myth and the Reality*. Berkeley and Los Angeles: University of California Press, 1978.

———. "The Myth and the Reality of Portuguese Rule in Angola: A Study in Racial Domination." Ph. D. dissertation, University of California at Los Angeles, 1975.

Bento Pimentel Castello-Branco, Bernardo. *Vida da Mulher Prudente*. Lisbon: Miguel Rodrigues, 1750.

Biker, Julio Firmino Judice, ed. *Collecção de tratados e concertos de pazes que o Estado da India fez com os Reis e Senhores com quem teve relações nas partes de Asia e Africa Oriental desde o princípo da conquista até ao fim do século XVIII*. 14 vols. Lisbon: Imprensa Nacional, 1882.

Bivar Guerra, Luis de. *Inventário dos Processos da Inquisição de Coimbra (1541–1820)*. 2 vols. Paris: Fundação Calouste Gulbenkian, 1972.

Blake, John W. *West Africa: Quest for God and Gold, 1454–1578*. 2d ed. (retitled). London: Curzon Press, 1977.

Boletim do Arquivo Histórico Colonial. Lisbon, 1950.

Borges Coelho, António. *Inquisição de Évora*. 2 vols. Lisbon: Caminho, 1987.

Boucher, Philip P. "France 'Discovers' America: The Image of Tropical America in Sixteenth and Seventeenth Century France and Its Impact on Early French Colonization." Ph.D. dissertation, University of Connecticut, 1974.

————. "French Images of America and the Evolution of Colonial Theories, 1650–1700." In *Proceedings of the Sixth Annual Meeting of the Western Society for French History*, ed. Joyce D. Falk, 220–28. Santa Barbara, Calif.: ABC-Clio, 1979.

Boxer, Charles R. "O Almirante João Pereira Corte Real e a construção da frota portuguesa das Indias Orientais nos princípios do século XVII." *Boletim do Instituto Vasco da Gama* 49 (1941): 1–21.

————. "Fidalgos Portuguêses e Bailadeiras Indianas." *Revista de História* (São Paulo) 56 (1961): 83–105.

————. *From Lisbon to Goa, 1500–1750: Studies in Portuguese Maritime Enterprise*. London: Variorum Reprints, 1984.

————. *The Golden Age of Brazil, 1695–1750*. Berkeley and Los Angeles: University of California Press, 1969.

————. "Portuguese and Dutch Colonial Rivalry, 1641–1661." *Studia* 2 (1958): 7–42.

————. *The Portuguese Seaborne Empire, 1415–1825*. London: Hutchinson, 1969.

————. *Portuguese Society in the Tropics: The Municipal Councils of Goa, Macao, Bahia and Luanda, 1510–1800*. Madison: University of Wisconsin Press, 1965.

————. "As Raízes de Portugal em Africa, 1415–1800." In *Balanço da Colonização Portuguesa*, 111–31. Lisbon: Iniciativas Editoriais, 1975.

————. "Reflexos da Guerra Pernambucana na India Oriental, 1645–1655." *Boletim do Instituto Vasco da Gama* 74 (1957): 1–36.

————. "Three Sights to Be Seen: Bombay, Tangier, and a Barren Queen." *Portuguese Studies* 3 (1987): 74–83.

————. *Women in Iberian Expansion Overseas, 1415–1815: Some Facts, Fancies, and Personalities*. New York: Oxford University Press, 1975.

————, ed. *Asia Portuguesa no Tempo do Vice-Rei Conde de Ericeira*. Macau: Imprensa Nacional, 1970.

Boyajian, James C. *Portuguese Trade in Asia Under the Habsburgs, 1580–1640*. Baltimore, Md.: Johns Hopkins University Press, 1993.

Boyer, Raymond. *Les crime et les châtiments au Canada Française du XVIIe au XXe siècle*. Montreal: Le Crecle du Livre de France, 1966.

Bragança Pereira, António Bernardo de, ed. *Arquivo Português Oriental*. 11 vols. Bastorá [Goa]: Rangel, 1936–1940.

Braganza, Alfred. *The Discovery of Goa*. Bombay: Brooks, 1964.

————. *Os Portugueses em Diu*. Bastorá [Goa]: Rangel, 1938.

Brásio, António. "Descobrimento/Povoamento/Evangelização do Arquipélago de Cabo Verde." *Studia* 10 (July 1962): 49–97.

————. "As Misericórdias de Angola." *Studia* 4 (1959): 106–49.

Brásio, António, ed. *Monumenta Missionaria Africana*. 11 vols. Lisbon: AGU, 1952–1971; second series, 1 vol. Lisbon: AGU, 1958.

Brasseaux, Carl A. "The Image of Louisiana and the Failure of Voluntary French Emigration, 1683–1731." In *Proceedings of the Fourth Meeting of the French Colonial Historical Society*, ed. Alf Heggoy and James J. Cooke, 47–56. Washington, D.C.: University Press of America, 1979.

Braz Mimoso, Ruy. "A Natureza Jurídica do Dote." *Revista da Faculdade de Direito da Universidade de Lisboa, Suplemento-Dissertações de Alunos-III*, 1952.

Brito Freyre, Francisco de. *Nova Lusitania, Historia da Guerra Brasilica*. Lisbon: Joam Galram, 1675.

Broadside on Resettlement of Persons from the Azores to Brazil. 1755.

Bulhão Pato, Raimundo António de, (vols. 1–5) and Antonio da Silva Rego, (vols. 6–10), eds. *Documentos Remitidos da India*. 10 vols. Lisbon: Academia Real das Sciencias de Lisboa and Imprensa Nacional, 1880–1982.

Bulhão Pato, Raimundo António de, (vols. 1–4) and Henrique Lopes de Mendoça, (vol. 5) and Lopes de Mendoça (vol. 6), eds. (no editor listed for vol. 7). *Cartas de Affonso de Albuquerque*. 7 vols. Lisbon: Academia Real das Sciencias de Lisbon/Imprensa Nacional/Universidade de Coimbra, 1884–1935.

Cabral de Mello, Evaldo. *Olinda Restaurada: Guerra e Açúcar no Nordeste, 1630/1654*. Rio de Janeiro: Forense-Universitária, 1975.

Caetano, Marcelo. *Do Conselho Ultramarino ao Conselho do Império*. Lisbon: AGC, 1943.

Caetano Braz de Albuquerque, Viriato António. *O Senado de Goa. Memória histórico-archeológica*. Goa, India: Imprensa Nacional, 1909.

Caetano Perreira e Sousa, Joaquim José. *Esboço de hum Diccionario Juridico, Theoretico, e Pratico (Remissivo)*. 2 vols. Lisbon: Rollandiana, 1825.

————. *Primeiras Linhas sobre o Processo Criminal*. 4th ed. Lisbon: Rollandiana, 1827.

Caio Prado Junior. *The Colonial Background of Modern Brazil*. Trans. Suzette Macedo. Berkeley and Los Angeles: University of California Press, 1969.

Campos, J. J. A. *Antiguidades Portuguezas em Mombaça e na Costa de Azania*. Bastorá [Goa]: Rangel, 1934.

————. *History of the Portuguese in Bengal*. Calcutta: Butterworth and Co., 1919.

Carreira, António. "Aspectos da influência da cultura portuguesa na área com-
    preendida entre o rio Senegal e o norte do Serra Leoa (Subsídios para o seu
    estudo)," *Boletim Cultural da Guiné Portuguesa* XIX (1964): 373–416.
Carvalho da Costa, Padre António. *Corografia Portuguesa e Descripção Topo-
    gráfica.* 3 vols. Lisbon: Valentim da Costa Deslandes, 1706–1712.
Castilho Barreto, António Maria de. *Indice Remissivo da Legislação Ultrama-
    rina desde 1446 até 1878.* Praia, Cape Verde: Imprensa Nacional, 1882.
Cervantes Saavedra, Miguel de. *Don Quijote de la Mancha.* Barcelona: Juven-
    tud, 1966.
Chauhan, R. R. S. "Crime & Punishment in 17th Century Goa." *Purabhilekh-
    Puratatva* 3, no. 2 (July–December 1985): 29–39.
Choquette, Leslie Phyllis. "French Emigration to Canada in the 17th and 18th
    Centuries." Ph.D. dissertation, Harvard University, 1988.
————. "Recruitment of French Emigrants to Canada, 1600–1760." In *"To
    Make America": European Emigration in the Early Modern Period,* eds. Ida
    Altman and James Horn, 131–172. Berkeley and Los Angeles: University of
    California Press, 1991.
Coates, Timothy J. *Degredados e Órfãs: colonização dirigida pela coroa no im-
    pério português. 1550–1755.* Lisbon: CNCDP, 1998.
————. "Early Modern (1500–1755) Sources in Portuguese and Goan (India)
    Archives and Libraries: A Guide and Commentary." *Primary Sources and
    Original Works,* 2–4 (1993): 229–56; published simultaneously in Law-
    rence J. McCrank, ed. *Discovery in the Archives of Spain and Portugal:
    Quincentenary Essays,* 229–56. Binghamton, N.Y.: Hayworth Press, 1994.
Cockburn, J. S. "The Nature and Incidence of Crime in England, 1559–1625: A
    Preliminary Survey." In J. S. Cockburn, ed. *Crime in England 1550–1800.*
    Princeton, N.J.: Princeton University Press, 1977.
Codigo Penal Português. Nova Goa: Imprensa Nacional, 1855.
Coelho, F. Adolpho. *Os Ciganos de Portugal.* Lisbon: SGL, 1892.
*Collecção Chronologica de Leis Extravagantes posteriores a Nova Compilação
    das Ordenações do Reino publicadas em 1603, desde este anno até o de
    1761 .... 6 vols. in 5.* Coimbra, Portugal: Real Imprensa da Universidade,
    1819.
*Collecção das leis, Decretos, e Alvarás, que comprehende o feliz reinado del rei
    fidelissimo D. José I nosso senhor desde o anno de 1750 até o de 1760 e a
    pragmatica do Senhor Rei D. João o V do anno 1749.* Lisbon: Antonio Ro-
    drigues Galhardo, 1760.
Collecção de Noticias para a história e geografia das nações ultramarinas.
    7 vols. in 3. Lisbon: Academia Real das Sciencias, 1813.
"Colonização do Brasil por Madeirenses." *Arquivo Histórico da Madeira* 5,
    no. 1 (1937): 49–54.

Compilação de Reflexões de Sanches, Pringle, Mouro, Van-Sweiten, e outros a cerca das causas, prevenções e remedios das doenças dos exercitos. Lisbon: Academia Real das Sciencias, 1797.

Conceição Rodrigues, Vítor Luís Pinto Gaspar. "A Guiné nas cartas de perdão (1463–1500)." In *Actas do Congresso Internacional Bartolomeu Dias e a sua Época*, 3:397–412. Porto: Universidade do Porto, 1989.

Cooke, James J. "France, the New World, and Colonial Expansion." In *Frenchmen and Indians in the Lower Mississippi Valley*, ed. Patricia K. Galloway, 81–92. Jackson: University Press of Mississippi, 1982.

Cordeiro, Luciano, ed. *Viagens, Explorações e Conquistas dos Portuguezes, Collecção de Documentos.* Lisbon: Imprensa Nacional, 1881.

Corrêa da Serra, José, ed. *Collecção de livros ineditos de história portuguesa.* 5 vols. Lisbon, 1790–1824. Vol. 3, part 3: *Fragmentos de legislação Portugueza extrahidos do livro das Posses da Casa da Suplicação.*

Correia-Afonso, John, S. J. "Postscript to an Odyssey: More Light on Manuel Godinho." *Studia* 49 (1989): 181–94.

———, ed. and trans. *Intrepid Itinerant: Manuel Godinho and His Journey from India to Portugal in 1663.* Bombay: Oxford University Press, 1990.

Correia-Afonso de Figueiredo, Propéncia. *A Mulher na India Portuguesa.* Nova Goa, India: Tipographia Bragança, 1933.

Cortesão, Armando. *History of Portuguese Cartography.* Lisbon: JIU, 1969.

Cortesão, Jaime. *A Expansão dos Portugueses na História da Civilização.* Rpt. Lisbon: Horizonte, 1983.

———. *O Ultramar Português depois da Restauração.* Rpt. Lisbon: Portugalia, 1971.

Costa, Alfredo. "Orfãs d'El Rei e as Mulheres Portugueses vindas à India durante o século XVI." *Boletim do Instituto Vasco da Gama* 47 (1940): 115–24.

Costa Mesquita Brito, António Pedro de. *Patriciado Urbano Quinhentista: As Famílias Dominates do Porto (1500–1580).* Porto: 1991.

Couto, Carlos. "Presença cigana na colonização de Angola." *Studia* 36 (July 1973): 107–15.

Couto, Diogo do. *O Soldado Prático.* Ed. M. Rodriques Lapa. 3d ed. Lisbon: Sá da Costa, 1980.

Cunha de Azeredo Coutinho, José Joaquim da. *Ensaio Economico sobre o comercio de Portugal e suas colonias.* Lisbon: Academia Real das Sciencias, 1794.

Cunha Rivara, J. H. da, ed. *Arquivo Portuguez-Oriental.* 6 vols. in 9. Nova Goa, India: 1857–1876.

Curtin, Philip D. *Disease and Imperialism Before the Nineteenth Century.* Minneapolis: James Ford Bell Library/University of Minnesota, 1990.

Degredados e Órfãs: colonização dirigida pela coroa no império português. 1550–1755. Lisbon: CNCDP, 1998.

Dellon, Dr. M. Charles. *Relation de L'Inquisition de Goa.* Paris: Horthemels, 1688.

Désoulières, Alain. "La communité portugaise d'Agra, 1533–1739." *Arquivo do Centro Cultural* 22 (1986): 145–73.

Dias, Jorge. "Algumas considerações acêrca da estrutura social do povo português." *Revista de Antropologia* (São Paulo) 3, no. 1 (June 1955): 1–19.

Dias Farinha, António. *História de Mazagão durante o Período Filipino.* Lisbon: CEHU, 1970.

Diffie, Bailey W. *A History of Colonial Brazil.* Malabar [Florida]: Krieger, 1987.

Documentação Ultramarina Portuguesa. 8 vols. Lisbon: CEHU, 1960–1983.

Documentos Históricos. Biblioteca Nacional de Rio de Janeiro.

Documentos Históricos do Arquivo Municipal, Atas da Câmara, 6 vols. Salvador: Prefeitura do Município do Salvador-Bahia, 1942–1949.

Documentos para a História do Açúcar. 3 vols. Rio de Janeiro: Instituto do Açúcar e Alcool, 1954–1963.

Documentos Sobre os Portugueses em Moçambique e na Africa Central, 1497– 1840. Documents on the Portuguese in Mozambique and Central Africa. 9 vols. to date. Lisbon: CEHU and the National Archives of Rhodesia and Nyasaland; after vol. 8– Zimbabwe and the Universidade Eduardo Mondlane, 1962–.

Donovan, Bill M. "Changing Perceptions of Social Deviance: Gypsies in Early Modern Portugal and Brazil." *Journal of Social History* 26, no. 1 (fall 1992): 33–53.

———. "The Politics of Immigration to Eighteenth Century Brazil: Azorean Migrants to Santa Catarina." *Itinerario* 16 (1992): 35–56.

Duffy, James. *Shipwreck and Empire: Being an Account of Portuguese Maritime Disasters in a Century of Decline.* Cambridge, Mass.: Harvard University Press, 1955.

Dumas, Silvio. "Les Filles du Roi en Nouvelle-France: Étude historique avec répertoire biographique." *Cahiers d'Histoire* (Quebec) 24 (1972).

Duncan, T. B. *Atlantic Islands; Madeira, the Azores, and the Cape Verdes in 17th Century Commerce and Navigation.* Chicago: University of Chicago Press, 1972.

Ekirch, A. Roger. *Bound for America: The Transportation of British Convicts to the Colonies, 1718–1775.* Oxford: Clarendon Press, 1987.

Elkiss, T. H. "On Service to the Crown—Portuguese Overseas Expansion: A Neglected Aspect." *Journal of the American Portuguese Society* 10, no. 1 (spring 1976): 44–53.

Esquemeling, John. *The Buccaneers of America*. 1684. Rpt., Glorieta, N.M.: Rio Grande Press, 1992.

Estaço da Silveira, Simão. *Relação sumaria das coisas do Maranhão . . . dirigida aos pobres deste Reyno de Portugal*. Lisbon: Geraldo da Vinha, 1624.

Faria Blanc Junior, Hermenegildo Augusto de. *O Depósito de Degredados*. Luanda, Angola: Imprensa Nacional, 1916.

Faria de Morais, Samoa Teixeira A. *Subsídios para a história de Timor*. Bastorá, India: Rangel, 1934.

Fernandes Brandão, Ambrósio, (attributed author). *Dialogues of the Great Things of Brazil*. Ed. and trans. Frederick Arthur Holden Hall. Albuquerque: University of New Mexico Press, 1987.

Fernandes Pinto Alpoyon, Joze. *Exames de Bombeiros*. Madrid: Francisco Martinez, 1748.

Figueiredo, José Anastásio de. "Memoria sobre a origem dos nossos Juizes da Fora." In *Memorias de Litteratura Portugueza*, 1:31–44. Lisbon: Academia Real das Sciencias de Lisbon, 1792.

———. *Synopsis Chronologica de Subsidios Ainda os Mais Raros para a Historia e Estudo Critico da Legislação Portuguesa*. 2 vols. Lisbon: Academia Real das Sciencias, 1740. (n.b.: the volume references in the index are reversed.)

Franck, Augustus Hermannus. *Pietas Hallensis or a publick Demonstration . . . of the Orphan House and Other Charitable Institutions at Glaucha near Hall in Saxony*. London, 1705.

Freire de Oliveira, Eduardo, ed. *Elementos para a História do Município de Lisboa*. 17 vols. Lisbon: Câmara Municipal, 1887–1911.

Ferreira, José Augusto (Padre). "Origem das Misericórdias ou institutição em 1498 da Misericórdia de Lisboa." In *Congresso do Mundo Português*, 5:11–29. Lisbon: Comissão Executiva dos Centenários, 1940.

Ferreira Martins, José Frederico. *História da Misericórdia de Goa*. 3 vols. Nova Goa, India: Imprensa Nacional, 1910–1914.

Fonseca, José Nicolau da. *An Historical and Archaelogical Sketch of the City of Goa*. Bombay: Thacker, 1878.

Franck, Augustis Hermannus. *Pietas Hallensis or a publick Demonstration . . . of the Orphan House and Other Charitable Institutions at Glaucha near Saxony*. London: 1705.

Freeman-Grenville, G. S. P. "The Portuguese on the Swahili Coast: Buildings and Language." *Studia* 49 (1989): 235–53.

Gama Barros, Henrique da. *História da Administração Pública em Portugal nos Séculos XII a XV*. 2d ed. Lisbon: Sá da Costa, 1947–1954.

Garcia, Carlos Alberto. "A Ilha de São Tomé como centro experimental do comportamento do Luso nos trópicos." *Studia* 19 (1966): 209–21.

Garcia, Rodolfo. *As Orfãs*. Rio de Janeiro: Imprensa Nacional, 1947.

Garfield, Robert. *A History of São Tomé Island 1470–1655. The Key to Guinea*. San Francisco: Mellon Research University Press, 1992.

As Gavetas da Torre do Tombo. 12 vols. Lisbon: CEHU, 1960–1977.

Gerson da Cunha, Joseph. "An Historical and Archaeological Sketch of the Island of Angediva." *Journal of the Bombay Branch of the Royal Asiatic Society* 11 (1875): 288–310.

———. *Notes on the History and Antiquities of Chaul and Bassein*. Bombay: Thacker, Vining, 1876.

Gomes, Olivinho J. F. *Village Goa: A Study of Goan Social Structure and Change*. New Delhi: S. Chand, 1987.

Gomes da Camara, José. *Subsídios para a História do Direito Pátrio, Vol. 1, 1500–1769*. Rio de Janeiro: Livraria Brasiliana Editora, 1954.

Gonçalves Pereira, Carlos Renato. *Tribunal da Relação de Goa*. Lisbon: 1964.

Gracias, J. A. Ismael. *Catálogo dos Livros do Assentamento da gente da Guerra que veio do reino para India desde 1731 até 1811*. Nova Goa: Imprensa Nacional, 1893.

Gracias, J. B. Amáncio. *Portugueses na India*. Bastorá [Goa]: Rangel, 1935.

Granada, Frei Luís de. *Guia de Peccadores e Exortação à Virtude*. Lisbon: Ignácio Nogueira Xisto, 1764.

Grande Enciclopédia Portuguesa e Brasileira. 40 vols. Lisbon and Rio de Janeiro: Editorial Enciclopédia, 1935–1960.

Guedes, Padre Baltasar. *Breve Relação da Fundação do Colégio dos Meninos Orfãos da Nossa Senhora da Graça*. Porto: Edições da Câmara, 1951.

Guimarães e Freitas, José de Aquino. *Colleção de Noticias para a história e Geografia das Nações Ultramarinas*. 4 vols. Lisbon: Real Academia das Sciencias, 1826.

Guimarães Sá, Isabel dos. "A casa de roda de Porto e o seu funcionamento (1770–1780)." *Revista da Faculdade de Letras, História* (Universidade do Porto) second series, 2 (1985): 161–99.

———. *Quando o Rico se faz pobre: Misericórdias, caridade e poder no império português 1500–1800*. Lisbon: Comissão Nacional para as Comemorações dos Descobrimentos Portugueses, 1997.

Gune, V. T., ed. *Assentos do Conselho da Fazenda*. Panaji, India: 1979.

Hanke, Lewis. "The Portuguese in Spanish America, with Special Reference to the Villa Imperial de Potosí." *Revista de História de America* 51 (1958): 1–48.

Hein, Jeanne. "Portuguese Communication with Africans on the Sea Route to India." *Terrae Incognitae* 25 (1993): 41–52.

Hemming, John. *Red Gold: The Conquest of the Brazilian Indians, 1500–1760*. Cambridge, Mass.: Harvard University Press, 1978.

Hespanha, A. M. "Da 'Justiça' à 'Disciplina': Textos, Poder, e Política no Antigo

Regime." *Boletim da Faculdade de Direito* (Coimbra), número especial (1986): 1–98.

História Geral de Cabo Verde: Corpo Documental. 2 vols. to date. Lisbon: IICT, 1988–1990.

Hromnik, Cyril Andrew. "Goa and Mozambique: The Participation of Goans in Portuguese Enterprise in the Rios de Cuama, 1501–1752." Ph.D. dissertation, Syracuse University, 1977.

Huetz de Lemps, Christian. "Indentured Servants Bound for the French Antilles in the Seventeenth and Eighteenth Centuries." In *"To Make America": European Emigration in the Early Modern Period,* ed. Ida Altman and James Horn, 172–203. Berkeley and Los Angeles: University of California Press, 1991.

Hughes, Robert. *The Fatal Shore: The Epic of Australia's Founding.* Rpt. New York: Vintage, 1986.

Isaacman, Allan. *Mozambique: The Africanization of a European Institution, The Zambesi Prazos 1750–1902.* Madison: University of Wisconsin Press, 1972.

Israel, Jonathan I. *The Dutch Republic and the Hispanic World 1606–1661.* Oxford: Oxford University Press, 1982.

Jacobs, Hubert, S. J., ed. *Monumenta Historica Societatis Jesu: Documenta Malucensia.* 3 vols. Rome: Institutum Historicum Societatis Jesu, 1974–1984.

Jennings, Ronald C. *Christians and Muslims in Ottoman Cyprus and the Mediterranean World, 1571–1640.* New York and London: New York University Press, 1993.

Kieman, Mathias C. *The Indian Policy of Portugal in the Amazon Region, 1614–1693.* 1954. Rpt. New York: Octagon Books, 1973.

Kol, Joaquim José Ciclia. *Statistical Report on the Portuguese Settlements in India, Extracted in the Year 1850 from Official Documents, to which are Added Copies of Treaties Concluded between Great Britain and Portugal between the Years 1661 and 1850.* Published with *Memoir of the Sawunt Waree State.* 1855. Rpt. New Delhi: Asian Education Services, 1995.

Landry, Yves. *Les Filles du Roi au XVIIe Siècle.* Ottawa: Leméac Editeur, 1992.

Laranjo Coelho, P. M., ed. *Documentos Inéditos de Marrocos: Chancelaria de D. João II.* Lisbon: Imprensa Nacional, 1943.

Leis Extravagantes Collegidas e Relatadas pelo licenciado Duarte Nunez do Liam per mandado do muito alto & poderoso Rei Dom Sebastião nosso senhor. Lisbon: Antonio Gonçalves, 1569.

Leite, Serafim, S. J., ed. *Monumenta Historica Societatis Jesu: Monumenta Brasiliae.* 5 vols. Rome: Institutum Historicum Societatis Jesu, 1956–1968.

Léry, Jean de. *History of a Voyage to the Land of Brazil.* Trans. and ed. Janet Whatley. Berkeley and Los Angeles: University of California Press, 1990.

Ley para se prenderem os deliquentes antes da culpa formada . . . (broadside dated 19 October 1754).

Leys e Provisões . . . *1570*. Lisbon: Francisco Correa, 1570.

Lîbano Guedes, João Alfredo, and Ribeiro, Joaquim. *História Administrativa do Brasil*. 4 vols. 2d ed. Rio de Janeiro: Imprensa Nacional, 1962.

Lima Cruz, Maria Augusta. "Exiles and Renegades in Early Sixteenth Century Portuguese India." *The Indian Economic and Social History Review* 23, no. 3 (1986): 249–62.

Lisboa, João Francisco. *Crônica do Brasil Colonial: Apontamentos para a História do Maranhão*. 1864. Rpt. Petrópolis, Brazil: Vozes, 1976.

Lista das Pessoas que das Cadeas deste Corte vão para o Estado da India e Rio de Sena servir a Sua Magestade no presente anno de 1755 em a Nao S. Fransciso Xavier comandada pelo Capitão Tenente Fransciso da Sa e Saldanha. Sentenceados pelo Supremo Tribunal da Casa da Supplicaçam, sendo pressos neste Corte e mais partes do Reino. Lisbon: Domingos Rodrigues, 1755.

Livro Primeiro do Govêrno do Brasil, 1607–1633. Rio de Janeiro: Imprensa Nacional, 1958.

Ljungstedt, Andrew. *An Historical Sketch of the Portuguese Settlements in China and of the Roman Catholic Church and Mission in China*. Boston: James Munroe, 1836.

Lopes Ferreira, Manuel. *Pratica Criminal Expedida na Forma da Praxe*. Lisbon: Carlos Esteves Mariz, 1742.

Magalhães Godinho, Vitorino. *Os Descobrimentos e a Economia Mundial*. 4 vols. 2d ed. Lisbon: Presença, 1984.

———. *A Estrutura na Antiga Sociedade Portuguesa*. Lisbon: Arcádia, 1971.

———. *História Económica e Social da Expansão Portuguesa*. Lisbon: Terra Editora, 1947.

———. "Portugal and Her Empire." In *The New Cambridge Modern History*, V: 384–97. Cambridge: Cambridge University Press, 1957–1979.

———. "Portugal and Her Empire, 1680–1720." In *The New Cambridge Modern History*, VI: 509–40. Cambridge: Cambridge University Press, 1957–1979.

———. "Portuguese Emigration from the Fifteenth to the Twentieth Century: Constants and Changes." In *European Expansion and Migration*, ed. P. C. Emmer and M. Mörmer, 13–48. New York: St. Martin's Press, 1992.

Malheiro Dias, Carlos, ed. *História da Colonização Portuguesa do Brasil*. 3 vols. Porto: Litografia Nacional, 1921–1926.

Malon de Chaide, Frei Pedro. *Libro dela Conversión de la Madalena en que se esponen los tres estados que tuvo de pecadora, y de penitente, y de gracia*. Valencia, Spain: Pedro Patrício, 1600.

Mandelslo, J. Albert de. *Mandelslo's Travels in Western India 1638–9*. Ed. M. S. Commissariat. London: Oxford University Press, 1931.

Marchant, Alexander. "From Barter to Slavery: The Economic Relations of Portuguese and Indians in the Settlement of Brazil, 1500–1580." *The Johns Hopkins University Studies in Historical and Political Science* 60, no. 1 (1942): 4–160.

Marinho Homem de Melo, Vasco. "O Degrêdo." *Boletim dos Institutos de Criminologia* 6 (1940): 131–97.

Martins da Silva Marques, João. *Descobrimentos portugueses: documentos para a sua história*. 3 vols. Lisbon: Instituto de Alta Cultura, 1944–1971.

Martins Vieira, Maria Eugénia. "Registro de cartas de guia de degredados para Angola (1714–1757): Análise de um códice do Arquivo da Câmara Municipal de Luanda." Thesis for the *licenciatura* in history, Faculdade de Letras, Universidade de Lisboa, 1966.

Mascarenhas, Jerónimo de. *História de la Cuidad de Ceuta*. Lisbon: ACL, 1915.

Matthews, George T., ed. *The Fugger Newsletters*. 1959. Rpt. New York: Capricorn Books, 1970.

Matos, Artur Teodoro de. *O Estado da India nos anos de 1581–88: Estrutura administrativa e económica. Alguns elementos para o seu estudo*. Ponta Delgada, Portugal: Universidade dos Açores, 1982.

———. "Origem e reminisências dos povoadores das ilhas atlânticas," *Actas do Congresso Internacional Bartolomeu Dias e a sua Época* (Porto: Universidade do Porto, 1989) Vol. III, 241–52.

McEvedy, Colin and Richard Jones, eds. *Atlas of World Population History*. New York: Penguin, 1980.

McKnight, Brian E. *The Quality of Mercy: Amnesties and Traditional Chinese Justice*. Honolulu: University Press of Hawaii, 1981.

McNeill, John Robert. *Atlantic Empires of France and Spain: Louisbourg and Havana, 1700–1763*. Chapel Hill: University of North Carolina Press, 1985.

McPherson, Kenneth. "A Secret People of South Asia: The Origins, Evolution, and Role of the Luso-Indian Goan Community from the Sixteenth to Twentieth Centuries." *Itinerario* 11, no. 2 (1987): 72–86.

Meintel, Deirdre. *Race, Culture, and Portuguese Colonialism in Cabo Verde*. Syracuse, N.Y.: Syracuse University Press, 1984.

Mello e Souza, Laura de. *Inferno Atlântico: Demonologia e colonização. Séculos XVI–XVIII*. São Paulo: Companhia Das Letras/Schwartz, 1993.

Mendes de Almeida, Angela. "Casamento, sexualidade e pecado—os manuais portugueses de casamento dos séculos xvi e xvii." *Ler História* 12 (1988): 3–21.

Mendes de Almeida, Candido, ed. *Ordenações Filipinas*. 5 vols. in 3. Auxiliar Jurídico, 2 vols. Rio de Janeiro, 1869. Facsimile ed., Lisbon: Fundação Calouste Gulbenkian, 1985.

Mendes Pinto, Fernão. *The Travels of Mendes Pinto.* Trans. and ed. Rebecca D. Catz. Chicago: University of Chicago Press, 1989.

Mendoza, Jeanine Anne. "Dowries and Membership in the Portuguese Order of Santiago, 1668–1706." In *Marginated Groups in Spanish and Portuguese History,* ed. William D. Phillips and Carla Rahn Phillips, 101–9. Minneapolis: Society for Spanish and Portuguese Historical Studies, 1989.

Meneses, Dom Luis de. *Asia Portuguesa no Tempo do Vice-Rei Conde da Ericeira (1717–1720). Correspondencia oficial do Conde da Ericeira.* Ed. C. R. Boxer. Macau: Imprensa Nacional, 1970.

Mesgravis, Laima. *A Santa Casa de Misericórdia de São Paulo (1599?–1884).* São Paulo: Imprensa Oficial do Estado, 1977.

Miller, Joseph C. "Angola in the Sixteenth Century—Um Mundo que o Português Encontrou." In *Empire in Transition: The Portuguese World in the Time of Camões,* ed. Alfred Hower and Richard A. Preto-Rodas, 118–31. Gainesville: Center for Latin American Studies, University Presses of Florida, 1985.

Moniz, António Francisco. "Relação completa das religiosas do Mosterio de Santa Mónica de Goa." *O Oriente Português,* first series 15: 177–98; 16: 284–94, 354–63; 17: 92–102, 188–97; second series 2–3: 111–19.

Moser, Gerald M. "Grumbling Veterans of an Empire." In *Empire in Transition: The Portuguese World in the Time of Camões,* ed. Alfred Hower and Richard A. Preto-Rodas, 97–105. Gainesville: University Presses of Florida, 1985.

Mott, Luiz. "Justiça e Misericórdia: a Inquisição portuguesa e a repressão ao nefando pecado da sodomia." In *Inquisição. Ensaios sobre Mentalidade, Heresias e Arte,* ed. Anita Novinsky and Maria Luziz Tucci Carneiro, 703–39. São Paulo: Universidade de São Paulo, 1992.

Mulher na Sociedade Portuguesa: Visão histórica e perspectivas actuais. 2 vols. Coimbra, Portugal: Instituto de História Económica e Social, Faculdade de Letras da Universidade de Coimbra, 1986.

Nazzari, Muriel. *Disappearance of the Dowry. Women, Families, and Social Change in São Paulo, Brazil, 1600–1900.* Stanford, Calif.: Stanford University Press, 1991.

Newitt, M. D. D. "Plunder and the Rewards of Office in the Portuguese Empire." In *The Military Revolution and the State 1500–1800,* ed. Michael Duffy. Exeter, Eng.: University of Exeter Studies in History No. 1, 1980.

———. *Portuguese Settlement on the Zambesi: Exploration, Land Tenure and Colonial Rule in East Africa.* New York: Africana, 1973.

———, ed. *The First Portuguese Colonial Empire.* Exeter Studies in History, no. 11. Exeter, Eng.: A. Wheaton, 1986.

Noonan, Laurence A. "The Portuguese in Malacca: A Study of the First Major European Impact on East Asia." *Studia* 23 (April 1968): 33–104.

Nunes de Leaõ, Duarte. *Descripção do Reino de Portugal*. Lisbon: Jorge Rodriguez, 1610.

Ogot, B. A., ed. *General History of Africa, Vol. V: Africa from the Sixteenth to the Eighteenth Century*. Berkeley and Los Angeles: University of California Press/UNESCO, 1992.

Olesa Muñido, Francisco-Filipe. *La Organización Naval de los Estados Mediterráneos y en Especial España durante los Siglos XVI y XVII*. 2 vols. Madrid: Editorial Naval, 1968.

Oliveira Marques, António Henrique de. *Daily Life in Portugal in the Late Middle Ages*. Trans. S. S. Wyatt. Madison: University of Wisconsin Press, 1971.

————. *História de Portugal*. 2 vols. 8th ed. Lisbon: Palas, 1978.

————. *Introdução a História da Agricultura em Portugal: A Questão Cerealífera durante a Idade Média*. 2d ed. Lisbon: Cosmos, 1968.

————. *Portugal Quinhentista (Ensaios)*. Lisbon: Quetzal, 1987.

————. *A sociedade medieval portuguesa. Aspectos de vida quotidiana*. 5th ed. Lisbon: Sá da Costa, 1987.

Ordenações de D. Manuel I. 5th ed. Lisbon: Manoel João, 1565.

Ordenações e leys do reino de Portugal Confirmadas, e establecidas pelo senhor Rey D. João IV impressas e accrecentadas com tres Collecções; a primeira de Leys Extravagantes, a segunda de decretos e cartas, e a terceira de Assentos da Casa da Supplicação, e Relação do Porto. Lisbon, 1767.

Orders Taken and Enacted for Orphans and Their Portions. 1580. Rpt. Amsterdam: Theatrum Orbis Terrarum, Ltd. 1973.

Paiva e Pona, António de. *Orphanologia Pratica, em Que se Descreve Tudo. . . .* Lisbon: Joseph Lopes, Ferreyra, 1713.

Parry, J. H., Philip Sherlock, and Anthony Maingot. *A Short History of the West Indies*. 4th ed. New York: St. Martin's Press, 1987.

Pearson, M. N. *Coastal Western India: Studies from the Portuguese Records*. New Delhi: Concept, 1981.

————. "Goa During the First Century of Portuguese Rule." *Itinerario* 8, no. 1 (1984): 36–57.

————. "The People and Politics of Portuguese India during the Sixteenth and Early Seventeenth Century." In *Essays Concerning the Socioeconomic History of Brazil and Portuguese India*, ed. Dauril Alden and Dean Warren, 1–25. Gainesville: University of Florida Press, 1977.

————. *The Portuguese in India*, Vol. 1.1 of *The New Cambridge History of India*. Delhi: Orient Longman, 1987.

Peregalli, Enrique. *Recrutamento Militar no Brasil Colonial*. Campinas, Brazil: Unicamp, 1986.

Pereira de Barredo, Bernardo. *Annaes Históricos do Maranhão*. 2d ed. São Luís, Brazil: Maranhense, 1849.

Peres, Damião. *História dos descobrimentos portugueses*. Rpt. Porto, Portugal: Vertente, 1982.

Peres, Damião et al., eds. "A Actividade Agrícola em Portugal nos Séculos XII à XIV." *Congresso do Mundo Português*, 2:463–86.

Perry, Mary Elizabeth. *Crime and Society in Early Modern Seville*. Hanover, N.H.: University Press of New England, 1980.

Pescatello, Ann M. "The African Presence in Portuguese India." *Journal of Asian History* (Weisbaden) 11, no. 1 (1977): 26–48.

Pieroni, Gerlado. "Detestáveis na Metrópole e receados na Colônia: os ciganos portugueses degredados no Brasil." *Varia História* 12 (December 1993): 114–27.

———. *Os Excluídos do Reino: A Inquisição Portuguesa e o Degredo para o Brasil Colônia*. Brasília: Universidade de Brasília Editora, 2000.

———. "Vadios, Heréticos e Bruxas: os degredados portugueses no Brasil-Colônia." M.A. thesis, Universidade Federal de Bahia, April 1991.

Pike, Ruth. *Penal Servitude in Early Modern Spain*. Madison: University of Wisconsin Press, 1983.

Pinheiro Marques, Alfredo. *Guia de História dos Descobrimentos e Expansão Portuguesa*. Lisbon: BNL, 1988.

Pinheiro da Silva, José. "A Capitania de Baia (Subsídios para a história da sua colonização na 2ª metade do século do XVII)." *Revista Portuguesa de História* 8 (1959).

Pinto, Jeanette. *Slavery in Portuguese India*. Bombay: Himalaya Publishing House, 1992.

Pinto Ferreira, J. A. *Recolhimento de Orfãs de Nossa Senhora de Esperança (fundada na cidade de Porto no século XVIII)*. Porto, Portugal: Câmara Municipal, 1971.

Pinto da França, António. "Influência Portuguesa na Indonésia." *Studia* 33 (December 1971): 161–234.

Pissurlencar, Panduronga S. S., ed. *Assentos do Conselho do Estado, 1618–1750*. 5 vols. Panaji, India: Imprensa Nacional, 1953–1957.

A Plea for the City Orphans and Prisoners of Debt, Humbly Offered to this Present Parliament. London: Randal Taylor, 1690.

Powers, Edwin. *Crime and Punishment in Early Massachusetts, 1620–1692: A Documentary History*. Boston: Beacon Press, 1966.

Prado Junior, Caio. *História Econômica do Brasil*. São Paulo: Editora Brasiliense Limitada, 1945.

Primor e Honra da Vida Soldadesca da India. Lisbon: Jorge Rodrigues, 1630.

Priolkar, Anant Kakba. *The Goa Inquisition: Being a Quartercentenary Commemoration Study of the Inquisition in India with Accounts Given* by Dr. Dellon and Dr. Buchanan. Bombay: Bombay University Press, 1961.

Pullan, Brian. *Orphans and Foundlings in Early Modern Europe*. Reading, Eng.: University of Reading Press, 1989.

Pyrard de Laval, François. *Voyage of Pyrard de Laval*. 2 vols. in 3. Trans. Gray and Bell. Hakluyt Society, first series, vol. 77, 1887; rpt. New York: Burt Franklin, n.d.

Qaisar, Ahsan Jan. *The Indian Response to European Technology and Culture (1498–1707)*. Delhi: Oxford University Press, 1982.

Rau, Virginia. "A Grande Exploração Agrária em Portugal a Partir dos Fins da Idade Média." *Revista de História* (São Paulo) 30 (1965): 65–74.

"Recolhimento da Nossa Senhora da Serra," *O Oriente Portuguêz* (first series) VII (1910): 140–42.

Recopilación de las leyes destos reynos, hecha por mandado de la Magestad Catholica del Rey Don Philippe Segundo nuestro señor. 2 vols. Acalá de Henares, Spain: Juan Iniguez de Liquerica, 1581.

Redman, Charles L., and James Boone. "Qsar es-Seghir (Alcácer-Ceguer): A 15th and 16th Century Portuguese Colony in North Africa." *Studia* 41–42 (1979): 5–51.

Registro Geral da Câmara da Cidade de São Paulo. Vols. 1–4. São Paulo, 1917–1923.

Ribeiro, Orlando. *Aspectos e Problems da Expansão Portuguesa*. Lisbon: JIU, 1962.

———. *Portugal o Mediterrâneo, e o Atlântico*. 4th ed. Lisbon: Sá da Costa, 1986.

Ribeiro, Orlando, Herman Lautensach, and Suzanne Daveau. *Geografia de Portugal*. 4 vols. Lisbon: Sá da Costa, 1987.

Ribeiro Coutinho, André. *O Capitão de Infantaria Portuguez com a theorica, e pratica das suas funções*. 2 vols. Lisbon, 1751.

Rodney, Walter. *A History of the Upper Guinea Coast, 1545 to 1800*. 1970. Rpt. New York: Monthly Review Press, 1980.

Rodrigues, L. A. "The Indo-European Miscegenation." *Boletim do Instituto Meneses Bragança* 108 (1975) separata, 1–20.

———. "The Mercy House of Goa." *Boletim do Instituto Meneses Bragança* 96 (1971): 1–16.

———. "Portuguese-Blood Communities in India." *Boletim do Instituto Meneses Bragança* 110 (1975) separata, 1–9.

———. "Portuguese Feminine Emigration for Colonization of India." *Journal of Indian History* 58, parts 1–3 (1980): 53–61.

———. "The Recluse Houses of Goa." *Boletim do Instituto Meneses Bragança* 106 (1974): 1–14.

Rodrigues da Silveira, Francisco. *Memórias de um Soldado da India,1585–98*.

Ed. António de Sousa Silva Costa Lobo. 1877. Rpt. Lisbon: Imprensa Nacional, 1987.

Rusche, Georg, and Otto Kirchheimer. *Punishment and Social Structure*. New
York: Columbia University Press, 1939.

Russell, P. E. "Galés Portugueses ao Serviço de Ricardo II de Inglaterra, (1385–
89)." *Revista da Faculdade de Letras* (Universidade de Lisboa) vol. 28 (second series), 1–2 (1953): 61–73.

Russell-Wood, A. J. R. *Fidalgos and Philanthropists: The Santa Casa de Misericórdia de Bahia, 1550–1755*. Berkeley and Los Angeles: University of California Press, 1968.

———. "Women and Society in Colonial Brazil." *Journal of Latin American
Studies* 9, no. 1 (1977): 1–34.

Saldanha, J. A. "Survival of Portuguese Institutions in British Western India."
Journal of the Bombay Branch of the Royal Asiatic Society 25 (1918–
1919): 153–60.

Sanceau, Elaine. *Mulheres Portuguesas no Ultramar*. Trans. Aureliano Sampaio. Porto, Portugal: Civilização, 1979.

———. "Uma familia portuguesa quinhentista na India." *Studia* 1 (1958):
101–10.

Santa Maria, Frei Agostinho de. *História da Fundação do Real Convento de
Santa Monica da Cidade de Goa, Corte do Estado da India, e do Império
Lusitano do Oriente*. Lisbon: António Pedrozo Galram, 1699.

Santos Júnior, António Alves dos. "O povoamento de S. Tomé." In *Elementos
de História da Ilha de São Tomé*, 71–78. Lisbon: Centro de Estudos de Ma-
rinha, 1971.

Sarkar, Jadunath. "Portuguese Christian Communities in Bengal, 1679 A. D.
(Report of the Augustin monks of Goa)." *Bengal Past and Present* 61
(1951): 1–6.

Saunders, A. C. de C. M. *A Social History of Black Slaves and Freedmen in
Portugal, 1441–1555*. Cambridge: Cambridge University Press, 1982.

Scammell, G. V. *Oceans, Ships, and Empire: Studies in European Maritime
and Colonial History, 1400–1700*. London: Variorum, 1995.

Schwartz, Stuart B. *Sovereignty and Society in Colonial Brazil*. Berkeley and
Los Angeles: University of California Press, 1973.

Serrão, Joel. *Cronologia geral da história de Portugal*. 4th ed. Lisbon: Horizonte, 1980.

———. *A Emigração Portuguesa*. 2d ed. Lisbon: Livros Horizonte, 1974.

Serrão, Joel, ed. *Dicionário de História de Portugal*. 6 vols. Lisbon: Iniciativas
Editoriais, 1963–1971.

Severim de Faria, Manuel. *Noticias de Portugal*. . . . Lisbon: Craesbeeckiana,
1655.

————. *Relaçam universal do que succedeo em Portugal & mais Provincias do Occidente & Oriente, de Março de [1] 625 atè todo Setembro de [1]626. Contem muitas particularidades & curiosidades.* Lisbon: Geraldo da Vinha, 1612.

Shastry, B. S. *Studies in Indo-Portuguese History.* Bangalore, India: Ibh Prakashana, 1981.

Shaw, A. G. L. *Convicts and the Colonies.* London: Faber, 1966.

Shirodkar, P. P. "Dutch-Portuguese Relations in the East (1580–1663) vis-à-vis Indian Peninsula." *Studia* 48 (1989): 123–44.

————. "Fort of Aguada." *Purabhilekh-Puratatva* 3, no. 1 (January–June 1985): 107–22.

————. "Fortress of Anjediv." *Purabhilekh-Puratatva* 2, no. 2 (July–December 1984): 119–33.

Silva, Chandra Richard de. *The Portuguese in Ceylon 1617–1638.* Colombo, Sri Lanka: H. W. Cave, 1972.

Silva Correia, Alberto Carlos Germano da. *História da colonização Portuguesa na India.* 6 vols. Lisbon: AGU, 1960.

Silva Cosme, O. M. da. *Fidalgos in the Kingdom of Kotte, Sri Lanka (1505–1656): The Portuguese in Sri Lanka.* Colombo, Sri Lanka: Evangel, 1990.

Silva da Natividade, José da. *Confortaçam para os Queixozos.* Lisbon, 1752.

Silva Rego, António de. *O Ultramar Português no Século XVIII.* 2d ed. Lisbon: AGU, 1970.

————, ed. *Documentação para a história das Missões do Padroado Português do Oriente: India.* 12 vols. Lisbon: AGC, 1947–1958.

Silva Telles, Francisco Xavier de. *A transportação penal e a colonização.* Lisbon: SGL, 1903.

Silveira Cardozo, Manuel da. "The Santa Casa da Misericórdia of Lisbon." *Revista de História* (São Paulo) 100 (1974): 217–55.

Slicher van Bath, B. H. "The Absence of White Contract Labour in Spanish America During the Colonial Period." In *Colonialism and Migration; Indentured Labour Before and After Servitude,* ed. P. C. Emmer, 19–32. Dordrecht, The Netherlands: Martinus Nijhoff Publishers, 1986.

————. *The Agrarian History of Western Europe A.D. 500–1850.* Trans. Olive Ordish. London: Edward Arnold, 1963.

Smith, Abbot Emerson. *Colonists in Bondage.* Chapel Hill: University of North Carolina Press, 1947.

Smith, W. H. C. "The Portuguese in Malacca During the Dutch Period." *Studia* 7 (1961): 87–106.

Soares, Manuel Lourenço. *Breve Explicaçam dos casos reservados nas constituçõens deste Arcebispado de Lisboa & em alguãs dos outros Arcebispados deste Reyno de Portugal.* Coimbra, Portugal: Manuel Rodrigues de Almeyda, 1679.

Soares de Sousa, Gabriel. *Tratado Descriptivo de Brazil em 1587.* 2d ed. Rio de Janeiro, 1879.

Sousa Campos, Ernesto de. *A Santa Casa de Misercórdia de Santos.* São Paulo: Elvino Pocai, 1943.

Sousa Dias, Gastão. *Ocupação de Angola (exploração, conquista e povoamento).* Lisbon: AGC, 1944.

Sousa Ferreira, Eduardo. *Origins e Formas da Emigração.* Lisbon: Iniciativas Editoriais, 1976.

Souza, George B. *The Survival of Empire: Portuguese Trade and Society in China and the South Sea, 1630–1754.* Cambridge: Cambridge University Press, 1986.

Souza, Teotonio R. de. *Medieval Goa: A Socio-Economic History.* New Delhi: Concept, 1979.

Spierenburg, Pieter. *The Prison Experience: Disciplinary Institutions and Their Inmates in Early Modern Europe.* New Brunswick, N.J.: Rutgers University Press, 1991.

Spindel, Donna J. *Crime and Society in North Carolina, 1663–1776.* Baton Rouge: Louisiana State University Press, 1989.

Stanislawski, Dan. *The Individuality of Portugal: A Study in Historical-Political Geography.* Austin: University of Texas Press, 1959.

Sturdivant, Sheila T. "Rich Man, Poor Man, Beggar Man, Thief: Frenchmen Exiled to Louisiana, 1717 to 1721." M.A. thesis, University of Southwestern Louisiana, 1971.

Subrahmanyam, Sanjay. *Improvising Empire: Portuguese Trade and Settlement in the Bay of Bengal, 1500–1700.* Delhi: Oxford University Press, 1990.

———. *The Portuguese Empire in Asia, 1500–1700: A Political and Economic History.* New York: Longman, 1993.

Tavernier, Jean Baptiste (1605–1689). *Travels in India.* Trans. V. Bell. 2 vols. 1889. Rpt. New Delhi: Oriental Books Reprint, 1977.

Teixeira, Manuel. *Galeria de Mulheres Ilustres em Macao.* Macau: Imprensa Nacional, 1974.

———, *Macau e a sua Diocese.* 16 vols. Macau: Soi-Sang, 1940–1982.

Teixeira da Mota, Avelino. *Some Aspects of Portuguese Colonization and Sea-Trade in West Africa in the 15th and 16th Centuries.* Bloomington: Indiana University Press, 1978.

Telles, Ricardo Michael. "Igrejas, Conventos, e Capelas na Velha Cidade de Goa, Real Mosteiro de Santa Mónica." *O Oriente Português,* second series, 1 (1931): 78–91.

Trinidade, Frei Paulo de. *Conquista Espiritual do Oriente.* 3 vols. Lisbon: CEHU, 1962.

Vallasciin Senatu, Thomae. *Livro da Reforma da Justiça: Explanationis in Novam Justitiae Reformationem*. Coimbra, Portugal: Imprensa da Universidade, 1677.

Varnhagen, Francisco Adolfo de. *História Geral do Brasil*. 4 vols. 4th complete ed. São Paulo: Melhoramentos, 1948.

Vasconcellos e Meneses, José de. "Armadas Portuguesas (séculos XV e XVI): Abastecimento e Alimentação." *Boletim da Sociedade de Geografia de Lisboa* 102, no. 7–12 (July–December 1984): 55–88.

Verlinden, Charles. *The Beginnings of Modern Colonization*. Trans. Yvonne Freccero. Ithaca, N.Y.: Cornell University Press, 1970.

Vianna, Helio. *Estudos de História Colonial*. São Paulo: Editora Nacional, 1948.

Vieira, Alberto, ed. *O Município no Mundo Português*. Funchal, Madeira: Centro de Estudos de História do Atlântico, 1998.

Viega Torres, José. "Uma Longa Guerra Social: Os Ritmos da Repressão Inquisitorial em Portugal." *Revista de História Económica e Social* 1 (1978): 55–68.

Vieria Ferreira, Fernando Luís. "O Degredo nas Ordinações do Reino e os degredados vindos com Pedro Alvares Cabral." *Revista do Instituto Histórico e Geográfico Brasileiro* 199 (1950): 127–31.

Viotti da Costa, Emília. "Primeiros povoadores do Brasil: O problema dos degredados." *Revista de História* (São Paulo) 13, no. 27 (July–September 1956): 3–23.

Waley-Cohen, Joanna. *Exile in Mid-Qing China. Banishment to Xingjiang, 1758–1820*. New Haven, Conn.: Yale University Press, 1991.

Weisser, Michael R. *Crime and Punishment in Early Modern Europe*. Atlantic Highlands, N.J.: Humanities Press, 1976.

———. "Crime and Punishment in Early Modern Spain." In *Crime and the Law: The Social History of Crime since 1500*, ed. V. A. C. Gartell, Bruce Lenman, and Geoffrey Parker, 76–96. London: Europa Publications, 1980.

Wicki, José, S. J., ed. "Duas relações sobre a situação da índia portuguesa nos anos 1568 e 1569." *Studia* 8 (1961): 133–220.

Wicki, Josephus, S. J., (vols. 1–13) and John Gomes, S. J., (vols. 14–18), eds. *Monumenta Historica Societatis Jesu: Missiones Orientales. Documenta Indica*. 17 vols. in 18. Rome: Institutum Historicum Societatis Jesu, 1948–1972.

Winius, George Davison. "India or Brazil—Priorities for Imperial Survival During the Wars of the Restoration." *Journal of the American Portuguese Cultural Society* 1, no. 4 (1967): 34–42.

———. "The Portuguese Asian 'Decadência,' Revisited." In *Empire in Transition: The Portuguese World in the Time of Camões*, ed. Alfred Hower and

Richard A. Preto-Rodas, 106–17. Gainesville: Center for Latin American Studies, University Presses of Florida, 1985.

———. "The 'Secret People' in Their Several Dimensions." Unpublished paper given at ISIPH-5, 1989.

———. "The 'Shadow Empire' of Goa in the Bay of Bengal." *Itinerario* 7, no. 2 (1983): 83–101.